Christopaganism
or Indigenous Christianity?

Edited by Tetsunao Yamamori and Charles R. Taber

William Carey Library

SOUTH PASADENA, CALIF

Library of Congress Cataloging in Publication Data

William S. Carter Symposium on Church Growth, Milligan College, Tennessee, 1974.
    Christopaganism or Indigenous Christianity?

    Consists of 12 lectures delivered at the symposium sponsored by Milligan College.
    Bibliography: p.
    1. Missions—Congresses. 2. Christianity and culture—Congresses. I. Yamamori,
Tetsunao, 1937-   II. Taber, Charles Russell.   III. Milligan College, Tenn. College. IV.
Title.
BV2391.M54 1974   266   75-6616
ISBN 0-87808-423-1

Published by the William Carey Library
533 Hermosa Street
South Pasadena, Calif. 91030
Telephone 213-799-4559

PRINTED IN THE UNITED STATES OF AMERICA

Dedicated to Mr. and Mrs. William S. Carter,
friends of Milligan College and pacesetters
in the
Christian World Mission

Editors

TETSUNAO YAMAMORI (Ph.D., Duke University)

Associate Professor of Sociology at Milligan College. Served as coordinator of the William S. Carter Symposium on Church Growth held at Milligan College, April 5-7, 1974. Dr. Yamamori was born and reared in Nagoya, Japan. He has traveled extensively for education and missionary research. His articles have appeared in such journals as *Practical Anthropology, Church Growth Bulletin, Journal of the American Academy of Religion* and *Japanese Religions*. He has contributed a chapter to *God, Man and Church Growth* (Eerdmans, 1973). He has authored *Church Growth in Japan* (William Carey Library, 1974) and has co-authored *Exploring Religious Meaning* (Prentice-Hall, 1973) and *Introducing Church Growth* (Standard Publishing, 1975). Currently he edits a missiological quarterly, *Milligan Missiogram.*

CHARLES R. TABER (Ph.D., Hartford Seminary Foundation)

Associate Professor of Anthropology and World Mission at Milligan College. Dr. Taber was born in France of missionary parents and reared in France and the then French Equatorial Africa. He served seven years as a missionary educator in the Central African Republic, and later for four years as a translations consultant of the United Bible Societies in West Africa. His writings include *French Loan Words in Sango* (Hartford, 1964), *A Dictionary of Sango* (Hartford, 1965), *The Structure of Sango Narrative* (Hartford, 1966), and (with Eugene A. Nida), *Theory and Practice of Translation* (Leiden, 1969) and *La Traduction: théorie et méthode* (London, 1971), as well as numerous articles on missionary anthropology, linguistics and translation. He was editor of *Practical Anthropology* (1968-1972), and is chairman of the editorial board of *Missiology.*

Participants

DONALD A. MC GAVRAN (Ph.D., Columbia University)

Senior Professor of Missions of the School of World Mission and Institute of Church Growth, Fuller Theological Seminary. Dr. McGavran was the founding dean, serving in that capacity from 1965-1971. Missionary to India under the United Christian Missionary Society, 1923-1955. Architect of the church growth school of thought now spreading widely in all continents. Authored *How to Teach Religion in Mission Schools* (1930), *Church Growth and Group Conversion* (1938, revised 1959), *The Bridges of God* (1955), *Multiplying Churches in the Philippines* (1957), *How Churches Grow* (1959), *Church Growth in Jamaica* (1962), *Church Growth in Mexico* (1963), *Church Growth and Christian Mission* (1965), *Understanding Church Growth* (1970), *Eye of the Storm: the Great Debate in Mission* (1973) and numerous articles in *International Review of Missions, Religion in Life, Christianity Today, World Vision Magazine*, etc.

JOHANNES CHRISTIAAN HOEKENDIJK (Th.D., University of Utrecht)

Professor of Missions, Union Theological Seminary, New York. Dr. Hoekendijk served as secretary for Evangelism, World Council of Churches, 1949-1953, and as professor of missions and church history at University of Utrecht, 1953-1965. Authored *World Missions During World War II* (1945), *Church and Nation in German Missiology* (1948), *Evangelism in France* (1951), *The Church Inside Out* (1964), *Horizons of Hope* (1970), and about 150 articles on missionary-ecumenical subjects in various magazines.

ALAN RICHARD TIPPETT (Ph.D., University of Oregon)

Professor of Missionary Anthropology, School of World Mission and Institute of Church Growth, Fuller Theological Seminary. Dr. Tippett held pastorates in Victoria, Australia, 1935-1940, and served as a missionary of the Australian Methodist Church to the Fiji Islands, 1941-1961. His missionary experience includes the superintendency of a theological seminary. Besides numerous missiological and anthropological articles, Dr. Tippett authored *The Christian: Fiji, 1835-67* (1954), *Solomon Islands Christianity* (1967), *Fijian Material Culture – Culture Context, Function and Change* (1968), *Verdict Theology in Missionary Theory* (1969), *Church Growth and the Word of God* (1970), *Peoples of Southwest Ethiopia* (1970), *People Movements in Southern Polynesia* (1971), *God, Man and Church Growth* (1973), and eight books in the Fijian language. Editor of *Missiology* for the American Society of Missiology.

PETER BEYERHAUS (Th.D., Uppsala University)

Director of the Institute for Missions and Ecumenical Theology at University of Tuebingen, West Germany. Before assuming the present position, Dr. Beyerhaus served as principal of Lutheran Theological College in Natal, South Africa. He is widely recognized for his contributions to the study of world missions and was one of the chief architects of the Frankfurt Declaration. His writings in English include *Missions: Which Way?* (1971) and *Shaken Foundations for Mission* (1972).

Table of Contents

Introduction

TETSUNAO YAMAMORI

Christopaganism or Indigenous Christianity? is a product of the William S. Carter Symposium on Church Growth. More than five hundred persons from around the nation gathered in East Tennessee for the three-day conference sponsored by Milligan College in April of 1974. The twelve lectures given then constitute the present chapters with only minor editorial changes. I am delighted that the William Carey Library is making these lectures available in book form, not only to those who gathered at Milligan, but, more importantly, to those who were unable to be there.

By way of introduction, I wish to explain briefly the metamorphosis and significance of the Carter Symposium, to elaborate on the plan of the book, and to give credits where credits are due in the preparation of this book.

Why should a small East Tennessee liberal arts college such as Milligan become the setting for a large symposium delving deeply into one of the most crucial issues in missions today? How did the Carter Symposium come about? What significance does the symposium have for Milligan and for the missiological world at large? The key to unlock these questions lies with the person of Jess W. Johnson and his dream. Milligan President Johnson once remarked: "The heart of Christianity resides in the mission which our Lord has committed to all his disciples. A college, if it be Christian, must be caught up in this mission."

Johnson wants Milligan to become *a college with a missionary vision.* It was this dream that brought me to Milligan College in 1972. When this dream was made known to them, Mr. and Mrs. William S. Carter of Dallas, Texas, provided a generous gift enabling us to carry the dream a step further. The first thing that was made possible by the gift was the appointment of Dr. Charles R. Taber for the academic year 1973-74 as the William S. Carter Visiting Professor of World Mission and Anthropology and Dr. Taber has now become a member of the permanent faculty. Second, the *Milligan Missiogram* (a missiological quarterly) was begun that same year and has now become self-supporting. Third, the William S. Carter Symposium was planned to stir up interest at the College on missions and church growth and to introduce *Milligan's* dream to the missiological world. The significance of the Carter Symposium is not limited only to those who assembled at Milligan in April of 1974. The Carter Symposium transcends the time and space categories. For Milligan College, it has a symbolic meaning. Granted, it was a declaration to the missiological world of Milligan's commitment to the Christian world mission, but, more than that, it will serve as a reminder to what is yet to be accomplished to realize Milligan's dream. The 1975 launching of Milligan's Institute of World Studies/Church Growth is only one among many services which the College will provide to the missionary world. For the missiological world, the Carter Symposium was significant because four highly qualified missiologists in different disciplines and with different areas of experience examined the perennial problem in the effective and sound communication of the gospel. This comprehensive, interdisciplinary approach in the setting of a conference paved the way for future cooperation among missiologists in solving the missionary problems of the first order. The accommodation-syncretism axis which the Carter Symposium took up as its central theme is not a new topic; the issue has remained problematic from the time of the Apostles to this day. That the topic keeps coming up indicates that each generation must wrestle with it utilizing the best insights gleaned from various disciplines. I hope this book will serve as a catalyst to the continuing debate on the issue of cultural accommodation and syncretism in missions.

Now I shall turn to the plan of the book. Perhaps an explanation on the format of the symposium will reveal the structure of the book. As symposium coordinator, I first settled on the topic to be the accommodation-syncretism axis which may be described in this way. The acts of God on behalf of men are, in their ultimate reality and significance, the same for every man. But they were concretely enacted on the human scene, and later reported and explained in terms of specific human cultures and languages. In order to make the message intelligible and relevant to people immersed in their various cultural settings, God became fully man and used exactly the same media and symbols as men used in everyday life. The same process of transposition necessarily occurs every time the gospel crosses a new cultural frontier. But it may happen as a result of careful, sensitive planning, in which case the form of the message is *accommodated* precisely in order to preserve the integrity of its meaning; or it may occur spontaneously, haphazardly, as a result of insensitivity and carelessness on the part of the evangelizer, in which case the message is often *syncretized* and thus distorted. The purpose of the Carter Symposium was to explore both the criteria by which one might distinguish legitimate accommodation from illegitimate syncretism and practical approaches designed to achieve the one and avoid the other. In short, the axis was thus defined: As Christianity spreads into the myriad cultures of the world, it must adjust to each culture to present an intelligible and relevant message, but what are the limits of such adjustments? Twelve lectures comprised the basic format of the symposium, with three main divisions: (1) the axis defined and illustrated, (2) principles applicable to the axis and (3) critical issues in the axis. Drs. Donald A. McGavran, J.C. Hoekendijk, Alan Tippett and Peter Beyerhaus were asked and agreed to address themselves to the axis, each incorporating his own discipline and area of experience. The following lecture assignments were given with each participant delivering three.

1. The terms defined (Tippett)
2. The axis illustrated from India (McGavran)
3. The axis illustrated from Indonesia (Hoekendijk)
4. The axis illustrated from South Africa (Beyerhaus)
5. Anthropological principles which apply (Tippett)

6. Biblical principles which apply (Beyerhaus)
7. Historical principles which apply (Hoekendijk)
8. Strategic principles which apply (McGavran)
9. My reactions to my colleagues (Tippett)
10. My reactions to my colleagues (Beyerhaus)
11. My reactions to my colleagues (Hoekendijk)
12. My reactions to my colleagues (McGavran)

The whole symposium was manuscript-based. Dr. Tippett had his first lecture on the definition of the terms circulated among the other speakers before they wrote theirs. Then lectures 2 to 8 were to be in my hand before Christmas of 1973 for me to distribute them to the other participants so that lectures 9 to 12 could be finished and in my hand by January 1, 1974. This was my suggested procedure. As the participants worked on their lectures, the concrete titles took shape and constitute the present chapters. To tie things together, I have asked my colleague, Dr. Charles R. Taber, to write a conclusion. In it, he will summarize the issues, delineate the range of opinions, identify the points of contact and disagreement and bring out the areas yet to be explored.

To thank all the people involved in the preparation of this book is a difficult task. I must thank the four lecturers, those who gathered at the symposium and the Milligan community which served as a cordial host to its guests. Appreciation must be expressed to Mrs. Freddie Smith, my secretary, who typed the manuscript and worked long, hard hours to see the book to its completion. To Dr. Taber whose willing help in this and other ventures is a source of inspiration, to President Johnson for his dream and to Bill and Liz Carter for their generous gift and exemplary missionary concern, I am grateful.

CHAPTER ONE

Christopaganism or Indigenous Christianity

ALAN R. TIPPETT

WHEN Dr. Yamamori supplied us with the terms of reference for this symposium, he spoke of the adjustments required in the spread of Christianity from one human culture to another as it takes root, and raised the question: What are the limits of such adjustments?

We agreed that the first chapter of the series should prepare the stage for our exchange, taking up a position in such a way that the other writers could react either positively or negatively, either by developing the argument further or by turning it in another direction. In any case, the first presentation, it was felt, should pinpoint the missionary problem which underlies the whole series — namely, how to avoid syncretism and to achieve an indigenous Christianity. So often the search for the latter leaves us with the former instead. The purpose of this presentation, then, after delineating the scope of the series and defining the terms, will be to demonstrate the character of the alternatives — Christopaganism or indigeneity.

THE SCOPE OF THE SYMPOSIUM

In popular missiological literature the theme of our symposium has been discussed under a number of terms. From the negative aspect it is spoken of as *syncretism* or as *Christopaganism*. Writers on the old Spanish Catholic colonies in particular have used the latter term. In both the Old and New Testaments the people of God were warned about the mixture of pagan religion with their own.[1] For this reason it is inevitable that any missionary whose roots are in Scripture will be predisposed to resist anything in the churches he plants which could lead to syncretism.

Yet the basic principles of anthropology and communication theory, indeed also of what we call incarnational theology, tell us that the churches we plant (and by churches here I mean the Christian fellowship groups, however simple) in cultures other than our own must be relevantly part of those cultures. We are continually (and quite rightly) warned of the danger of planting foreign western Christianity on what we have for so long called "the mission field."

Thus, on the one hand, we try to preserve "a pure faith and an essential gospel," and on the other, we seek to give it "an indigenous garment." For example, the moment we translate a portion of Scripture into a language which has hitherto built its vocabulary only for a pagan worldview and belief, we are confronted with the problem not only of translation, but of *reception*. Yet unless the written word of God can be incarnated in the linguistic flesh of the receptor people, the saving experience is not likely to be transmitted.

The basic problem, therefore, would seem to be how to communicate the essential *supracultural*[2] core of the gospel to new believers in other cultures without having it contaminated by the non-Christian forms with which it must be communicated and shared. This contamination may be manifested in any aspect of Christian ministry — apostolate, proclamation, fellowship, service or teaching, all of which in the last analysis are culturally conditioned.

It was partly the fear of this which hindered early missionary efforts in the fourth century. Ulfilas, for instance, had little support for his translation proposals, as it was thought the pure gospel could not be transmitted in the impure tongue of the Goths.[3]

This raises a whole nest of problems and questions that are within the orbit of these presentations. Perhaps the first of them is: what exactly is the essential core of the gospel which has to be transmitted? As we look at the Scriptures within their Hebrew and Greek garments, just what is supracultural, and what is cultural? The history of the translation of the English Bible is a story of the struggle for cultural relevance in communication, a struggle for meaning, not only across cultures (Hebrew and Greek to English)[4] but across generations of semantic change (Elizabethan, Victorian and Modern Man). Likewise, in every mission field over the last century, Scripture translation reminds us that the gospel, which is *above* culture, nevertheless has to be presented in a meaningful cultural form.

If the mission of God was achieved by the incarnation of his Son, culture-bound as a Jew, and a Jew of Galilee, and a speaker probably of Galilean Aramaic, and by occupation a carpenter in the tradition of his earthly father, and he in turn said, "As the Father hath sent me into the world so send I you into the world," thereby giving us a model for mission (Tippett 1970:64-65); I think we may assume that we are bound to work within the limitations of the cultural forms of the people to whom we are sent.

On the other hand, as we examine the churches of the 19th and 20th century mission fields, we frequently find one of two situations. First, they may be thoroughly western in form, teaching and values and quite unrelated to the cultural ethos, so that people live a borrowed, foreign kind of existence, or a dichotomous one which compartmentalizes the religious and secular. Or second, we may have the tragic manifestation of syncretistic worship, Christopagan, more animistic than Christian, because the thinking is animistic and the ritual magical. In all these manifestations, Christian missions have been sorely criticized by the anthropologists, and although this criticism has been grossly generalized, one cannot dispute that we have frequently deserved it.

Destructive or cynical criticism is both unkind and useless, but criticisms may be valuable if they lead us to take a hard look at our methods and correct our mistakes. No secular anthropologist has yet proved his ability to sit where we sit, and therefore has little right to speak. Given the biblical mandate of the Christian mission and the scientific principles and methodologies of anthropology and communication science (without which no man should go to Christian missions today), how do we plant Christian communities that are at the same time both truly indigenous and truly Christian? Or, as our frame of reference puts it, "What are the cultural limits to the adjustments" that have to be made with the passage of the supracultural message from one culture to another?

This is a *missiological* subject. It has a theological dimension, but is not confined to theology. It has a historical dimension, but is not confined to history. It has an anthropological dimension, but is not confined to anthropology. It has a strategic dimension, but is not confined to strategy. For this reason, we participants will approach the subject, each from one of these four dimensions, but the common bond between us is missiology. We stand now at a formative period in "the history of the expansion of Christianity," as Latourette spoke of it. An old era of mission has passed, and we are suffering the birth pangs of a new one. We look into Scripture and ask what are our basic underpinnings and our divine directions. We look into the past and ask what history has to say to us today. We examine the new insights and dimensions of anthropology and linguistics and try to analyze the transition we seek to achieve. We explore missionary strategies and relate methods to results: acceptance or rejection, growth or non-growth, understanding or misunderstanding, foreignness or indigeneity. Although we approach our basic problem from four quite different angles, nevertheless, we each trespass on the other's ground at some point or other. We may well tangle with each other at times. But we begin from a common base — the task of bringing Christ cross-culturally to the nations.

I would hope that each of us would bring the perspectives of his particular discipline to bear on the general subject in a way which forces the others to take alignments with his information and opinion, not that we need necessarily be led into heated debate, but that we may relate to each other in a symbiotic rather than a reactive manner.

DEFINITION OF TERMS

In current popular missiology, apart from the writing of members of our panel, several standard works for the missionary deal with our subject. The first of these is a translation from Dutch: Bavinck's *Introduction to the Science of Mission* (1964), in which he devotes chapter 9 to this topic. The second is Luzbetak's *The Church and Cultures* (1963), in which chapter 13 has the same title as the book. From the linguistic point of view Nida (1959: 1960), Smalley (1955:58-71), Reyburn (1957:194), Kraft (1963a:109-126), and others have written on the ethnotheological problems in communication. A number of anthropological analyses of Christopaganism are in existence, perhaps the best of them Madsen's *Christopaganism* (1957), and there are biblical studies like Visser't Hooft's *No Other Name* (1963), which describe the identical problem which Paul met with in the first century church.[5]

All these writers have written independently of each other. Apparently there never has been any attempt to coordinate these various researches and to formulate a common terminology as a basis for discussion. In the same way, we who will exchange our ideas during these sessions, have come to the subject, not only from different perspectives and experiences, but with different preferences in terminology. Even the word *syncretism*, which has long been in use in all disciplines, may give us trouble.

Syncretism may be defined as the union of two opposite forces, beliefs, systems or tenets so that the united form is a new thing, neither one nor the other.[6]

With critical consideration, however, we observe that either of two kinds of mixtures may be defined as syncretism: on the one hand, a distortion of Christian theology by mixing it with pagan myth to form a new kind of teaching; on the other hand, the singing of, say, a western Calvinist theology in an unfamiliar chant to a drumbeat previously used only for pagan dances. Yet at this point I wish to make a distinction between them. In the former we are dealing with a basic concept, a matter of thought and belief. In the latter we are dealing with the cultural forms in which it is expressed. Until this differentiation is clearly recognized, we will never be able to draw a line between these quite different processes. This is implied in our opening question about the "limits of our adjustments."

It seems necessary, therefore, that we find a new term for the second of these. We thus retain syncretism or Christopaganism for confusions in the essential content, the metaphysical, the theological, for the fusion of belief systems so that the supracultural gospel is contaminated, leaving us with a new kind of animism. The second, which covers the cultural adjustments that have to be made to achieve the indigeneity of the newly planted Christianity, we may consider briefly now.

Luzbetak's term for this is *accommodation,* which he defines as

the respectful, prudent, scientifically and theologically sound adjustment of the Church to the native culture in attitude, outward behavior and practical apostolic approach (1963:341).

Bavinck starts his discussion with the use of *accommodation* and *adaptation* as alternatives, and before long is involved in a lengthy discussion of various types of accommodation — external, aesthetic, social and juridical, intellectual, religious and ethical (following Thauren). He points out that accommodation is one thing to a missionary and quite another set of problems to the people of the recipient culture. He also differentiates between the Catholic and Reformation viewpoints. After eleven pages of discussion (169-179), he rejects the term *accommodation,* saying,

the Christian life does not accommodate or adapt itself to heathen forms of life, but takes the latter in possession and thereby makes them new.

He prefers the term *possessio,* "to take possession." For the next twelve pages (179-190) he discusses the practical problems of "possessing" a culture, or the entire life, so that a young church, living close to Christ and the Scriptures, may hope for fresh dynamics. He grants the need for expressing faith in forms of the old cultural heritage, but demands it be achieved without denying Christ (190).

The linguists with their incarnational theology prefer the term *transformation,* maintaining the constancy of the supracultural and the variability of the cultural forms with each society. They see God "starting with people where they are," and guiding man in the process of culture change "the People of God in partnership with God," using "culture to serve as a vehicle for Divine-human interaction" (Kraft 1973c:395). Kraft comes to grips with Bavinck and argues that *possessio* suggests the capture of a culture by force from without, rather than a possession from within. As an observer I see in Bavinck and Kraft the Calvinist and Arminian views of the sovereignty of God.[7]

I would hope that we can avoid devoting too much of our time to semantic discussion at the expense of practical confrontation with the missiological problems themselves. Whether we speak of adaptation, accommodation, possessio or transformation, we are using the term over against that of syncretism or Christopaganism — and to this extent I think the issue is clear. It is this basic dichotomy we seek to illuminate in order to draw a line somewhere between the supracultural and cultural, the gospel and the form.

As our discussion continues and we look at concrete situations, two questions will continually arise: Is the gospel influencing the cultural form or is the cultural form influencing the gospel? As we strive to employ a factual missiological data base for our arguments, we shall not only operate within the values and criteria of our respective disciplines, but we shall draw our data from different geographical regions and cultural systems, incorporating our different areas of experience: India, Indonesia, Europe and Oceania. Because we have no representative from Latin America, I shall commence in this chapter with a case study of syncretism from that continental region.

SYNCRETISM OR CHRISTOPAGANISM

Perhaps it would be appropriate in an introductory study like this to analyze a specific case of syncretism and to delineate some of its anthropological ingredients. I seek a locality where Christianity has been established long enough for the existing structures to have crystallized in a form stable enough for objective analysis. That is, I am not seeking so much a case of new religious formulation in which syncretism is currently emerging, but rather a stabilized and functioning religious form in which the process of syncretization is more or less complete and has resulted in a currently operating pattern of faith and practice.

My data base is the case study of a real character, one Juan, a small peasant village official, who considered himself a

Christian and left his autobiographical record (Pozas 1962), from which I borrow at length. Even where length has necessitated abbreviation, I have retained Juan's own terminology, to reduce the possibility of my being a misinterpretive middleman. Many years ago Spaniards invaded his homeland and forced their well-known form of Christianity on his forebears. But Spanish Christianity suffered a considerable degree of modification in the process of transmission, and at the time when the autobiography was written, Juan considered himself a normal Christian, and as a village leader his life was pretty well what the "Christian" villagers expected it to be. In point of fact it was so thoroughly Christopagan as to be hardly Christian at all.

On a basis of Juan's autobiographical statements, I shall enumerate a few anthropological concepts which throw light on the character of this syncretism, and raise some questions about their origin, for they certainly have both theological and missiological (strategic) significance. Time will confine me to four ideas, and these I can only pinpoint: (1) the capacity of cohesive cultural complexes for survival, (2) the orientation of mythical thinking and belief, (3) the demand for a therapeutic system, (4) the notion of the living dead. In discussing the character of this specific case of Latin American Christopaganism from each of these points of view, I want to point out that none of these is confined to Latin America or to the present day. These experiences must have been shared by those incorporated into Christianity in the movements of the first century and the middle ages. I have often wondered whether historians should not re-examine these great movements with a new interpretive analytical tool based on the known dynamics of present day movements both *into* and *out of* the church.[8]

(1) The Capacity of Cohesive Cultural Complexes for Survival

A cohesive cultural complex is here a notion embodied in a cultural form with its regular behavior pattern — a practice which continues and a set of ideas which survives with the practice. Thus in a descriptive passage Juan tells us:

> Three hours later the sky grew bright and the sun came up behind the mountains. My mother put some coals into the clay incense burner and went out to greet the first rays of the sun. She

dropped some pieces of copal into the burner, knelt down to kiss the ground, and begged the sun to protect us and give us health (p. 47).

This is sheer nature worship, both in its faith and practice — an offering to the sun at the moment of appearance of morning light. The sun is greeted. The earth is kissed. The act of prayer for human protection is directed to the sun whose warmth and light give healing and health. This man considers himself a Christian. Yet he worships the creation, not the Creator.

The point I wish to make in this particular instance is that this is *not* a corruption of his Christianity but a survival of a discrete cultural unit, an animistic cohesive cluster of both faith and practice which co-exists with his so-called Christianity, and represents a compartment of this pagan life he never surrendered to Christ. He sees no contradiction in it. It has persisted for several centuries. It has resisted disintegration. It has rejected absorption. And Christian education has failed to communicate a doctrine of God the Creator which would have corrected it. So the first point I want to make about Christopaganism is that it is not always a fusion or intermingling of Christian and pagan ideas. It is often an agglomerate with cohesive animistic units embedded in it. A number of these units may co-exist, in spite of the fact that they represent flat contradictions to one another. They are cohesive and they change or survive cohesively as units like a phonetic pattern in linguistic change (Sapir 1949:186-187).[9] It should not be impossible to deal with them.

(2) The Orientation of Mythical Thinking and Belief

No part of the religion of a people shows up its basic animism more quickly than its mythology — in other words, its faith formulation. We return again to Juan.

He tells us that the Savior watches over people on the road. He died on a cross to save the wayfarer from the Jews, whom he equates with devils, and who were supposedly cannibalistic. Originally the sun was as cold as the moon, but it grew warmer when the Holy Child was born. He was the son of a virgin among the Jews, who sent her away because they knew the Child would bring light. St. Joseph took her to Bethlehem where the Child was

born. The sun grew warmer and the day brighter. The demons
ran away and hid in the mountain ravines. Their activity is
confined to night because the Savior watches over the day, for the
sun is the eye of God. After three days the Holy Child started
work as a carpenter. He made a door from a log. The log was too
short so he stretched it out like a rope to the required length.
Fearing him the people determined to kill him and the family fled
from village to village across the mountains. In one village he
planted a cornfield. The people were bitten by a swarm of flies.
The Savior said, "Don't eat them, eat me instead." He visited the
afterworld and then they nailed him to a cross so the people
would remember that demons would be punished and would
stop eating people (pp. 94-96, summarized).

Let us backtrack briefly over this completely confused but
supposedly Christian account of the life of our Lord. It covers
the journey to Bethlehem, the nativity, the flight into Egypt, the
carpenter of Nazareth, the vicarious death on the cross. There is
a suggestion of the sacramental partaking of the body of Christ,
and his descent into hell.

Within this structure are woven a number of animistic
features — the role of the sun and moon, the cannibal demons,
their residence in the mountains, traditions of the origin of the
cornfield and the swarm of flies.

There is no coherent relation between the details of the story,
but there are clear equations: the biting flies, demons and Jews;
the light and warmth of the sun with the light of Christ; the
conflict of light and darkness, and of Christ and demons; the
vicarious character of being bitten by flies and of being nailed to
the cross.

We could not ask for a better (or more appalling) example of
syncretism than this, or anything which cries out more
pathetically to the strategy of mission. The educational
follow-up of conversion was so defective as to permit this fusion
of the gospel narrative with ancient traditions of the origin of the
cornfield (their main subsistence staff of life), and some ancient
epidemic of biting diptera. The fear of cannibalistic demons,
equated with the role of the Jews as the enemies of our Lord in
his last days on earth, is obviously an example of the problem of
meaning in cross-cultural gospel communication. Juan reminds

us that the meaning ascribed to the message by the receptor may be quite different from that ascribed by the advocate (Barnett 1953:339).[10]

Moreover, an anthropological principle is involved here. Behind this strange belief structure inherited by Juan from his Christian forebears lies a mythical orientation, a preference for the narrative or pictorial faith formulation. It should have provided no problem to the pastors of the first converts. The simple biblical narrative would have delighted these converts and would have served as a perfect functional substitute to their mythology. One can only assume that the Spanish teachers of the early converts failed to do this, with the result that the converts who cherished the narrative form, tried to weave together the old and the new, grasping at the points which were open for equation. This is a basic principle of innovation. People will accept readily new ideas which reinforce or coalesce with existing ideas, and in many cases the meaning ascribed to the new is derived from the old in the same way that (in a completely different context) many Greek words in the New Testament have Hebrew, rather than Greek, meanings.

Once again this facet of syncretism reminds us of the fundamental importance of the teaching program in the follow-up of conversion. The great commission, after all, said both: "Make disciples" and "teach them."

(3) The Demand for a Therapeutic System

Another area of cultural analysis which exposes any inherent syncretism is the whole field of belief regarding sickness and healing. When I find myself within an animist community for a few days, I usually try to ascertain their basic theories of sickness.

After the burial of his father, Juan was sick of *komel* (a sickness caused by fear) and called an *ilol* to diagnose it. He demanded candles, copal resin, *aguardiente,* a rooster and flowers, and returned the next day for a healing ritual. Juan explains the theory of sickness (greatly abbreviated) thus:

> Each person has a *chulel* (a representative animal in the mountains) which shares his fortunes — health, sickness, fatness, hunger and so on. Some hostile chulels prey on those of

ordinary people, so that the latter sicken. If a demon ties up a chulel, the person whose chulel it is sickens. The ilol had to sacrifice a rooster to untie the chulel and set him free. The flowers had to be picked before sunrise and put on a small altar, the rooster hung up by its feet, the candles lit, the resin put on hot coals in the incense-burner, and a prayer had to be offered to the demon concerned to appease his feelings against the victim. The aguardiente drink would be spilled on the ground and the following prayer offered:

> Holy Earth, Holy Heaven; Lord God, God the Son, . . . take charge of me and represent me; see my work, see my struggles, see my sufferings. I place the tribute in your hands. In return for my incense and my candles, spirit of the Moon, virgin mother of Heaven, virgin mother of Earth, in the name of your first Son, your first glory, see your child oppressed in his spirit, in his chulel.

During this prayer the ilol killed the rooster by twisting his neck and Juan records, "Suddenly I felt free!" He knew that, his chulel having been seriously mistreated, he himself was not yet well, but that he would recover now (pp. 88-91).

The therapy, belief structure and psychology are all thoroughly shamanistic. The only trace of Christian borrowing are the references to the Virgin and the Son, and this was probably a case of protective borrowing. The divinitory diagnosis, the sympathy of patient and forest creature, the shamanistic process of curing, the psychological moment of release, the libation of liquor — all these are animistic survivals from the pre-Christian society. In no way whatever has Christianity changed or "possessed" this therapeutic configuration or its philosophical base.

Whatever Christianity brought to Juan's people, it completely bypassed this aspect of life. It raises one of the basic questions of missionary failure. If religion is to fulfill the role that has been ascribed to it in a communal society as "integrator" (Radin 1937:15, Malinowski 1948:53), "governor" (Wallace 1966:4), the "universal feature" (Lowie 1952:xiv-xvi), the "sanctioner of the mores" or "the part of the mores which rules" (Sumner & Keller 1927), etc., it must both recognize and provide ways of dealing with the basic *felt needs* of the society. The animist has a confidence in the shaman and regards him as a benefactor and an essential person. When a new religion neglects its therapeutic ministry in a communal community, that society will inevitably retain its shamanic configuration. Either religion and healing will become compartmentalized and religion will lose its function as integrator of society, or the configuration of animistic diagnosis and healing with its philosophical underpinnings will be incorporated into the new religion. This is another way in which Christianity has often become syncretistic — by failing to meet the basic felt needs of the society. These long-standing needs often arise from the environment or physical condition of the converts and continue after conversion, and Christianity is effective only as it meets the needs of its adherent. Neglect of these physical environmental and cultural needs forces the newly converted community to seek solutions elsewhere. When these solutions have pagan overtones, the Christianity becomes syncretistic.

(4) The Notion of the Living Dead

"Everything is the same as when I was little," says Juan. "When I die and my spirit comes back here, it will find the same paths I walked when I was alive, and it will recognize my house" (p. 7).

Then there is the ritual of the *Day of the Dead*, when special bowls are taken from a chest for offerings of food to the souls of the dead, which Juan describes in the following way:

> One of my brothers went to the village to ring the bell . . . to call the souls. I went to the graveyard with my father, to clear the weeds from our family graves and to mark a little path in the direction of our house so the souls wouldn't get lost when they went for their offerings . . . "My parents died here in this house," my father said, "and my father's parents also. The souls of your mother's parents will go over to the other house, because they lived and died there."

Here we are confronting the animistic concept of the living dead, which is the basis of ancestor worship. The conceptual structure is based on kinship and inheritance, and the dead are still recognized as part of the life of those who continue to live in the traditional place of abode and work the lands of the lineage. The dead still must eat the produce of the land and receive the services of the present occupants of their lands.

"In every house there is a table set with food for souls," says Juan, and goes on to add that theirs "was spread with pine needles and wild orchids." These are protective taboos against the mysterious power (cf. *mana*) associated with the things of the dead. The souls were offered tamales with beans and a gourd of cornmeal beverage. Juan's mother prepared the meal and set it out on the table. They thought of the souls as those who left an inheritance and the mother called

> Come and eat!
> Come and taste the flavor of the food!
> Come and enjoy the fragrance of what you eat!

They burned candles in all the houses that night. Juan is certain the souls do come and partake of the food left for them.

The conversation this night concerns the sun and moon and ties in to the ancient pre-Christian worldview and origin myths (pp. 48-51).

When Juan's father died, the symbolism of the burial was based on the notion of his departure on a journey across a lake infested with frogs. He takes food with him — chicken, tortillas and salt. Every time he rests, the living dead share some of his food. He also has clothes and money to buy fruit on the journey, and when the ceremony is over the mourners wash in proper animistic fashion (pp. 87-88).

What does Christianity, the new religion, say with respect to death and the life after death? Was the Christian eschatology credible to Juan's forebears when they became Christian? Are the dead still living and continually concerned with the cohesion and perpetuity of the tribe which they founded? How does Christianity preserve the entity of the lineage, the strength and stability of the family, the continuity and security of tribal lands — all part of what Sir Henry Maine called the *concept of perpetuity?* In communal society it is the faith formulation of the living dead and the cycle of associated ritual practices which preserve this.

If Christianity does not provide a *vital* eschatology (by "vital" I mean a living one, that is actually believed and is the base of actual religious performance), it runs the risk of perpetuating the animistic notion of the living dead — which leads, of course, to Christopaganism or co-existence with polytheism.[11]

I have pinpointed four anthropological notions which show how syncretism may impose itself on Christian missionary effort. They are not exhaustive nor confined to Latin America. On the surface Spanish Christianity defeated animism and imposed its western Christian structure on the defeated, leaving the animists no option of rejecting it. In the main the animists found Spanish Christianity incredible. This forced acceptance was not a meaningful one, and, therefore, they preserved their old values and faith formulation at the heart. The continued morning worship of the sun, the shamanistic ritual of healing and the theory of sickness on which it stood, and the ritual of the day of the dead all demonstrate that the conqueror was, in point of fact, the conquered.

Examination of case histories like that of Juan also shows how anthropological or ethnohistorical investigations raise important questions for missionary strategy, and demand theological evaluation of missionary effort. So I feed these illustrations "into the hopper" in the expectation that we will want to discuss some of the points I raise.

To this point I have been taking a hard look at the negative aspect of our subject: namely, what must be avoided in cross-cultural missionary activity. But there is another side to which I must refer briefly.

THE ALTERNATIVE: INDIGENOUS CHRISTIANITY

It would be a tragedy to see cross-cultural church-planting as merely a negative thing. After all, the gospel is positive not negative, an experience to be entered into and shared. Somehow the supracultural core of truth, in both the written and the living Word of God has to be incarnated in the culturally-bound churches or fellowships. We seek an assurance of salvation, when worshippers may say as individuals that they *know* him whom they have believed and are persuaded of his ability to keep what they have committed unto him against that day, and as communities they share the experience. We need in each cultural unit a written word of God in the vernacular language, for public and private use (reading, hearing or memorizing). The gospel has to come through in indigenous rhythm and speak its message to the heart. For the man from the forest, the worship must have the capacity to vibrate with the beat of the drum. The arts and crafts of the group must be employed to absorb the energy, skills and dedication of the artists and craftsmen of the group, that their manual and mental competencies may be expressive of spirituality, and help the group to worship the Lord in what, to their eyes and ears, may be described as "the beauty of holiness," even though discordant or grotesque to the westerner. We need a meaningful faith which holds together the daily life within the cultural structures, however strange may seem their modes of tilling the soil and plowing the deep. The universal human problems — finding one's way in the darkness, comforting the bereaved, encouraging the discouraged, preserving the family, solving the personal disagreements — will all have their peculiar formations in any culture different from our own. No religion can be indigenous unless it comes to grips with these universal problems in their culture-bound forms. When the laughing and crying, the feasting and mourning, the instructing and singing are truly culturally patterned, then we are looking at indigenous Christianity — here the gospel is at work in an experience of incarnation. And this is a far cry from syncretism.

Communication is a two-way process. God may be omniscient, but I am not. He may speak to me, but I must hear and understand. The limitations in the process are with me. He is supracultural but I am culture-bound. Therefore, there must be an incarnation. The space about me is alive with vibrations and impulses of which I am completely ignorant. I touch a button on my TV and in a few moments these vibrations are transformed into sounds and pictures. They are immediately meaningful because the sounds are in my own language and the pictures are of things I recognize. The problem of communication is one of meaning. That is why if the gospel is to be meaningful in any given culture, it must be expressed and experienced in the forms of that culture. Syncretism is frequently due to what Barnett calls "the subliminal striving for meaning" (1953:117),[12] the meaning the convert ascribes to the new religion being an expansion only of his old frame of reference. The expansion may be one of two kinds. Either he will innovate with new (foreign) religious forms while retaining the old conceptual framework, or with the Christian gospel using meaningful cultural forms for expressing it. The former I have called syncretism, and the latter I am calling indigenous Christianity.

Now, lest you imagine that I have been unfair to Latin America in my exposure of its Christopaganism, let me give you an example of indigenous Christianity which I witnessed myself in the same part of the world. Juan lived in Mexico. This account comes from Guatemala, but the people in it are from another sub-group of the same great Maya tribe as Juan. I merely transcribe here a passage from my own field notes:

Somewhere about mid-day, after an hour of very dusty driving we arrived at the market town for the area, and after cleaning up we went down to the church. It was a long and commodious building with a narrow frontage on a cobblestone street, which led onto the plaza, where a hugh Catholic structure dominated the skyline. The street was alive with people with every kind of merchandise, with tables, carts and music, for the fiesta was in full swing. The evangelical church boasted an upper room and a back yard. The local women's group had prepared food in the yard and stood behind their pots and containers. Each visitor took a plate and passed along the line for a serving of tamales, tortillas and baked sweet bread. One concoction was said to be a culinary peculiarity to that locality alone — which made it a social talking-point. There was meat in the tamales and this was wrapped in banana leaves. All the members of the congregation were involved and we all ate together as a community.

After the meal we observed the Sunday school in session. I went to the adult men's class in the upper room, which was crammed to the door. I sat with the others on the floor and nobody seemed to notice I was a foreigner. The class was mostly illiterate, but the peasant teacher used the blackboard and demonstrated pictori-ally the story of Cornelius from Acts. The class participation was good, and sometimes the leader was asked to read a point from the Bible. The singing was hearty. The prayers were multi-individual — everyone talking to the Lord at once regardless of his neighbor.

Subsequently the groups went into church for the united worship service. The building was already full. I counted a sample of ten seats and figured there were about a thousand people present. Normally the congregation was about 300, but this was fiesta week and the country groups were in town. Special Christian services serve as a functional substitute for the old festival, the best values of which are preserved, the gathering at the market center, the joyful celebration, the fellowship that is wider than the town itself. The seating of the congregation reflected sex and age-grade groupings rather than regions. The presence of extended-families was apparent. Annually they change their officiating elders during fiesta week, as was done in their old pre-Christian priesthood.

The opening of the service was dramatic — guitars, bass, small organ and rattles. The singing was lively and in the vernacular. They borrowed Western artifacts but used them in their own way. They amplified the music and preaching in the street outside so that it mingled with the jingles of the market as a witness. The ceiling was decorated with streamers of all colors and the walls with epiphites, which must have required a lot of congregational preparation and participation. There was a table of vernacular literature at the door for any who could read.

The service was led by one of the elders, appointed by his colleagues for the day. He does not preach, but calls on one of the congregation. This reflected the local pattern of social organization. That day he happened to call on an old man, who not having the preaching skills of the young preachers, preferred to give his testimony. He had been the first convert in the locality, and narrated how the evangelical religion came to the district and how the church grew there. (After this there follows a description of how the pattern of leadership reflected the social structure.)

The meeting was now open for testimony and folk from the small rural groups shared their experiences. This made me aware of a widespread Christian movement in the area, and a people excited about what the Lord was doing in their midst. For the duration of the fiesta a different kind of church meeting was planned for each evening — praise and testimony one night, a baptismal service on another, appointment of officials and so on. Their turning away from the secular festival had left no cultural void here: their own program was a real functional substitute.

To me the most exciting episode of the worship service was the introduction of five men, who had determined to become evangelicals. They were already receiving Christian instruction, and would be baptized before the fiesta finished. I saw each of these men in turn hand over his personal fetish. To this week it had been a fearful and powerful thing. Now, before the congregation of people who had known him all his life, he "cast it from him" as a mere thing, a "not-god" as the prophet Isaiah might have said. One of these I noticed was an old Mezoamerican female figurine, an ancient fertility fetish — face, head and breasts — whose creator lived long before the Spanish had come.

The description goes on for four more pages, but I must leave it and make the point I wish to emphasize. Not at any point was there a foreigner in charge. Everything was done by the people in their own way. This differed from the ways I was myself familiar with, but I saw no one there who seemed to be bored or out of touch. The whole thing was obviously exciting and meaningful, intensely cultural and indigenous. It was as far removed from the faith formulations of Juan as it could possibly have been.

In my next chapter I shall probe more deeply into the dynamics of this kind of indigenous Christianity which I have set up as over against Christopaganism. Before you read that chapter you will have heard from each of my colleagues, who is quite free, of course, either to build on what I have suggested or to draw our discussions out into some other dimension he might wish to discuss.

Notes

1. This is one of the basic themes of the whole Bible. The People of God are to be the people of One God, who will not tolerate any polytheism or syncretism. In the revelation through Moses we have it in the first law of the Decalogue (Ex. 20:2-6) and again in the last long message of Moses to Israel, when he tells them to "go in and possess the land," he warns them to have no traffic with the idols or fertility cults of Canaan (Deut. 4:14-19; 5:6-9; 6:12-15; 13:29-30; etc.). For the prophets also, "I am the Lord thy God, there is none else, there is no God beside me" (Isa. 45:5, 22 &c.), and for failing to observe this warning there is judgment (Jer. 7:17-31).

In the New Testament church again the People of God are tempted, but as there is to be only one God, so there is to be only one way of access to him (John 14:6, Acts 4:12). Yet in the Corinthian church, for example, the congregation has to be told they cannot take both the cup of the Lord and the cup of devils (I Cor. 10:21) (See Tippett 1973:25-33). This is not the only warning against syncretism Paul gave to that congregation (see also Visser't Hooft, 1963:50-82).

2. The term *supracultural* in this sense comes from the linguistic ethnotheologians. The earlier form, supercultural (Smalley 1955:58-71), has been abandoned because of possible ambiguity. The recent writings of Charles H. Kraft (1973a:118-120) have distinguished between the cultural and supracultural.

"God," says Kraft, "is supracultural. He stands outside of culture, and is not bound by culture unless he chooses to be bound by it. Man, however, is immersed in culture and unable to escape his culture-boundness."

3. Ulfilas (c311-388) worked as a pastor and leader among the Visi-Goths, and for 33 years as Bishop of the Trans-Danubian Goths. His great achievement was the translation of the Bible for which purpose he had to create a written form of the language. According to Moeller (1893:32) this was "the foundation of the Christian civilization of the Goths, the foundation stone of German literature." Christianity had spread among the Goths through Christian prisoners captured from Cappadocia (Fisher 1945:92; Kidd 1922, 2:364-365). Ulfilas was familiar with Latin, Greek and Gothic, and served as a go-between. "He was completely one with the Goths," says the *Oxford Dictionary of the Christian Church* (Cross 1957), "both in language and sympathy." Many historians have been so concerned with his Arianism that they have failed to appreciate Ulfilas's methods and skill as a cross-cultural communicator. For further sources on Ulfilas see Ayer's *Source Book for Ancient Church History* (1952). (See also Wand, 1954:181-182.)

4. Work in this area is proceeding under the name of *ethnolinguistics*, in which the missionary is involved in biblical translation and interpretation, as Kraft points out, not in two, but three or four cultural frameworks. He says:

The Bible records God's revelation as it was perceived in Hebrew, Aramaic, and Greek language and culture. Our own perception of this revelation, however, is pervasively affected by our Euro-American culture. We translate and interpret the revelation into appropriate linguistic and cultural forms of still another culture (1973b:233).

He goes on to relate this to planting churches which are conceptually indigenous (p. 234).

5. Visser't Hooft's *No Other Name* (1963) has a whole chapter on the struggle of the New Testament church with syncretism. He deals with Antioch, Ephesus, Corinth, Rome, Samaria, Lystra, Athens, Colossae and Pergamos.

6. I believe the etymological derivation of the word takes us back to political events in early Crete where two parties coalesced *(sunkretizo)* thus giving birth to a noun meaning the union of opposites (two Cretan parties united against a third, forming a new unit, *sunkretismos);* hence "syncretism" as defined above.

7. These phrases are cited from the typescript draft of a manuscript now awaiting publication, from a chapter entitled "Tranformational Culture

Change," but Kraft has written elsewhere of conceptual transformation in language in missionary situations (1973b:237-247).

8. Latourette calls the period from 500 A.D. onwards "The Thousand Years of Uncertainty." I doubt if he really explores the cultural dynamics of the period. True, he allows for the "inward vitality" of expanding faiths, and he comes back to the "hidden springs of conduct" of the conquering faith with a self-protective sentence or two that this may

> carry us far beyond the domain to which the historian is supposed to be restricted. At the most he can only recognize the possible existence of realms into which the canons of his craft forbid him to venture (1966:14).

This fine historical study which ethnohistorians could have given further depth is incomplete. Men like Wallace and Barnett, who have pondered the dynamics of the innovative process and stress situations in historical reconstructions have improved our tools. My contention is that we should turn the information we have on the dynamics of contemporary religious movements and the diffusion of Christianity onto the documents of the middle ages, which so often have been interpreted in the light of the heresies or the politics of Graeco-Roman Christendom. I disagree that these "hidden springs of conduct" are "beyond the domain of the historian" and think that our missiological insights on modern people movements should be brought to bear on the experiences of Boniface and Patrick.

9. The linguist Edward Sapir who laid many of the foundations of ethnolinguistics demonstrated the cohesion of phonetic clusters. A single consonant — p, t or k — will resist change until the whole set p-t-k changes as one thing. He shows how the English series

| $p\ t\ k$ | $b\ d\ g$ | $f\ th\ h$ |

correspond point for point with the Sanskrit

| $b\ d\ g$ | $bh\ dh\ gh$ | $p\ t\ k$ |

The analogy serves to illustrate how cultural clusters survive in Christopaganism. The whole complex of faith and practice is a discrete unit, and has to be confronted as such in Christian education, with a Christian doctrine of creation and a worship pattern which expresses it for the convert.

10. Barnett points out that when the advocate (novelty introducer — evangelist in our case) or an observer conceptualizes acceptance (conversion) in terms of his own thought processes instead of those of the acceptor (or rejector), it can only lead to "confusion and artificiality" — the observer's fallacy (1953:339). On my recent trip to New Guinea I found many cases of native converts who had accepted Christianity because they thought that thereby they would acquire the prosperity and power of the white man whose religion it was. Now they are passing through a stage of disillusionment, as also are the missionaries who had assumed they understood the gospel.

11. Some attempt has been made recently by the African theologian, John S. Mbiti, to relate traditional and Christian eschatology (1969:159-184), but theologians have not yet had much exchange on the subject, which certainly bears on the issue of syncretism and indigenous Christianity.

12. Barnett says that this subliminal striving for meaning is "a central need of the ego system," and is drawn from an individual's "unconscious struggle to understand his universe in terms of what he already knows." As he configurates it he ascribes meaning only on a basis of "the frames of reference available to him, namely, those provided by his past experiences" (1953:117-118). This is why the follow-up of conversion requires a careful period of Christian instruction. Without this the convert ascribes meanings predetermined by his pagan preconceptions of what religion is.

CHAPTER TWO

The Biblical Base from Which Adjustments Are Made

DONALD A. MCGAVRAN

DR. Tippett's chapter breaks the subject open in a splendid way. He makes perfectly clear, first, that as the Christian religion spreads from one culture to another, it must correctly adjust to each; and second, that such adjustments have their limits. He has pointed out that incorrect adjustments are frequently made. Christopaganism frequently results. He has given some examples of appalling syncretism. All this raises questions such as the following. What adjustments are correctly made? What are illegitimate? Where does honoring the culture become dishonoring Christ? Where shall we draw the line? What is the base from which adjustments are made?

THE PURE FAITH

Dr. Tippett repeatedly speaks of a "a pure faith" and "an essential gospel." He believes that the goal is an "indigenous *Christianity.*" He assumes that what Christianity says in regard to life after death *ought* to have replaced the pagan concepts of the old Indian culture. He points out that prohibitions concerning mixing pagan religions with that revealed by God in the Old and New Testaments are "one of the basic themes of the Bible. The People of God are to be the people of One God who will not tolerate any polytheism or syncretism."

I presume that such a concept of the Christian faith is shared by my colleagues in this symposium. But if these chapters are to speak to the enormous confusion which marks our day in regard to Christianity and cultures, each of us will have to attempt a more definitive statement of what constitutes a pure faith, an essential gospel and "the uncontaminated core." I shall devote the first part of this chapter to carrying further what Dr. Tippett has begun so well and attempt to define more exactly what "the pure faith" is.

At the outset, let me point out that such a faith has underlain Christianity down through the ages. Each church has formed a clear concept of what that faith is, and has defended it against all comers. Indeed, some concept of what "the faith once for all delivered" (Jude 3) has generally been a chief cause for the expansion of the Church on new ground. Men turn from old faiths to new faiths because of what they conceive the new faith to be. Their first understandings of what Christianity means are often biblically inadequate, but nevertheless powerfully convincing to those becoming Christian. If the first formulations affirm belief in the Bible as God's Word, the only sacred Book, then the new church gradually is taught all things whatsoever Christ has commanded. The Bible brings the church to sounder and sounder formulations of the faith.

Who Determines Pure Faith?

The ultimate authority which determines the pure faith (which I shall also call "the core" and "essential Christianity") has been conceived in three main ways.

(1) For Roman Catholics, *the Church* has been ultimate authority. It rested on tradition and the inspired and inerrant Bible, which included the apocryphal books, interpreted by the hierarchy and voiced ultimately by the Pope in council.

(2) For Protestants, the ultimate authority has theoretically been the Bible alone, the canonical books, but practically — since the Bible is a very extensive record from which many things can be proved — the ultimate authority has been the Bible plus the great creeds, plus the practices of each empirical fathering church. By "church" I mean an association of like-minded

congregations. These usually constitute themselves into a denomination — sometimes large and impressive, sometimes small and weak. As through missions or directly, empirical churches establish congregations, they tend to rule that the faith once for all delivered to the saints includes essential biblical Christianity as formulated by their written or unwritten creeds, plus those of their practices which can readily be carried over into the daughter congregations. It is at this last point that missiological error occurs.

(3) Some Christians today (both Roman Catholic and Protestant, both Latfricasians and Euricans),[1] seeking to free Christianity from all "western cultural accretions," advocate that the ultimate authority which determines the essential core of the faith is neither the Pope nor the Bible but the direct experience of "Christ". Provided *that* is there, they seem to say, Christian faith is there and must be encouraged to clothe itself in cultural forms natural to its adherents. Christ can operate in any culture. Christ within will express himself in culturally relevant ways. We ought not tell new converts what to do. We should trust that the indwelling Christ, with or without the Bible, will lead new Christians into all truth. Furthermore, Christ may use some element of their culture to reveal new truth, not in the Bible, but particularly needed by them. To me, this position is unacceptable. It dismisses God's revelation which comes to us in and through the Bible, and depends entirely too heavily on "inner light" and human reason.

I shall maintain that the faith once for all delivered to the saints, for which Christians must contend, is to be known strictly from the Bible. I hold that all later understandings and formulations, such as the great creeds, while useful, are not inspired documents. They should be learned by leaders of new churches, for each creed is based on thorough study of the Bible and speaks to the universal human condition though voiced in the culture of one particular period and people.

I shall affirm that the practices of the fathering church or mission should be used, or *not* used, according to circumstances. Frequently such practices are both biblical and practical. Then they ought to be used. Sometimes they are heavily characteristic of the alien culture of a distant church and impractical — then they should be discarded. Wearing shoes into village churches in India is a case in point.

Granted that difficulties dog the steps of anyone who tries to describe accurately the pure faith, the task must nevertheless be undertaken.

The Bible Affirms the Pure Faith

Such a faith is clearly recognized by the New Testament. The Epistle to Jude says: "I found it necessary to write appealing to you to contend for the faith once for all delivered to the saints" (Jude 3 RSV). The Apostle Paul declared, "I delivered to you as of the first importance that which I also received" (I Corinthians 15:3). The New Testament frequently refers to "faithful words" worthy of all acceptance. These carried the essential gospel. As men placed their faith on Jesus, were baptized and formed into Christian churches, they were known as "followers of the Way" and became different from other men. They believed a common gospel and were stamped with a common stamp and indwelt by the same Holy Spirit. The faith once for all delivered was inextricably bound up with Jesus Christ, both the historical Jesus and the Christ of experience. It was He who proclaimed "I am the Way, the Truth and the Life, no man comes to the Father but by me" (John 14:6). In like vein, the first Epistle of John declared "He who has the Son has life, and he who has not the Son of God has not life" (5:11, 12). The Logos who was in the beginning with God, through whom everything was made that has been made, "became flesh and dwelt among us . . . the law was given through Moses, but grace and truth came through Jesus Christ" (John 1:14, 17). Paul writes that all men of all tribes and cultures have sinned. God put forth Jesus Christ as propitiation for sin, and forgiveness is available only through faith in him.

God Has Revealed the Pure Faith

This faith once for all delivered, this pure gospel, this source of grace and truth is known only through the words revealed by God, written by inspired men and recorded in the canonical books of the Bible. This pure gospel was not perceived by men so much as it was revealed by God. Men guided by the light of reason alone did not calculate that a crucified Lord who bore our sins would be a rather convincing Savior and consequently perceive and proclaim God's love in the cross. No! God himself put Jesus Christ forward as a propitiation for our sins. God "spoke through" the authors of the New Testament those wonderful words — which could never have been conceived in any human culture. God commanded Christians to proclaim them to all men and persuade as many as possible to put their faith in Jesus Christ.

I am emphasizing the point that "the pure faith and essential gospel" Dr. Tippett has mentioned and we all take for granted was *made known by God*. The missionary does not take his own culture-bound invention to other lands. He is an ambassador taking the message of the King. That is its overwhelming importance. It is *God's* message.

Someone has said that the word "God" should be banned from intelligent discourse, because today it has come to mean so many different things. The word "God" is an expletive, a process, the ground of being, the personification of a value system, a cunning invention to control the masses, an impersonal force, an unknowable prime mover *and* the God who chose to reveal himself in and through the Bible. I use the word "God" to mean exclusively the Triune God, the only God there is, who created the vast and enormously complex universes without us and within us, God who speaks and acts throughout the Bible, God as he manifested himself to men in the historical Jesus and continues to manifest himself in the Christ of experience.

Man Sent to Discover Some Things

I have been emphasizing that God *revealed* the faith once for all delivered. Man did not invent, discover or perceive it. To be sure, man can discover some kinds of truth. Man is, in fact, the great discoverer. God made him that way and purposed for him to discover much truth. God gave him "dominion over all the earth" (Genesis 1:26) — dominion over a real world. What we see about us is not *maya jal* or illusion, but a real world about which the truth can be discovered. For example, the development of human knowledge limped along for tens of thousands of years without an effective way to record and transmit discovered truth, until about four thousand years ago in the turquoise mines of the Sinai peninsula men discovered that written marks could be used for sounds. Suddenly an alphabet was born. From that one alphabet all the alphabets on earth have gradually been fashioned. Few discoveries have been of greater moment and none are basically more simple. One sound can be represented by one written symbol! Man is a great discoverer.

In the world of sense, it appears that God *sent* man to discover. There in the world of sense, man discovered factual truth. God may indeed have said, "In the world of sense, I shall not reveal. You, my creatures, are sent to find out." In the world of ultimate questions, however, God apparently has said, "Here, you are incapable of discovering ultimate truth. Even when I disclose it to you, in your wickedness you stifle the truth, you refuse to honor me, and hence all your thinking has ended in futility (Romans 1:18-21). I speak to you wherever you are, but your mortality, transiency and fallen nature are such that despite my efforts, you misunderstand me. You speculate, but your religious thinking, together with a little that is sublime, contains much that is foolish, and some that is gross. So I shall progressively *reveal* truth to a chosen race and culminate my revelation in One Sinless Incarnation who will usher in a new age."

Christians are well aware that unbelievers find it incredible that God (who created the innumerable galaxies of the universe and, no doubt, other universes besides this and who formed man in his own image and endowed him with tremendous powers of thought and self consciousness) should have made his definitive revelation to a tiny tribe in an inconsiderable country through a peasant carpenter. Christians agree that this is very strange, but believe that that is exactly what happened. They are willing to bet their lives on it. That is what makes them Christians.

I have taken time to develop this point, because as Christianity spreads from culture to culture, where we draw the line depends very greatly on whether what I have said truly portrays the nature of the pure essence of the gospel. I have been maintaining that the essential faith is something *given*, revealed, locked up in the Bible, not to be discerned outside the Bible, inextricably bound up with *Jesus Christ according to the Scriptures*.

We must, of course, state this truth accurately. I, therefore, explain what it does not mean and then what it does. The faith once for all delivered is not exactly my faith or your faith. It is not a systematic theology, not an organization, not a man-made creed, not the way my church does it or your church does it. Rather, it is that central essential revelation of God's nature and of his will for man which impregnates every one of the 66 canonical books and streams from the risen and reigning Lord, who acts in ways in harmony with those so faithfully recorded in the Bible.

The Core of the Pure Faith Defined

This essential core of the Christian religion is broadly and briefly definable. Anything which damages this core is forbidden syncretism. Anything which leaves this core intact is permissible adjustment. To be sure, different churches will draw the lines in slightly different places, but the outlines of the faith once for all delivered to the saints will be clearly visible. As each denomination draws its fine line, the multitude of fine lines will together make one wide line clearly identifying the pure faith. I now attempt a very brief definition of this, trusting that my readers will not rush off to sharpen sectarian scalpels, but will themselves *frame brief definitions*. As they do so, I am confident that their pictures will reinforce mine.

(1) The core of the Christian religion is belief in and allegiance to the Triune God only. Christians cannot worship God and mammon, or God and Baal. "You shall have no other gods before me." "There is no other name . . . given among men by which we must be saved" (Acts 4:12).

(2) The core of the Christian religion is belief in the Bible as the only inspired Word of God, the infallible rule of faith and practice. The only certain knowledge which man has of the Triune God is that which he has chosen to reveal in the Bible and in Jesus Christ according to the Scriptures.

(3) The core of the Christian religion consists of those great central facts, commands, ordinances and doctrines which are so

clearly set forth in the Bible. Provided this three-fold core is faithfully communicated and *honored*, almost any custom, belief, symbol or configuration can be adopted into Christian worship, conduct and daily life.

Furthermore, if a church faithfully transmits the first two parts of the core, a degree of elasticity in regard to part 3 can be tolerated. Great elasticity in regard to part 3 cannot be tolerated. No change in a central fact, ordinance or doctrine is acceptable which negates or damages points 1 and 2. However, even substantial changes in doctrines, made *in accordance with the biblical revelation, Christ's teaching and the guidance of the Holy Spirit*, have historically been acceptable. For example, the Friends' Church — on the ground that the Bible's clear teaching emphasizes inward not outward things — observes neither the Lord's Supper nor baptism. Most other churches feel that the Friends are mistaken in their conviction, but (seeing their unqualified acceptance of Jeus Christ as God and Savior and of the Bible as the authoritative inspired rule of faith and practice) count them as validly Christian. Indeed, provided a church is sound on points 1 and 2, the common practice in the latter half of the twentieth century among most churches is to rate it as validly Christian. The degree of elasticity permitted in forming the great central doctrines varies from denomination to denomination. Some allow a great deal. Some allow very little.

I hold rather precise doctrinal beliefs. I subscribe to the Fuller Seminary statement of faith — and hold it without mental reservation or evasive inner interpretation which says the words but means something else. I commend it. I am confident that the doctrines it sets forth express the clear teaching of the Bible. They are parts of the core of biblical truth, to alter which in order to agree with some other system is unacceptable syncretism. Nevertheless should any church make changes in some of these doctrines — in my statement of faith — and make them *in order to be truer to the Bible and more loyal to the Lord*, I might call the changes mistakes ; I would not call them syncretism.

THREE FAMOUS ADJUSTMENTS

With the biblical foundations of "the faith once for all delivered to the saints" beginning to come into view, let us observe what adjusting it to cultures has meant in the life of the Church or her missions. I shall present three illustrations, the first from the modern Eurican world. I choose it because the process of making adjustments is substantially the same in every continent and every age. Ethnotheology is constantly being formulated in all cultures, in all *ethne*. When it is correctly formulated, the church accepts it as valid. When incorrectly, the church rejects that ethnotheology as heresy. We err when we describe adjustments solely as they take place among animists or polytheists. God has made of one blood all *ethne* who dwell on the face of the earth, so that what the church ought to do in regard to Eurican cultures will be normative for her as she turns to cultures across the seas. Something very like that is what churches ought to do in Latfricasia.

Secularism

For illustration one, I use an adjustment which Christianity is currently making to the secular culture, about which everyone in this room has perforce thought deeply. The greatest adjustments which Christianity is making today are to contemporary cultures and philosophies in Eurica, not to those of Stone Age tribes in Irian. Avalanches of scientific facts, unparalleled development of historical and critical thinking, vast new discoveries concerning the age of the solar system, staggering implications of the atomic furnaces which fuel the stars, the awesome power of gravity which may produce "black holes," and the tremendous increase of knowledge about the thousands of ingenious and sensible manners of life which men have fashioned to fit the various environments and circumstances in which they have had to live — all these and many more have created the secular cultures of contemporary man. Secular, self-sufficient man believes that he has come of age and outgrown the notion of a Creator. He confidently proclaims that there is no God "out there." No god exists other than the rather remarkable process by which inanimate matter has become conscious of itself and of the universe about it which wheels through vast spaces quite oblivious of the speck which is human consciousness.

This modern culture, which I am sketching so hastily and inadequately, has many facets. One, it gives birth to a conviction that life is meaningless. This is well described by Camus. He believes that life, though utterly absurd, must be lived with style and faced with courage. Another facet is the way the media steadily portray all new discoveries of science as if they happened by themselves. The media never suggest, for example, that *God* created man on planet earth and may have created millions of other earths with millions of other races of beings made in the image of God to praise and glorify their Creator.

Another facet is that some philosopher-theologians believe a radically new form of Christianity must be created. Traditional Christianity (creed, cultus, organization and customs) is outworn. Since such philosopher-theologians believe the personal God revealed in the Bible is utterly incredible to contemporary men, the new form they propose is substantially humanism. Paul Tillich, John T. Robinson, the authors of the ''God is Dead'' way of thought, and many more are well-intentioned men trying to adjust Christianity to twentieth century culture. Their followers defend them on the ground that Christianity must adjust to each culture it enters and must be made credible to the men of that culture. If it be objected that this involves radically changing Christianity, they reply that it is better to change Christianity so that the old forms continue on filled with new meaning, than to have men gradually turn from Christianity to other religions and ideologies.

That the adjustments I refer to sound reasonable to many modern Christians and fit the humanistic mood of contemporary man is beyond debate. Tillich is quoted with approval in ten thousand pulpits weekly — though his adjustment is less and less convincing to Christians. *Honest to God* has sold hundreds of thousands of copies and been translated into many languages. Those adjustments to contemporary Eurican culture — those ethnotheologies — were devised by Christians to commend Christianity to today's secularists and to our American Christopagan peers. Whether they actually do so is another matter.

If this skillfully wrought tissue of thought — this adjustment to culture — imperils the faith which God has once for all delivered, it has gone too far; it is syncretism. It should be rejected by intelligent Christians on the grounds that instead of revelation judging culture, in such adjustments the culture has weighed revelation, found it wanting and moulded it into a syncretistic form agreeable to modern man.

When, in adjusting to culture, Christianity becomes unlike itself, takes on the color and genius of another religion and loses its soul, then its power to save is destroyed. Perhaps it does not even attract others. If it attracts them, they belong to its churches but do not meet Christ and are not transformed. When the Roman Catholic Church calls the great industrial areas of France "mission territories," it is saying that in them, while infants are still baptized in Catholic churches and grow up counting themselves in a vague way Catholic, the bulk of the population has really ceased to be Christian. Large sections of Protestant countries are in a similar position. Christianity in such cases has become a culture religion. It has become so closely identified with the culture, it has adjusted so largely and uncritically to the culture, that it has ceased to exist as powerful transforming religion. Culture churches on occasion repeat the words of the Bible like "If anyone is in Christ, he is a new creation" (II Corinthians 5:17 RSV), but the reality of *being* a new creation is unknown to them.

Churches on new ground and on old ground must adjust to cultures, but neither uncritically nor stupidly. Christianity must remain itself. In Eurica today, the pure faith must not be contaminated by secularism. It must speak to secularists, yes. It must use their language and thought forms, yes. It must seek their company and converse with them, yes. It must appreciate the good it finds secularists doing, yes. But it must not become secularism or humanism. Secularism Christianity must reject, for that whole system is built on the conviction that God does not exist or at least does not matter and that the Bible and other god-talk are strictly irrelevant to the good life.

The Bible says it tersely. Christians are to be *in but not of* the world. Missiology must emphasize both parts of that beautiful sentence. Christians *are to be in* each culture of the world. That is important. Christians are *not to be of* any culture in the world. That also is most important.

Under some circumstances missiology should emphasize adjusting to cultures, estimating them highly, avoiding an arrogant ethnocentric posture to the effect that our culture, just because it is ours, is better than your culture. In these circumstances, missiology rightly stresses that missionaries should learn languages thoroughly, identify with the people to whom they go and help converts continue all their good cultural practices.

Under other circumstances, however, when the Christian faith is being so changed by adjustments that it ceases to be Christian, ceases to bring men to a personal knowledge of Jesus Christ, ceases to believe in biblical truth, loses contact with the living God and begins to live life as if there were no revelation in the Bible, missiology must emphasize preserving the faith once for all delivered to the saints. Missiology must make sure that as Christianity spreads from culture to culture, it is "the pure gospel" which is believed and transmitted, and the inspired authoritative Word of God written, which is given and received.

Deism

For illustration two, I turn back a couple of centuries to the deistic culture which swept Europe and America after the discovery of the unchangeable laws which seemed to govern all of life. Mathematics, physics, chemistry, geology and astronomy, all were shown to be ruled by immutable laws. Knowing these laws gave man more control over nature than any amount of prayer or incantation. As it spread, deistic culture did not ban God, it simply assigned to him the role of a far-off original Maker of the Laws. Laws, not God, were seen to govern the universe and everything in it. Any intervention in the closed nexus of law was unthinkable. God never intervened. At most, he might use a law heretofore not discovered by man to achieve his purpose. Miracles were impossible. Prayer was meditation. Its good effects resulted from changes it produced within the men who prayed, not in any action of a personal God outside the process.

This in barest outline was deistic culture. This symposium knows that Christianity ought to adjust to each culture in which it finds itself. Let us see how it ought to have adjusted to deistic culture. According to the Bible, God made this universe. The laws he used in creation were conceived by him. When God said, "Let there be light" (Genesis 1:3), only a wooden literalism would hold that he pronounced these four English words and in somewhat less than two seconds of time, light burst forth. A more reasonable view of the Bible is that those four words tell us that God created light. The processes by which he wrought the creation may well have taken aeons of time. Recent discoveries as to the way in which God gave our sun and other suns nuclear fuel, which burns for billions of years and thus made light and heat, add to our reverent understanding of his glory and wisdom. Furthermore, the rule of law has enabled men to control nature, rivers, diseases, fertility, heat and cold, and thus add immeasurably to the welfare of men. Since God desires the welfare of men, a culture which emphasizes the means for enhancing human welfare is certainly in the will of God. Christians consequently rejoice in such control and teach God's laws in churches and schools. Deistic culture has much truth and goodness in it, and Christianity ought to incorporate many of its components into itself.

However, this symposium also knows that adjustment can go too far. Whenever adjustment imperils the essence of the faith, syncretism has taken place. Whenever Christians, counting culture of higher value than revelation, cloud the clear teaching of the Bible concerning the nature of God and his will for man and thus adulterate the pure biblical faith, the process of adjustment has gone too far.

As we apply this principle to the intercourse of Christianity with deistic Eurican culture during the last two centuries, we see that some segments of the church made such large adjustments to it that, among their members, they all but destroyed "the faith once for all delivered to the saints." Their Christians grew cold in the grip of iron law. Among them, the vivid experience of meeting the living God occurred rarely. The icy impersonalism of deism emptied their churches. They scorned evangelism. Ethics and law replaced a bubbling joy in the Lord. Prayer seemed futile — they really believed that there was no one out there to hear. All these adjustments to the deistic culture were syncretisms. Under the guise of adjusting Christianity to a rational culture, theologians and leaders of these segments of the church gave birth to a new syncretistic religion. They still called it Christianity. It used the old familiar words. It met in church houses and listened to robed choirs. It sang hymns and employed ministers trained in seminaries which devoted themselves to hastening the adjustment to deistic culture. It looked very like Christianity — but it radically disbelieved the Bible, had little faith in the resurrection of our Lord and had little power. It converted few sinners. In America, it maintained itself by proselytizing out of the orthodox churches Christians whose faith had grown cold. It emphasized ethics — partly because righteousness was the one component of the pure faith in which it yet believed, and partly because, having lost the vertical dimension, it had to compensate by stressing the horizontal. Missiologists do not have to go abroad to observe the tragic futility of syncretism.

We should note that these major wrong adjustments to deistic culture did not have to take place. They could have been avoided. Many segments of the church did avoid them. It is clear to all thinking men that as far as the rule of law is concerned, God made the laws and is not bound by them save as he wills to be bound. God is not a helpless prisoner of the universe he has made. If puny man can so manipulate law as to hurl rockets weighing hundreds of tons clear of global gravity, God the Father Almighty, Maker of Heaven and Earth, can easily find ways to do anything he wants. If a mortal man by the power of his thought alone can set his ten pounds of blood pounding in his veins, surely the Great Thinker can cause all sorts of changes in inert matter, and even more easily in thinking willing men.

The arguments from reason, just tendered, are not the Christian's strongest. His strongest arguments are from revelation. God's revelation assures him that God has given him dominion over all the earth and directs him to get wisdom to enable him to rule well. The Bible also assures the Christian that the earth is the Lord's, the whole universe holds together in Christ, not a sparrow falls to the ground without the Father's will, and God hears and answers prayer. Missiologists adjusting Christianity to a culture dominated by the rule of law must leave such biblical faith intact.

That the biblical faith, when presented to unbelievers in the culture, seem credible is important, but not most important. The task of the Christian *is* to make his faith seem reasonable to men, but more important than making it seem reasonable, is that he present it *faithfully*. He must always be sure that — like his Lord — he says only that which God gives him to say. He must not tamper with the revelation. Even the new light which God gives him from time to time through the Word, must be brought into harmony with the Light which entered the world in Jesus Christ and lies enshrined in the Bible.

In making adjustments to fit different cultures, to be particularly avoided as essentially evil is the process by which old sacred words are filled with radically different meanings and used without making it clear that their content has been thoroughly changed. When one speaks of "prayer" and means meditation, or speaks of the "atonement" and means what man does for himself, or talks about "revelation" but means what man has discovered by his unaided reason, then hypocrisy and dishonesty are abroad in the land. Some cynical Christians announce that they practice "morphological fundamentalism." By this, they mean that they use the old forms, the dear words which time and usage have made sacred and powerful, but use them with radically new meanings. In effect, they perpetrate a pious fraud on the church and defend it on the ground that Christianity must always adjust to culture. New knowledge must indeed be added to the golden store of wisdom, and truth must be expressed in meaningful current terms, but it must be *truth* which is expressed. Plain honesty demands either that new words be employed to convey new meanings, or that the changed meanings of the old words be called sharply to the attention.

Arianism

My third illustration of the way in which Christians should and should not make adjustments to culture goes back to the third and fourth centuries A.D. As Christianity spread around the Mediterranean, it encountered many cultures, many philosophies and many religions in which incarnations, saviors and god-men of various sorts were worshipped. Garbe believes that Mahayana Buddhism, teaching many reincarnations of the Buddha, was well-known around the Mediterranean (1959:71,

78). If one realizes that the Greek word *gnosis* would inevitably be used for the Sanskrit *buddhi* and Buddhism would necessarily portray itself as a gnosticism, Garbe's belief seems reasonable. Indeed, gnosticism may be the form in which Buddhism appeared when it spread into the West. There are some remarkable parallels. Be that as it may, the cultures of that day (except for the growing Christian culture) were generally friendly to the idea of incarnations and saviors and salvific rites and ceremonies. Saviors were conceived as emanations of the One, the Supreme, the Monad, the Unknowable. A characteristic feature of gnosticism was that of the Primal Man, who existed before the world, a prophet who went through the world in various forms and finally revealed himself in Christ and other saviors. Manicheism also taught that the God of Light begot the Primal Man and sent him to fight against Satan — Primal Man in the character of Christ disseminated the true *gnosis.* But none of the gnostics would have claimed that the saviors they knew were God, the One, the Absolute, or were of one substance with the Absolute.

In the Mediterranean culture I have been describing, the presbyter-theologian Arius about A.D. 320 was trying to explain the doctrine of the Trinity in a gnostic or neoplatonic way in order to preserve the uniqueness of God the Father. Arius taught that Christ was created by God the Father and was less than God, though higher than man. Arius was describing the relationship between the Father, the Son and the Holy Spirit (all clearly taught in the apostolic writings) and describing it in an intellectual climate shot through and through with ideas of saving emanations, who were created by and were less than God. In short, Arius was formulating an ethnotheology, or adjusting Christian theology to contemporary gnostic culture. Jesus Christ, he felt, could be best understood were he to be seen as created by God. Arius did not want to ask men to believe that Jesus Christ was One with the Father — an idea alien to gnostic culture and difficult for men of that century to conceive. While by 325 (the date of the Council of Nicea) the battle against gnosticism was being won, gnostic ideas were still common coin. They appeared reasonable to men both within and without the church. Floyd Filson, the New Testament scholar says,

The ancient world was a ferment of competing philosophies and religions. Denunciations of false teachers in the New Testament show that not every Christian teacher avoided the danger of surrendering to the world something essential (1973:707).

So Arius taught that Christ was not God. Some passages in the New Testament, taken by themselves, supported his position and he and his many followers leaned heavily on them.

The Arian accommodation to the culture of the early fourth century had two fatal weaknesses. First, it allowed for the existence of other emanations. Perhaps the Arian preacher did not advertise these. We may hope that he advocated Christ. But by teaching that Jesus Christ was created by God, he opened the door to the thought that God had created other Primal Men, prophets, teachers and saviors. The Arian formulation permitted doctrines to arise which flatly contradicted the pure faith. Second, Arius brushed aside and explained away the many passages of the Bible which imply the trinitarian faith. The Bible does not clearly set forth trinitarian doctrine, but many passages lead straight in that direction. They cannot be understood save on the hypothesis of God the Father, God the Son, and God the Holy Spirit, all uncreated, all existing from before time and all constituting one God. Stated in any language, adjusted to any culture, these biblical affirmations must come through.

As the Arian adjustment to gnostic culture spread and flourished, many orthodox leaders of the church believed that a vital part of the biblical evidence was being suppressed, the pure faith was being altered, syncretism was occurring. The apostolic faith was being displaced and adulterated by the non-Christian culture. These leaders gathered to draw the line, to state in contemporary terms (which were also true to the teaching of the apostles in the canonical books of the New Testament) the faith once for all delivered to the saints. They took with utmost seriousness both the passages which affirm the humanity of Jesus Christ and those which affirm his deity. The issue was a most important one. It concerned the very center of the faith. It also concerned the authority of the Bible. Was John's prologue, for example, just an awkward passage voiced in an earlier Greek culture which had little meaning for men in the fourth century?

Or was it an integral part of what God had revealed? Would the prologue stand for all time? The Council deliberated at length and finally pronounced Arius' adjustment — his ethnotheology — a heresy. The Nicene creedal statement ends with these plain words:

> As for those who assert that there was a time when He was not, and that before He was begotten He was not, and that He was made out of nothing, or that He is of a different substance or essence, or that the Son of God is created, changeable, mutable — these men the universal Church declares anathema (Musurillo 1962:598).

Sound Christology, adjusting to any culture whatever, must satisfy all the biblical data — not just some of them, not just those which state the Lord's humanity. Every low Christology falters at this point. It can appear reasonable only if it warps or by-passes those passages which speak so clearly of Christ's divinity and tie the Holy Spirit so closely to him and to the Father.

It is worth noting that the same church which pronounced anathema on Arius' adjustment to the dangerous gnostic culture, instructed the missionary Boniface in discipling the German tribes to allow or rather to engineer many minor syncretistic adjustments to their weak and disappearing former pagan faith. Of these the most famous is the celebration of the winter solstice as the birthday of the Lord and the use of a tree sacred in the pagan faith as part of the festivities. I am preparing this chapter during the Christmas season and I must confess that I am grateful for this bit of ethnotheology, for the instructions which the Pope sent to missionary Boniface.

CONTRASTS BETWEEN DR. TIPPETT'S ILLUSTRATIONS AND MINE

Dr. Tippett chose his illustrations of faulty adjustments exclusively from one rather narrow segment of churchly experience. I have chosen mine from a much wider segment lying at the opposite pole. Four contrasts thus afforded will help us see the real issues involved in our subject.

First, the faulty adjustments he cited could easily have been prevented by the Roman Catholic Church in Latin America. It was wealthy, powerful and in full control of the situation. At its top levels, it would certainly have judged then (as it judges now) that these adjustments were erroneous. The resulting religion was not Roman Catholic Christianity. Faulty adjustments were allowed, however, partly through inertia, but mostly through a race pride which despised the ignorant Indians and permitted them to do whatever was culturally agreeable to them as long as they paid token respect to the church. One might almost say that sensitiveness to tribal beliefs and reluctance to replace them created the Christopaganism which Dr. Tippett and other missiologists today find appalling.

The faulty adjustments to secularism, deism and gnosticism I have presented could not have been prevented by the churches concerned. No one church was in charge. The adjustments rose within the churches and were only gradually recognized as wrong. At first they appeared to be merely restatements of Christian faith in the thought forms of the dominant culture. It was argued that they would benefit Christianity, indeed, that they alone would enable it to survive. Only gradually did it become clear that they distorted or denied the clear teaching of our Lord and his apostles as recorded in the canonical books.

Second, the erroneous accommodations Dr. Tippett describes were made by the conquered Indian tribesmen — depressed and illiterate men, who knew very little of Christianity and nothing of the Bible. Those I have set forth were made by highly educated men, most of them ordained ministers, who knew the Christian system thoroughly well.

Third, in the Indian populations of Latin America, faulty adjustment was caused by criminal neglect on the part of a wealthy powerful church, which did not approve of Christopaganism but winked at it. In the Eurican populations of the last two hundred years, by way of contrast, faulty adjustments were caused by intelligent Christians and the churches they controlled consciously adjusting to culture and consciously slighting portions of Scripture which were inconvenient to their purposes.

Fourth, Dr. Tippett was portraying the adjustment-syncretism axis of dominantly non-Christian countries. I have been portraying it in dominantly Christian lands, believing that the principles of correct adjustment are the same everywhere. Ethnotheology is being framed in Eurica just as much if not more than in Latfricasia. Each *ethnos* in which the church forms requires a statement of biblical truth in its thought forms and idioms. When we think of adjustment solely in terms of tribal peoples, often the victims of Eurican imperialism, we confuse the issue. We rush to champion the oppressed. The Eurican guilt complex deprives us of good judgment. We emotionally declare everything Eurican no better than everything tribal. As a result, the question to which we address ourselves soon becomes: Should Euricans oppress Latfricasians?

This is scarcely the subject of the Carter Symposium! The question facing us is: Granted that Christianity should adjust to each culture from which men become Christians, when does legitimate adjustment become illegitimate syncretism? I have turned our attention away from victims of Eurican exploitation, away from tribal populations, so that we can see the real question. I trust that this change of direction has enriched our understanding of the vast and intricate subject before us.

CONCLUSION

In this chapter I have not been engaging in a theological digression. The subject is inescapably theological. The right questions must be theological and the right answers must be theological. Christians being who they are and the Bible being what it is, the Carter Symposium must be built upon theological and biblical considerations.

From among the many emphases let me, in conclusion, call attention to four of great importance. First, Christianity necessarily adjusts to cultures. Such adjustment goes on ceaselessly in every age and at every level. The revelation God has given us in the Bible is a progressive revelation culminating in his Son, our Savior. The living church, constantly meeting new conditions, lives in a constant tension between the biblical given and the changing culture.

Second, erroneous adjustments are easy to make. The men who make them are fallible. The problems they face are complex. The church lives in the midst of ambiguities. Good

Christians differ in regard to what the revelation is. Sin within effectively misleads us. As a result, Christian leaders often make grave errors in adjusting to cultures, jeopardize the health and welfare of the church and become what Jude calls "enemies of religion" (v. 4 NEB).

Third, these errors arise mainly from failing to take all the biblical data seriously. The Bible, we believe, contains all that is necessary for our guidance, but the *whole* Bible must be our guide. The apostolic faith is built on the total witness of the whole Bible, considered as a unity, each part contributing to the one revelation given by God which is the Christian faith.

Fourth, that the right formulation of any adjustment to culture will be in harmony with all the biblical evidence as well as be couched in terms understandable by men in that culture. The right formulation does not have to be pleasing to that culture, but it does have to be understandable. The exclusiveness of the Nicene position, for example, must have been highly displeasing to gnostic culture, but it was beautifully clear.

Note:

1. Latfricasia: *Lat*in America, *A*frica and *Asia*; Eurica: *Eur*ope and North Ame*rica*. Readers will kindly forgive the inconvenience caused by these contractions. When it is necessary as in this chapter, to refer repeatedly to these areas, much time is saved by the contractions.

CHAPTER THREE

A Perspective on Indonesia

J.C. HOEKENDIJK

OBVIOUSLY, *Indonesians* should speak about this theme. The western, middleclass, male, missionary syndrome is a thing of the past. The only excuse I have for my anachronistic transgression into somebody else's territory is the following combination of facts:

I was born in Indonesia of missionary parents and grew up there; studied in a missionary training institute preparing for service in my mother-country; *hominum confusione et Dei providentia* "because of the confusion of humankind (wars, etc.) and the providence of God," I have only been able to serve in various short-term ministries in Indonesia.

So I do not pretend to be an expert. In the true sense of the word, I consider myself to be an amateur.

INTRODUCTION

(1) Pick up a book, any good book, on Indonesia and you will very soon come across words like "complexity", "diversity", "unpredictability" (Cooley 1968:9ff; Neill 1973). To be sure, the national motto now reads, "Diversity Becoming Unity" *(Bhinneka Tunggal Ika)*. Gratefully admitting a growing awareness of common nationhood ("Indonesianhood"), in various places this slogan seems to be an ideological program or a mythical dream, rather than a statement of a sociopolitical fact.

(2) The official *lingua franca (bahasa Indonesia)* has, without doubt, been a unifying factor. But the regional vernaculars (the

number varies in estimates between 150 and 250, without counting dialects) are by no means dead. They seem to be very much alive in "ethnic churches" (Cooley 1968:50).

(3) For more than a century cultural anthropologists have used the term Indonesia (Indian islands) for good reasons: "10,000 islands, 3000 of them inhabited, 5 among the largest in the world." Along with isolated, "ethnocentric" groups, Indonesia is made up of merchants who took part in the international Asian trade, mainly concerned with the powers that rule the waves (thalassocracy).

(4) By population Indonesia is the fifth nation; by area, the sixth nation of the world. Demographic statistics are not always reliable. A minimum guess suggests 120 million people; the figure is expected to double in the next 20 years.

(5) Not only the magnitude of Indonesia is staggering. The depth of Indonesia's history (pre-, proto-, recorded) is very impressive indeed. Found there are relics of primal man (500,000 B.C.?); survivals of Veddoid folk; immigrants from the Asian heartland (China?) via Vietnam (Dongson culture, 8th century B.C. to first century A.D.); the "Proto-Malays" (Altvoelker, who still count for about 10% of the present population?); followed by the "Deutero-Malays" (Jungvoelker). Ancient contacts with Africa are hypothesized, and the Malagasy peoples and languages are, several of them, clearly from Indonesia. This is an eldorado for archeologists.

(6) In recorded history we hear about Chinese monks who came to Indonesia for their post-graduate studies in Buddhism, long before the Christian faith had made any significant impact on northwestern Europe; infiltration and later occupation by Indian powers ("the Indian period"); about the expansion of Islam, now the dominant religion; about the conquistadores of Spain and especially of Portugal, who brought their missionaries, about 200 in a time span of 80 years (among them Xavier, "one of the greatest missionaries in the whole history of the church" (Neill 1964:148). These were followed by the Dutch, at first in the style of "theocratic mercantilism" of a trading company (1599-1795); later as colonial imperialists (1815-1942). In between came a brief British intermezzo (1811-1815), and finally the Japanese (1942-1945). In its idiom the bahasa Indonesia

reflects exposure to this cascade of foreign cultures and languages.

(7) In the nationalist movements (probably first among students in 1918?), the very word "Indonesia" has shifted from a cultural-geographical term (as in point 3 previously) to a *political* slogan. It came to stand for the struggle for independence and the celebration of selfhood. Nurtured by the glorious past, the name Indonesia sometimes carries associations of being a significant world power. Famous, and often quoted, are the words of the father of the Republic, Sukarno: "The MA of *Ma*laya, the MA of *Ma*nilla and *Ma*dura, the MA of *Ma*dagascar, and the MA of *Ma*oris, all are the same." After independence, Indonesia continues to be an expression of rediscovered grandeur.

(8) The Republic of Indonesia (August 17, 1945) is unique as it pretends and intends to be "a secular state with a religious basis." The core of the official ideology is expressed in the Five Principles *(pantjasila):* the state is based on belief in One Deity; nationalism; internationalism as manifested by respect for human rights; representative government (democracy?); social justice.

The first principle is "a multi-interpretable formula, providing a real possibility for people to agree while disagreeing" (Boland 1971:39). By definition, an Indonesian is "somebody with a religion"; through all levels of education, religious instruction is compulsory. The secular state has committed itself "by means of its Ministry of Religion to promote religions and religious activities in a positive way." This "positive neutrality," with freedom of religion guaranteed, was definitely less than some orthodox Muslim groups desired. In the revolts of these groups, e.g. the Darul-Islam uprising (1945-1965), one might see an expression of the will to change the Constitution and to make Indonesia into an Islamic state.

(9) "Just as the period of the fight for freedom (1945-1950) can be typified as the era of relative unity-in-the-struggle, so the years 1950-1955 can be characterized as the period of strife between the parties" (Boland 1971:47). Sukarno tried to maneuver himself into a position of complete control by means of the concept of "guided democracy"; this was the alliance of

the three main sources of motivation for the Revolution: nationalism (NAS), religion (Agama) and communism (KOM), giving rise to the acronym NASAKOM.

In a tragic coup, September 30, 1965 (the 30 September Movement, *Gestapu*), leftist elements tried to break this delicate balance between parties that were ideologically so radically opposed to one another. The coup failed. In an outrageous reaction hundreds of thousands of (alleged) Communists were killed, or arrested and exiled. Muslim youth groups participated in this massacre.

General Suharto took command as President of the Republic. What has developed since has become known as the New Order (ORBA: *orde baru*), strictly based on *pantjas:laism*. Atheism, in whatever form, is now suspect as a possible manifestation of communist tendencies; every Indonesian (including those who hold on to "primitive" religions) is supposed to choose one of the registered religions (Islam, Protestantism, Roman Catholicism, Hinduism-Buddhism). Within this sociopolitical context we have to try and understand the people movements towards the Christian church (*Christen baru*, "New Christians").

SOME ASPECTS OF MISSIONARY HISTORY IN INDONESIA

This is, of course, not the occasion to repeat once again the history of missionary movements in Indonesia. Surveys of this enterprise, including the significant role of laypeople, e.g. in East Java, are available; unfortunately only very few exist in English. Many more data are still hidden in archives waiting to be uncovered.

But, as in most "younger-church histories," the facts are almost without exception organized in a missio(nary)-centric perspective. We have access to diaries of the messengers of the good news; we are allowed to read their correspondence; we find policy statements galore. Also reports *about* the Indonesia response, but these reports are usually written by missionaries who use (and nobody is to blame) the stereotypes of their current orthodoxy. They overdraw the course of events so that things fit neatly. An Indonesian theologian, after studying this kind of materials, has stated, "almost everything we have available might be used for writing *Western* church history, carried into effect in another, foreign, part of the globe. It is not helpful to reconstruct *Indonesian* church history" (Abineno 1956, ch. 1).

For all of us, who are not willing simply to parrot the great historiographers of missions (Warneck, Richter, Latourette, Walter, etc.) this poses a problem. Walter Holsten urged us, some years ago, to use a different canon (1953:61ff; see also Manecke 1972:15-63). If we go on along the same "classical" lines, he stated, we will project a specific (19th century) model on other eras; "organized missionary efforts" (with societies, etc.) become the yardstick to measure where and when authentic missionary work occurred. He tried to minimize the lamented "missionary vacuum" in Reformation theology, so often ridiculed by Catholic polemicists of the time, e.g. Bellarmine (Neill 1964:221). In the same vein, Gensichen has suggested that the missio-centric procedure is as absurd as "asking Napoleon what he thinks of nuclear warfare" (1960:119).

In principle, I think that we all agree. The real *theme* of missionary or church history should be the kerygmatic event *(Geschichte, die sich da vollzieht, wo in Auslegung der Heiligen Schrift das Zeugnis von Jesus Christus laut wird)*. But is this possible? Holsten obviously forgot his own canon when he made his significant contribution to missionary history (1949). Skeptics have asked for a long time, and they continue to do so, whether he really understood the kerygmatic event to have taken place wherever a solid orthodox Lutheran church was planted. And Gensichen's recent design of a theology of missions is definitely cast in missio-centric terms (1971).

A kerygmatic event cannot be reduced to correct words *(was laut wird)*. In the act of proclamation a missionary never is simply a speaker. His or her whole life is part of the story. We also have to know what was and is heard and experienced on the receiving end: heard with such compelling force that words spoken are accepted and will lead to an obedience of faith (Rom. 1:.5); and obedience expressed in the hearer's own authentic way. This part of the communication process has, until very recently, been only recorded by outsiders. It is safe to assume that what has been documented as "curious deviations," "syncretism," "Christopaganism" or even "heresy" might very well have been the undetected beginnings of an "indigenous theology." Statistics are not sufficient to trace the story of kerygmatic events, and, admittedly, missionary statistics have not always proved to be quite correct.

This whole discussion on the right *theme* of church history seems to be ignored in the very best treatise on Indonesia. As if we still lived in the days of Warneck, the author states that whatever happened in the 200 or so years prior to the "Great Century" should be (dis-)qualified as mere *Vorgeschichte*, a preface to the real thing (Müller-Krüger 1968:61f).

I often wonder how these same historiographers, using Holsten's canon, would write church history in general, or European church history in particular. If they would be consistent, the "real thing" might only be supposed to begin with the establishment of their own denomination composed of the *beati possidentes* of THE Truth.

How do we combine the parable of the Seed as recorded in the two versions of Matthew 13 and Mark 4? The seed (the witness of Jesus Christ) is sown, most of it wasted, unproductive; in some cases people "hear the word and *understand* it, bearing fruit" (Mt. 13:23). And again, "This is how it is with the reign of God. Somebody throws out seed on the ground (and waits), and automatically (*automate*, all by itself, 'without the help of anyone' NAB) the soil produces fruits" (Mk. 4:26-29). We have the story of the sowers pretty well documented. What happens in the soil we can only guess and wait to see. Something might be going on, of which the sower is not a part.

With the aforementioned *caveats* in mind (careful, mainly missio-centric materials), we still have to try and elicit some sense out of the abundant mass of data, looking for the Indonesian part of the story. And, of course, making use of Dr. Tippett's very helpful frame of reference.

A report about Christian headhunters might not be quite acceptable. The story of a baptized family who decided to commit suicide, rather than being exposed to Muslim pressure, has, perhaps, a better chance. In neither case are we adequately informed about the motivations. We had better leave the *judicium fidei*, the judgment on faith, where it belongs, with God.

(1) Portuguese Patronate (1511-1615, or 1512-1612, or ?)

In a magnificent gesture, Pope Alexander VI exercised his authority as a *cosmarch* (ruler over the cosmos). In one of the most fantastic comity arrangements of all times, he divided the world (which was yet to be "discovered" and explored — Columbus had still not set foot on the mainland of his new world, nor had da Gama crossed the Indian Ocean) into two equal spheres of interest. He prescribed a demarcation line, running from pole to pole, 370 leagues west of the Cape Verde Islands; conquests to the west were to be Spanish and to the east, Portuguese.

The Catholic monarchs of the Iberian peninsula found themselves in the roles of pontifical patrons, carrying out that a pope is supposed to do *(patronate)*. Sometimes they preferred to be known as vicars of the vicar of Christ on earth *(vicariate)*.

Indonesia was destined to become the area where east and west *did* meet. The Portuguese rounded Africa and continued on an eastward course, arriving in India, Malacca, the Moluccas (1511-1512). The Spaniards sailed west beyond the Americas and showed up on the same scene. Whatever arrangements were made back home, the Christian confraters engaged in a brisk little war, until the Spaniards were summoned to withdraw, to make the Philippines their headquarters. As obedient sons of the Holy See, they occasionally sent missionary expeditions to the Indian archipelago. But, in principle, Indonesia became part of the *Portuguese Patronate*.

Contemporary observers, unimpressed by what was decreed in ecclesiastical high places, soon passed the word that the Portuguese were really after "pepper" and "souls" (Plattner 1955). Adding insult to injury, Spaniards spread the rumor that their Christian brethren had set out to find *esclavos, no clavos* (slaves, not cloves).

It is significant to note that for centuries to come Europeans, under whatever flag, had to enter into what has become known as "the International Asian Trade System." There was no other way to do profitable business ("pepper"). Asian merchants of various nations had used the same communications network. They carried their cargoes from one trading post to the next, without real-life contact with the cultures and languages in the hinterland of their several *rendez-vous*. Without undue exaggeration, it can be said that these trading posts (the Portuguese introduced the name "factories") were extra-territorial, international bridgeheads of the Trading System.

It is only in the last few decades that historians, Indonesians among them (see Abineno 1956) have begun to investigate the implications of this system. In a very provisional list one can summarize some of the findings:

(a) Unlike the Spanish imperialists, the Portuguese mercantilists were not interested in owning more land than was needed to build up and protect their factories.

(b) A commercial language was the means of communication in these international posts. As far as Indonesia is concerned, this was a kind of pidgin Malay ("low-Malay") or Portuguese.

(c) The missionary enterprise ("souls") was concentrated on the "people in and around the castle" (this was a standing phrase). People living inland did not figure on the missionary agenda.

(d) Although they often reported so, European Christians were not in sole command of the seas (thalassocracy), and consequently had to face fierce competition. In the rush for the Spice Islands, the Portuguese found, to their horror, Muslim competitors on every stretch. This intricate story of almost simulataneous expansion of Islam and Christianity towards Eastern Indonesia is often cast in terms of another clash between *jihad* (holy war) and crusade. All the ingredients of such a classical confrontation are there. Perhaps people of the Crescent and people of the Cross had the same objectives: pepper and souls.

There are no indications that intra-Muslim or intra-Christian warfare was less bitterly fought than the conflagration between adherents of different religions.

(e) And, to repeat, this whole drama is only an imported facet of European history, a story of the "sowers" (of whatever brand). The things that happened "automatically" in the soil are only on record insofar as they affected the alien intruders.

(f) Finally, all these hermeneutical guidelines for interpreting the texts are true, with *exceptions*. History is too amorphous to be caught in a few paragraphs.

We have become used to stereotypes. So we pretend to know (with eyes shut and minds closed) that the Portuguese Patronate could only produce "superficial" or "nominal" Christians. These used to be the accepted adjectives to welcome our Indonesian sisters and brothers in their homecoming party.

Leaving the *judicium fidei* to those who feel comfortable in their role of inquisitors, I simply want to lift up two facets of the story.

First, we know the missionary *methods*, and they were wrong: Europeanization instead of accommodation;[1] a *tabula rasa* way of dealing with the Indonesian cultural heritage (their table had, supposedly, nothing worthwhile to offer for the upbuilding of the church); assimilation and all the wrong words missiological nomenclature may offer. Just an attempt at expanding the *corpus christianum*, that strange mix of faith-culture-and-power. The invitation to accept the gospel must have been heard and understood, most of the time, as: join US, be good proselytes. "Souls" can, apparently, be extricated from the fabric of society and transplanted into another society which one might term Christian, or civilized, or powerful — in this case Portuguese society. Don't waste time: baptize the souls; they are *naturaliter christianae* anyway, "naturally Christian," waiting to be harvested.

Before the Portuguese arrived on the scene there were, in fact, rumors about the Indonesian fields white for harvesting. This euphoria gradually diminished when they came closer to the field (see Visser 1925 and Visser 1934).

In this rubric, we have, I guess, to put together most of the reports about mass baptisms without previous instruction, like the famous story of sailors, tired of riding at anchor off the shore of Buru, who decided to go ashore, baptized 4000 people, in good old conquistador style, leaving a cross as a "sacrament". And that is only one instance.

Second, there is another facet, mostly ignored by Protestants and glorified by Catholics. This concerns what missionaries of different religious orders tried to pass on of the Words of Liberation. The language used was, as Indonesians say now, perhaps the wrong one, more an obstacle than a means of communication. The very outspoken Xavier once wrote, "It is very hard indeed to translate the mysteries of faith into a language one does not understand."

This was a style of missionary work one could, I think, best describe as an attempt at a mass catechumenate. However carelessly others had (ab-)used the holy sacraments, some priests were adamant in teaching the basics of the Christian faith (the Decalogue, the Creed, the Our Father, and occasionally, the Ave Maria). Looking over the whole history of missions, this is not a very bad *shibboleth*.

We know the instructions of Xavier, a latecomer (1546f). We might conjecture that some of his confraters conceptualized their tasks in a similar fashion. To oversimplify: the gospel has to be sung and played out in daily processions and parades, mainly by children and teenagers, probably in an idiom not quite (or not at all) understood by either the messengers or those to whom the message was addressed.

We know of at least one instance when a priest refused to administer the sacrament of baptism because he was not sure that the (necessary) post-baptismal catechumenate could follow (Enklaar 1947:27). There might have been other such instances.

How do we summarize the life stories of hundreds of thousands of people in a few cold paragraphs? I have no way of knowing. Counting Christian noses is a hazardous experiment; there may have been somewhere between 60,000 and 150,000. It is more important to remember that the rhymed catechism became part of Amboinese folk music and that the Christian display of pomp and power may have had a lasting effect. We had better add a postscript to the sorry story of the Crusades. Müller-Krüger speaks of the "last Crusade" (1968:26f).

Countless Indonesians were baptized. It is not for us to sniff out motivations.

As everywhere else, Christian conquest was accompanied by apostasy; as many as 60,000 may have defected. One of the reasons for this decline is the sobering fact that there never was a sufficient number of gospel messengers, and the means of transportation in this island world left much to be desired.

"Honoring our fathers," we have to pay tribute to all those who "put their bodies on the line" (Rom. 12:1). Names may have been forgotten. The presence of missionaries can, in some places, only be documented by their graves (Müller-Krüger 1968:145, referring to Halmahera).

(2) Dutch Theocratic Mercantilism (1599-1795)

Merchants in the Low Countries joined the rush for spices, without pontifical blessing, to be sure. They set sail while they were engaged in a life and death struggle with the Christian monarchs of Iberia (until 1648).

Imagine the surprise of these sturdy republican Calvinists when they finally (the voyage took fourteen months; more than half the crew did not make it) arrived at their first Indonesian port of call and were told by their Asian colleagues/competitors: "We have visited your king in Rome." Response: "We are Christians, all right, but we are not so particularly fond of the Pope" (Van Leur 1934:6; trans. 1955).

The theological rationale for this mercantile enterprise was spelled out in the Dutch Confession (1561; art. 36). It was an article of faith that the whole of society was redeemed in Christ, and consequently should be reformed according to Scripture. In this theocratic commonwealth, the "Christian Magistrate" had the privilege and the obligation of exercising the *jus reformandi*; in practical terms: to protect the citizens against erroneous ("popish") superstitions; to fight false religions and, wherever possible, to spread the gospel among the heathen "sitting in darkness" and among the Moorish Muslims.

The United East Indies (Trading) Company (VOC, founded in 1602) was charged to act on behalf of the reformed magistrate "in the whole of Asia." The arrogance of such a small nation projecting its own ideology on a vast continent may be difficult to understand now. Theocracies are, by definition, global ("The earth is the Lord's and those who dwell in it."). Sensitivity to pluralism is not one of the fortes of their set of mind. The VOC was also present in India, Ceylon, Formosa, Japan, etc. What happened in these other cultural settings influenced the policy in Indonesia and vice versa. The only possible way to cope with such a diversity of situations, so it was thought, was to set strict rules from the home base.

Historians have pointed out that these Dutch adventurers (scholars and pirates among them) brought a survival kit of three books: a Bible (theocracy), an atlas (universality) and a cashbook (profit). This trinity of scriptures may raise some questions for us now. It seems to have been a problem then only occasionally. The many public prayers of this period make it clear that profit was God's best friend.

If we can speak of a missionary *method,* then it was clearly a classic method of *assimilation.* Everything had to be done in strict conformity with *patria*, the fatherland. Sometimes missionaries requested the synods back home "to close their eyes once in a while because things are so different here." No such thing: "We keep our eyes wide open."

This obsession with uniformity led to ludicrous decisions. A *cause célebre* was the issue of hymn singing. Somebody reported that, without adequate supplies of hymnals and in congregations where the majority of the members were illiterate anyway, he used the "English mode." He read the text line by line, to be repeated in song by the church members. Uninformed members of a synod in Holland were quite upset: "Why English melodies; are our own not good enough?" One shudders to think what might have happened if someone would have had the audacity to suggest Indonesian melodies (Abineno 1956:40).

Operating within the trammels of the VOC policy and always subjected to strict censorship, missionaries had hardly any room to move. Innovative Indonesian expressions of the Christian faith were simply taboo.

Missionary work as we understand it today was mainly delegated to a *clerus minor* ("comforters of the sick," "exhorters"). They were allowed to preach (somebody else's sermons), to teach and to baptize. Extempore prayers were frowned upon. The sacrament of the Holy Supper was the privilege of the *clerus major*, the theologically qualified, ordained minister. These were always in short supply. We know of cases in which people had to wait 28 years to partake of the sacrament. This separation of sacraments had in Indonesia, as elsewhere, a disastrous effect (Enklaar 1947).

Faithful to their confession, Dutch merchants tried to eliminate "popish superstitions" and to do battle against "false religions," principally Islam. Most of the time Roman Catholics of the Portuguese era were simply re-labelled Calvinists. Christianity became known as the *agama Kompeni*, the religion of the Company (VOC), and baptism was sometimes referred to as *masuk belanda*, to enter the Dutch system.

Not much is known about organized efforts to reach out to the Muslims. They were, I guess, more often regarded as potential enemies than as prospective converts. Even in *our* century one of the outstanding missionary Bible translators (Adriani) suggested concentration of all missionary forces on the "not-yet-Islamized" parts of Indonesia (the "prophylactic method"). The "inconvertibility of Muslims" has been for long centuries a nightmarish axiom im missionary thinking (Bijlefeld 1959).

Missiological purists cannot look upon these two centuries of theocratic mercantilism as something resembling anything like a golden age. Almost the whole catalogue of things one ought *not* to do can be documented and abundantly footnoted. Increasing corruption in the VOC and the erosion of the Calvinist ethos in the course of the 18th century do not help to arrive at a positive appreciation. What was conceived as *theocratic* mercantilism deteriorated into mercantilism *sec*. In the 17th century VOC servants were urged to root out "false religions." In the next century (18th) some were known to have been involved in a profitable trade in idols.

So the policy was wrong. The citizens of the Kingdom who were scattered in this particular part of the field, the world (Mt. 13:38), were truly committed servants of the cause or the dregs of the nation, with everything possible in between. Unless we want to fall into the trap of a Donatist heresy and only accept certified saints as the real *dramatis personae* in the history of the expansion of Christianity, hardly any word of positive appreciation can come from our lips, only a "preface to the real thing." A couple of solid facts may, however, be remembered.

The church in the Moluccas, especially Amboina, is on record as "the first evangelical Protestant church in Asia" (Müller-Krüger 1968:107, 125, etc.). This "Calvinist Commonwealth" has no great prestige in our current frames of missionary reference (Kraemer 1958:13ff; Cooley 1961). But still, however deficient, there was a church that weathered the storms to come, developed a model of Christian life to be emulated in other parts of the archipelago ("the Amboinese pattern" Abineno 1956:54f) and offered servants for the evangelization of other regions in Indonesia (Hogerwaard 1953:258-65).

It was in Indonesia that "the oldest examples of a printed translation of a biblical text for missionary purposes" was published, a herald of many other translations to come (Koper 1956). Hot debates about translations of the Bible (and of the creed, catechism, etc.) were a common item on the theological agenda. Portuguese-speaking Christians got sacred Scriptures in their own language. One seems not to have been too successful with Chinese texts. This linguistic accommodation is, to say the least, a hopeful exception to this enterprise in which assimilation seems to have been the key word.

All missionary and church work (including schools, etc.) was paid for by the Trading Company. A minimum estimate suggests that the Company paid for about 250 ministers and 800 assistant ministers. Other estimates by experts set the number much higher and invite us to compare the VOC with the English East India Company.[2]

During the 17th and 18th centuries, theologians *in patria* were very often deeply involved in missionary problems. Voetius (1589-1676), one of the pioneers of the Dutch Evangelical Revival, wrote what has become known as the "first evangelical missiology" (Van Andel 1912).

In the course of the renowned 18th century of Enlightenment, ominous portents of an imminent change in ideology became increasingly evident. We had better ignore the many partial, unicausal "interpretations". They deal with *epiphenomena*. The real thing, so very hard to identify in precise categories, is now usually referred to as "The Crisis of the European Conscience" (Hazard 1935). It occurred presumably around 1700, with a long prelude of a continuing erosion of the *corpus christianum* and a protracted postlude, that eventually led to the first real (French) revolution.

Among the interpreters of this transition, E. Beyreuther has, it seems to me, made the most significant contributions, especially with regard to the implications for the missionary enterprise. He insists that the two groups who in our current babel of tongues are labelled "evangelicals" and "ecumenicals" arrived on the scene simultaneously. The two were, in fact, one community of believers who tried to express their newly discovered freedom *for* the world in their own authentic way (Beyreuther 1958). The institutional embodiments of this commitment were still provisional and embryonic. Heralds of a new time were not wholly absent, even *in patria* (Van Boetzelaer 1947).

Indonesian theologians are sometimes rather skeptical about this reconstruction of history: "Maybe this was true in the West; *we* had our own churches in some areas, however deficient; Scripture, maybe not in the best possible translation, *à la* King James Version; and the Holy Spirit did not leave us because the fabric of society changed in another corner of God's world." The one obvious sign of a loss of substance is the multiplication of rules and regulations; a poor substitute for the diminishing number of missionaries.

(3) *New Beginning (1795ff)*

We can be brief about the complex sociopolitical developments in the Netherlands. The VOC was corrupt and moribund: "theocracy" turned into an empty term of sacred rhetoric.

The Low Countries were occupied, then annexed by the revolutionary French. The British took command of Indonesia. After the war was over, it became clear that the old theocratic syndrome could not be restored. A variety of missionary models was available and different groups set out to experiment with them in the years to come.

(a) As in other European communities, a post-revolutionary *monarchy* was established in the Netherlands. To be sure, no longer an incarnation of the Christian (i.e., Reformed) old-style magistrate, with all its mystique, and not yet quite imperial sovereignty, new-style. The King was a Father (and later, a Mother) figure, trying to take care of the needs of loyal subjects, spiritual needs included. Paternalistic monarchy was mixed with colonial bureaucracy.

The King, William I, felt conscience-bound to provide the necessary means for the pastoral care of the neglected Christian constituencies of the VOC period. By decree, he instituted *one* Protestant Church (1816) "to increase knowledge of the Christian faith; to promote a Christian style of life; to protect law and order; and to bring about love for the government and the country." Ministers were civil servants. The administrative separation of the Protestant Church from the colonial government came only in the 1930's. Financial separation was effected in 1950, after independence.

The Indonesian *Protestant Church* is now a federated body, composed of the Moluccan Protestant Church, The Timor Evangelical Christian Church, The Minahassa Evangelical Church (all based in Eastern Indonesia) and the Western Indonesia Protestant Church (mostly members of the 3 other churches living in the western diaspora). With few exceptions, the church language is Malay. They are a conglomerate of folk churches, jealously protecting their old traditions.

(b) The colonial government, with its "obsession for religious neutrality" (Kraemer), closed off whole areas from Christian evangelism, confiscated Bibles in regional languages (like the Javanese Bible translation) and was, in general, particularly concerned about interdenominational competition ("double missions") (Beaver 1962:195f). Where a missionary agency was licensed to work, others were, by definition, excluded. These "comity" arrangements by government were, on the whole, not very successful. Indonesia had begun to be part of a mobile society. Comity only makes sense in stable cultures.

(c) In the "miraculous years" following 1790, supradenominational, evangelical missionary societies sprang up in Euramerica. Some of this new breed of evangelists, with their riotous variety of theologies, found their task within the framework of the established folk churches as "revivalists" (e.g. Joseph Kam, the apostle of the Moluccas). Others moved inland, beyond the coastal fringes of the International Asian Trade System, as lonely pioneers, sometimes oblivious to the government regulations. In the second half of the Great Century denominational societies followed, and, of course, "tent-making missionaries" who served as pioneers in various places (e.g. New Guinea).

(d) Christian lay people have played a decisive part in founding some of the evangelical churches, especially in Central and East Java. They did not need a license issued by the government to be able to evangelize as all the "missionaries" did, so they gossiped the gospel in their own style in otherwise "closed" areas.

(e) Neo-evangelical groups of all sorts began their organized missionary efforts in Indonesia during the 20th century without concern for comity arrangements.

(f) Since the early 1930's, a movement toward ecclesiastical independence gathered momentum. In 1950 a Council of Churches was founded with the express intention of creating "the One Church of Christ in Indonesia." Although the Council has initiated several projects of cooperation, the goal of union remains remote. The variety of Christian communities seems to be on the increase, both because of schismatic movements in the Indonesian churches and because of recent imports from Euramerica.

(4) Summary

It is obvious, even in this very sketchy overview, that one might detect all the stages/aspects of Dr. Tippett's axis paper amply documented in Indonesia. It all depends on where one decides to look for evidence and upon the degree of cultural myopia one finds oneself blessed with. There is the whole spectrum: a transplantation of western-style church life; attempts at "Christianizing the vernaculars" (Adriani) so that they become the vehicles of the gospel; experiments with local modes of communication and celebration; trends to understand and present the evangel as the ultimate truth mystics have been searching for. In some instances, we might find small groups of authentically indigenous Christians, who stay away from the sacraments because these were so central in imported church life. In other cases, pre-Christian mythologies are used without inhibition to bring Christology close to the heart of people (e.g. the Javanese "Messianic" expectation of the coming *ratu adil*, the liberating Lord of justice. See Van Akkeren 1970). Some work has been done recently in developing a fresh theological understanding of one's own traditional background *(adat)* (Schreiner 1972). On the whole, it seems safe to assume that in terms of a truly indigenous theology, too little has been done too late. An Indonesian theologian says: "The Churches in our nation seem to be obsessed by questions of organization and survival . . . whatever theology is available is mostly imported from Europe and America" (Latuihamallo 1966:151ff).

Acknowledging that "the Spirit blows where it will; you hear the sound it makes, but you do not know where it comes from and where it goes" (Jn. 3:8), we ought to remember some simple sociopolitical facts and stay away from pious rhetoric.

(a) After the 1965 massacres in which, allegedly, Muslim youth groups played such a dominant role, one might expect a serious self-examination in Muslim circles: "What and where is the real mainstay of our souls?" (Boland 1971:232). Some Muslim leaders have suggested that one should distinguish between mere "statistical" (90% plus of the population) and "authentic Muslims" (perhaps 40% of the population, who knows?).

As far as analogies go, one might think of something comparable to the Evangelical Revival in Christendom during the 18th century, after an often sterile orthodoxy, emphasis on *praxis pietatis,* solid education and new ways of Muslim apostolate (Bakker 1969:121-136).

(b) Hindus on the island of Bali have assured me that in the post-gestapu wasteland, many (5-10?) millions of Indonesians have "come home" *(datang kembali)* to where they originally belong: Hinduism-Buddhism.

(c) Adherents of "primitive" religions seem to find themselves in the greatest identity crisis. Suspect and, sometimes, not quite aware of "being with" the New Order, they are under pressure to adopt one of the "registered religions." Which one they choose depends very much on the sociopolitical situations where they find themselves. Muslims, as well as Hindus and Christians, can (and do) boast about the rapid expansion of their respective faiths in predominantly "primitive" areas. And, as elsewhere in the world, people in some of these regions have reacted to this "conquest" by outsiders by producing counter-theologies, in which they reaffirm and update the *raison d'être* of their tribal religion and celebrate it in unprecedented liturgical fashion (e.g. among the Karo-Bataks).

(d) Within this context, we have to reflect upon recent church growth or, as some Indonesians prefer to call it: "the advent of the New Christians" *(Christen baru)*. Accurate documents are scanty; promotional stories with almost hysterical superlatives are easy to find. "Statistical analysis of church life and growth in Indonesia is difficult and risky because of the paucity of data" (Cooley 1973:86). And motivations for joining the minority Christian community are, always, not for us to decide on. Humble agnosticism is one of the key words of our current missiological vocabulary.

One might humbly surmise a few factors, keeping in mind that the Holy Spirit is the true factor in the story. To become humble, we should first of all remember that there are no *prima donnas* in these *Opera Dei*, either in Indonesia or in Euramerica. So this cannot be an exact chronicle of the sowers. It rather has to be a story of the soil producing fruits "automatically". Whoever appropriates this story as representing the result of his or her endeavors is out.

When people tell how all this came about, one can hardly trust one's ears. Missiologists will be very suspicious, skeptical or even cynical.

The Christian community served, apparently, as an asylum or refuge for the persecuted and for those who lost their direction in life, for a church, a beautiful role to be in. A Muslim informant said, "You Christians can have them (ex-Communists). We don't want a fifth column within Islam" (Boland 1971:232ff).

One could go on and on with an evaluation of these "New Christians": What is their motivation? What personal commitment do they have to the Christian faith? Do they really know what they are doing? And so forth.

It is very likely that we will find our sisters and brothers on different steps of the axis ladder. So what? We Euramericans are somewhere on the same ladder, unless someone is arrogant enough to pretend that he or she has reached the top.

Notes

1. The distinction between accommodation/adaptation and "Europeanization"/assimilation has been familiar since A. Vath (1932). A detailed history of the Portuguese Patronate in Indonesia can be found in Visser (1925) and Wessels (1926).

2. Van Boetzelaer (1947:5) states that the VOC had sent out more than 900 ministers and thousands of assistant ministers and teachers, and suggests a comparison with the English East India Company.

CHAPTER FOUR

The Christian Encounter with Afro-Messianic Movements

The Possessio-Syncretism Axis
illustrated from South Africa

PETER BEYERHAUS

THE SOUTH AFRICAN CONTEXT

The task of this chapter is to give the third of the three regional illustrations of the possessio-syncretism axis, the missiological implications of which have been pinpointed so ably by the introductory chapter of Dr. Tippett. My illustration is taken from South Africa. Against this background the two key terms give a very peculiar ring. It is difficult to speak of "possessio" in South Africa and not to think of the historic instrusion of the white man which led to the fact that 85% of the land became his possession. And it is equally difficult to speak of syncretism in South Africa without thinking at once of the 3000 new religious movements, often called "African Independent Churches," of which so many render a perfect illustration of a complete blending of Christian concepts with the basic tenets of African Traditional Religion.

I am, of course, aware that I am not yet using the word "possessio" in the missiological sense in which it was coined by J.H. Bavinck[1] and adopted by Dr. Tippett as the basic term for the adaptation-accommodation-assimilation-transformation complex. But as Bengt Sundkler has pointed out in his *Bantu Prophets in South Africa* (1961:33), the Native Land Act of 1913 had a lot to do with the rapid increase of separatist movements of what he called the Ethiopian, the Zionist and the Messianic types. For by that new law it became virtually impossible for Africans to acquire land which had been occupied by the white population. This led to a tremendous repercussion in the religious outlook of the Bantu population: "Once you had the Bible as we had the land. Today we have the Bible and you have the land." To some degree the syncretistic movement in South Africa can be explained sociologically as "reaction to conquest," expressing itself in the revitalization of traditional tribal religion under the stimulus of some concepts of the new western religion. The latter had proved so powerful to its white adherents, but impossible to be appropriated by the African native.

Such a sociological approach to the so-called African Independent Church Movement has its credits. But if it is employed exclusively or one-sidedly, it would not do justice to the very complex nature of our problem. For there are other aspects, taken from the fields of comparative religion, of church history and of missiology, which are equally important to be considered. Only then can we come to a fuller understanding of the emergence of groups like the Afro-messianic movements, which are a most peculiar expression of syncretism within the bulk of the "African Independent Churches."

This reflection determines the procedure of this chapter. In the *first* part I want to describe the phenomenon of the Afro-messianic movements in the categories of anthropology and comparative religion. In the *second* part I want to identify the syncretistic forces working in these movements from the missiological point of view. In the *third* part I want to indicate how an improved missionary communication could counteract syncretism by taking in possession the legitimate questions in it, and thus pave the way for a truly indigenous Christian church in South Africa.

THE AFRO-MESSIANIC PHENOMENON

The messianic movements and groups in Africa are one specific manifestation within the new social formations which are taking place in African Traditional Religion. We also find them in Central Africa (e.g. the early Kimbanguist and Matswa movements [see Anderson 1958]), but there is a particular concentration in Southern Africa, i.e. in the Republic of South Africa, in Lesotho and in Rhodesia. They have developed a magnetic attraction and vitality, a fact which in the stationary religious and missionary situation in their South African environment makes them an exciting phenomenon. The rush into the "churches" of Lekganyane in Transvaal and Shembe in Natal is enormous.[2]

(1) The Anthropological Approach

How can we explain the sudden appearance of such post-Christian ethnic religious movements? The first people who found themselves confronted by them were the missionaries and colonial administrators. While missionaries regarded them as a falling away from the new religion, the government officers suspected concealed rebellion and, in some cases, interfered in a violent way. Quite early reports in missionary periodicals stirred up the interest of sociology and anthropology. The sociologists here discovered a chance to study the emergence of completely new social organizations in the realm of the apparently rather static primitive cultures. The parallelism of the cases caused scholars to assume that behind those seemingly spontaneous and incidental movements, quite definite sociological laws were hidden.

Soon they recognized that the reason for the origin of these movements was the so-called "reaction to conquest" (see M. Hunter 1964), i.e. the clash between the colonial expansion and the primitive ethnic society for which the political and economic annexation of their country meant rape and exploitation. Against this total threat the indigenous society defends itself by recalling its traditions and by the desire to expel the white man and his culture. In view of what Dr. Tippett calls "the capacity of cohesive cultural complexes for survival," such reaction must necessarily always be religious and social at the same time. This characterizes these movements as *nativistic*, a term which was defined by the American anthropologist R. Linton (1943:230) as "any conscious and organized attempt by the members of a society to revive or perpetuate selected aspects of their culture." The hope which is expressed by these attempts is, according to some ethnologists, predominantly of a socio-economic nature. Primitive messianism, according to Barber (1941), is the reaction of a people being deprived of their possessions and rights.

A profound socio-psychological approach is offered by the important essay of Anthony Wallace on "Revitalization Movements" (1956). According to Wallace, such revitalization movements are "any intentional organized and conscious attempts by the members of a society to construct a more satisfactory culture." Wallace describes the psychological stages which follow each other when the communal consciousness of a primitive society sees itself threatened by inevitable disintegration in consequence of the cultural clash. Under this stress the primal community reacts with an urgent desire either to reconstruct their old culture or to substitute for it a new superior culture. Such revitalization movements can bear rather different characters depending on the respective culture and situation. They can appear as *revival movements* which try to give a new validity to values of the old culture which seem to have been lost: a typical case is the Mau Mau Movement in Kenya. Revitalization movements can also appear as *cargo cults* or *chiliastic movements*. Another important type, finally, is the *messianic movement*. Here the decisive feature is the part played by an apotheosized savior who is expected to bring about the cultural revolution. In these movements the person of the founder, who impresses his adherents by his prophetic appearance, gains central significance. According to his sensitive nature, the conflict of his community is condensed in him. He receives in dreams, visions and auditions a vocation experience which transforms his personality and designates him to be the savior of his people.

The anthropological approach has contributed substantially to explaining the character of the messianic movements in their nativistic aspect as "reaction to conquest." The economic, social and psychological factors which are pointed out here must be taken very seriously. This approach explains convincingly why messianic and other nativistic movements appear in such a multitude, especially in South Africa. For here the cultural clash has been especially extensive and intensive. A nativistic reaction is, as B. Malinowski (1949:47) has pointed out, very frequently the result of an "integral rejection" of members of an inferior culture by the members of a technically and economically superior civilization. The enticement to join the European society in the enjoyment of a more "saturated" standard of living is not fulfilled as soon as expected, or is not fulfilled at all. Thus the disappointed members of the deprived society react either in a militant or an escapist way. Amongst the nativistic movements, however, a major attraction is developed only by those movements which not only arouse utopian hopes but also offer social protection to their adherents and effective help in mastering the new problems in the midst of rapid social change. This can be confirmed especially in the messianic communities of Lekganyane in North Transvaal and Limba (see Mqotsi and Mkele 1946) in Port Elizabeth. Both have established small settlements where some of their adherents can make a living. The question, however, is whether such sub-cultures which put themselves beside modern civilization can be of long duration.

(2) The Approach of Comparative Religion

The approach of the anthropologist has to be complemented by that of the scientist of religion. Here special interest is taken in all those features which show common ground between the nativistic movements and the animistic mother religions: the roles of the cultic key persons like divine chiefs, shamans and healers, the tabu, the concepts of witchcraft, the magical means, rituals. They all relate to Dr. Tippett's three categories: "mythical thinking, therapeutic system and the living dead."

It can easily be discovered that in their decisive presuppositions the adherents of the Afro-messianic movements have remained faithful to the old animistic worldview. Among them as well as among the pagan Africans, the key concept for explaining the world is the idea of the mystico-magic life force which fills the universe and which gives to each part its own quality and ability. African religion is the desire, in contact with the ancestors and mediated through the familiar or communal ritual, to channel the life force both to the individual member of the clan and to the whole community in order to strengthen them against the threats of enemies. Originally all African rituals had their ideological frame of reference in ancient mythology. Today those mythological notions have fallen into oblivion; the ritual practices, however, persist.

Highly important is the demand for a therapeutic system. According to Bantu conviction any misfortune, any illness, any death is the result of the diminishing of one's vital force caused by the interference of the superior force of somebody else. There are, besides ritual pollution, three major reasons for illness:

(a) Minor diseases like catching a cold or measles can be ascribed to *natural causes*. All other illnesses and misfortunes, however, are believed to be caused by witchcraft or interference by the ancestral spirits.

(b) The *sorcerer* or the *witch* is an evil person who by technical or biochemical manipulations and spiritist contacts gains power over his fellow man and thus prevents his psychological or bodily organs from functioning normally.

(c) But also the *ancestors* can interfere disastrously in the life of their posterity if they feel neglected. To avoid such misfortune the wrath of the ancestors has to be appeased by ritual sacrifices. The Bantu spend much time and attention to reveal the causes of disasters. This constitutes the power and authority of the witch doctor. He is first of all a witch finder and secondly a destroyer of witchcraft. For the Zulus, these two functions are separated into two professions, *isangoma* and *inyanga*.

Any study of the messianic movements in Africa will show how central to them are the concepts of magical forces, magical harm and magical restitution of life. This explains, first of all, the position of the head of the community. For he unites in himself the powers of divination and of healing in the highest potency. In a lower degree also the minor prophets, installed by him, participate in this ability. They are to be understood more in analogy to the traditional diviners and healers than to the biblical prophets. Such judgment would, of course, be sharply resented by the official representatives of the movements. They try to find a biblical cover for every phenomenon of their cult, however striking the actual parallels in traditional tribal religion might be. In some cases a process of transculturation has led to modern substitutes for the ancient means, and this usually goes together with the ostentatious renunciation of the "heathen practices" of the tribal environment.

It is interesting to note that several founders of messianic movements acted in their earlier life as diviners or mediums, or came from families of witch doctors. Usually they recruit their "prophets" from the range of pagan diviners and magical practitioners. This former contact with ancestral spirits (Zulu: *idlozi*) from which they received their clairvoyance forms an obvious counterpart to their present claim as nativistic prophets to have contact with "angels" or to be filled with the "Holy Spirit," which gives them the power of divination. This transcendental relationship constitutes the religious or magical authority of the Bantu messiahs. It leads their adherents to blind submission and makes them immune to missionary influences.

Lastly I want to refer to the parallelism between the institution of *divine chieftainship* and the office of the head of the messianic movement (Oosthuizen 1966:94-96; 1968:91). Traditional African Religion was a religion of the tribe and, therefore, had to carry out its main function in the frame of the community of blood and soil. The objects of religious invocation in prayer and sacrificial ritual were the ancestors of the clan, and especially of the family of the chief. The chiefs were the high priests who mediated between the tribal community and their own forefathers, who were the real national gods. In view of the dispersion of the tribal fellowship and the emergence of new social entities in urban areas, the only religion which proves its efficiency and reality is that which can transcend the former African particularism in its worship and its sense of fellowship. The Afro-messianic movements do this by substituting new religious authorities and forms for the traditional ones and by making large concessions to the traditional worldview. The cultic relationship between John Galilei Shembe, the present leader, and his deified father Isaiah Shembe, the founder of the Shembe community, forms a striking parallel to the royal ancestral ritual of Zulu chiefs. To this extent Afro-messianism is the most comprehensive attempt of a traditional African religion threatened by dissolution to save itself and to enter into the modern age by means of certain terminological and ritualistic transformations.

THE MOTIVES OF THE SYNCRETISTIC PROCESS

There are central aspects of the messianic movements which cannot properly be explained in the categories of religious phenomenology either. How could it happen that in the office of the chief-prophet-healer the traditional sacred king was transformed into an eschatological figure? The early adherents of Kimbangu expected that in connection with a marvelous event he would suddenly return from captivity on a great ship on the Congo river as a national liberator, heading all the old kings of the Congo Empire and the resurrected ancestors (Andersson 1958:228f). Shembe and John Masove are believed to stand at the Last Day at the gate of the coming Jerusalem granting entrance only to their adherents. For these roles there is no place in the cyclical worldview of the Bantu. East African languages, e.g., do not even have an equivalent for the word "future", as Dr. John Mbiti has shown (1969b:15-28; 1971:24-31).

The Afro-messianic movements, therefore, cannot be fully understood if we overlook the fact that these communities, even in their nativistic determination, remain oriented towards the Christian church, from which they took their point of departure. Secretly they also remain oriented towards the person of Jesus Christ, although they do so in a relativistic sense (see Damman 1965). The answer to the cultural clash remains a pseudo-Christian religious one: church and Messiah. Never has a nativistic messianic movement wholly become a nationalistic party. Rather the Afro-messianic movements claim to be the real manifestation of the Christian church among their people, possibly even for the whole world.[3] Thus we can say that the Christian church, both in its form and in its teaching, became not only the impulse but also the stumbling block for the messianic movements in Africa.

This is exactly the moment when missiology comes into its own and has to prove its character as a theological discipline. Missiology is concerned with the communication of the gospel to non-Christian people. Therefore, it has to trace the causes of the tragic breaking apart of mission church and Afro-messianic movement. In the first step we have to make ourselves advocates of the Afro-messianic movements and to put some searching questions to our western missions. In a second step we will use spiritual discernment to unveil how far the wrong answers of the Afro-messianic movements originate not merely in an inevitable misunderstanding, but also in an existential contradiction to the message proclaimed.

(1) Western Christianity Cross-Examined

There are many questions which, in view of the emergence of messianic and other nativistic movements, must be directed to western missions and "their" churches. Let us select five central ones:

(a) The Congolese people who had been healed by Simon Kimbangu returned to their home with the exclamation: "We have found the God of the black people!" Sundkler reports a sermon of John Galilei Shembe, in which he described the significance of his father in the following words: "You, my people, were once told of a God, who has neither arms nor legs, who cannot see, who has neither love nor pity. But Isaiah Shembe showed you a God who walks on feet and heals with his hands and can be known by man, a God who loves and who has compassion" (Sundkler 1961:278). These two examples make it quite clear that the preaching of the missionaries at one decisive point did not reach its aim. It could not convince many Africans that in Jesus Christ the Immanuel, the "God with us," has really appeared. John V. Taylor (1963:121ff) has tried to elucidate this tragic failure of the missionary's message and of the church established by him. He claims that the most important experience of the African listeners was the encounter with the personality, nearness and holiness of the transcendent God. This nearness, however, can only be tolerated if, at the same time, the merciful love of this God as revealed in Jesus Christ, the second Adam, is not only preached, but also testified to by the life of the Christians for each other. Otherwise God will return into the indefinite distance of the *deus otiosus* which characterizes the African belief in a supreme God.

(b) The Afro-messianic movements present themselves as eschatological communities of salvation. They either urgently expect salvation to happen with the immediate *parousia* of the Messiah, or they do already enjoy the *shalom* of a realized eschatology (Martin 1964:123; Oosthuizen 1968:83-84). Christian hope has been perverted here. But the idea of an eschatological expectation as such had been introduced by the preaching of the missionaries. The question directed to the missions, therefore, is this: What has been the object of their own hope to which they testified to the people of Africa? Into what relationship did the missionaries set the futuristic and the present aspects of the New Testament hope? Was it the psychological state of inner peace and harmony — which must have appeared rather strange to animistic listeners? Or did the missionaries not bother at all about the realization of the final aim of Christian hope because they were only concerned with the planting of the indigenous church? Or did they represent that apocalyptic type of mission in which everything is acclaimed as total but imminent future? Or did they secularize the Christian hope resolutely in the sense of a social gospel? I am afraid that the history of modern missionary preaching cannot offer any additional reply to this question. But none of all these eschatological concepts is really fully representative of the eschatological message of the New Testament. This is all the more painful since in Protestant missions the essential motive has always been the eschatological one.

(c) In all missiological writings about the messianic movements we find agreement that their prophesying, speaking in tongues and ecstatic dancing reveal a hunger for genuine religious life. Sundkler and Martin call it a "hunger for a revelation here and now" (Sundkler 1961:30; Martin 1964:167ff). Christian Baëta speaks of the "desire to probe the reality of spiritual things" (1962:5). African religiosity puts the emphasis not so much on the intellectual or ethical sides, but rather on the emotional aspect of the relation with God. Members of Afro-messianic movements often talk about the coldness which has driven them away from the main-line churches. Without overlooking the opposite danger of being raptured by an unhealthy enthusiasm, we may ask: does this not indicate that the charismatic life of the early church has been impoverished and that we have failed to develop a relevant pneumatology in general?

(d) In the present debate about the shortcomings of western missions in the light of the religious expectations of the Africans, it is sometimes stated sweepingly that missions have been too spiritualistic. In their attempts to save the souls, it is said, they have forgotten the human body. The pioneering enterprises of medical missions give the lie to such accusations. But there is an element of truth hidden in this self-accusation. It is that missions treated the body and the soul of man in different departments, the soul in the church and the body in the clinic. Such a tearing apart is impossible in view of the concept of wholeness which we find in primal thought, especially as it is manifested in the magical diagnosis and therapy. The black messiah as a healer and prophet stands in the tradition of the Bantu philosophy (Tempels 1959:27-46) of wholeness. But does he not also stand nearer to the biblical view about the psychosomatic unity of man and of his salvation, at least structurally?

(e) As our ethno-sociological analysis has shown, Afro-messianism is the outcry of a community which has broken down in the cultural clash. The place of the traditional unity of life in the tribe will be taken by the modern pluralistic society. Even the church today has already accepted its place in the pluralistic society as one segment which is competent for the cultic claim of man. The uprooted African looks back to his community, in which he had his protecting home in all respects, social, economic and cultic. The Afro-messianic movement is a last, though utopian, attempt to restore the lost unity under the present sociological conditions. Is it thus not at the same time an accusation against the western church which has not been able as *koinonia* in the *diaspora* to penetrate the totality of our pluralistic life and to claim it for the *basileia tou Christou?*

Our five questions which we as missiologists have directed to the western missionary movement have clarified two points:

(a) Not all differences between the messianic movements and the main-line churches are a conscious rejection of the Christian faith. Many phenomenological and psychological peculiarities of the messianic movements can be explained simply by the

African's inability to overcome the difficulties of the cultural clash.

(b) Neither can we plainly identify the historic manifestation of the church (i.e. in our case the mission church in Africa), with the *ekklesia* of the New Testament. Some features of the messianic movements show a greater phenomenological similarity with those e.g. of the congregation in Corinth, than the mission churches can present. Probably the messianic movements from their primal background sensed intuitively that the God of creation originally put together certain things which the God of redemption wants to join anew. But they did not realize that this junction has to pass through the crisis of the Cross and that the units have to be renewed by the power of the *Creator Spiritus* who is to be received by faith.

(2) Afro-Messianism Under the Crisis of the Cross

Having listened humbly to the questions of the messianic communities, or to questions which anthropologists and theologians might ask on their behalf, the missiologist is now entitled in return to put some questions to the Afro-messianic movements. We want to formulate them rather cautiously:

(a) Could it be that many responsible members in the messianic movements did indeed hear the call of the Crucified to believe in him, but stumbled over this call because they preferred a new national hero?

(b) Could it be that some of these later Bantu messiahs, in their original choice to use their genuine Christian charisma in an obedient way, could not resist the temptation to yield to the sudden desire of their adherents to treat them as God?

(c) Could it be that the people, who in the cultural clash discovered the fantastic new possibilities of civilization but at the same time also heard the message about the coming kingdom of peace, did not tolerate the eschatological tension between the "already" and the "not yet" any more, and preferred to take a secularist short-cut?

(d) To summarize it briefly: Is not in the deepest analysis Afro-messianism just another new expression of the old offense which natural religious man finds with the *theologia crucis*? A Zulu pastor once stated in a lecture: "The syncretistic sects in our country are the way of the African to by-pass the Cross." If he is right, Afro-messianism reveals itself as a new post-Christian religion which, as Freytag[4] has shown, necessarily must turn anti-Christian.

RESPONDING TO THE AFRO-MESSIANIC CHALLENGE

How should the apostolic agents of the Christian church in South Africa react to those searching questions put to us by the emergence of Afro-messianic movements? They will have to reconsider all expressions of church life, *kerygma, leiturgia* and *koinonia* in constant confrontation with the challenge of their Christopagan counterpart and to work for a reformation.

(1) Preaching and Teaching in Africa

Mission means translation. The fact that the doctrinal terminology of the church is syncretized by the Afro-messianic movements constitutes a double challenge to our theology, an *apologetic* and a *kerygmatic* one.

Our *apologetic responsibility* forces us to discover what those familiar words, whose content is determined for us by the history of Christian interpretation, mean if they are received without this guidance into an African frame of reference. "The Gospel heard is different from the Gospel preaching," said Walter Freytag. This could be illustrated by a careful analysis of the understanding of any Christian key term by "unenlightened" African listeners. Let us take as an example the concept of the Holy Spirit.[5] He is the real principle of life for all African sects and nativistic movements. He is identified with the life force of the African Traditional Religion, but sometimes also with the spiritistic forces that take possession of diviners. He is the principle of continuous revelation. He is the power of healing and of biological and professional strengthening. He is the protecting force for all critical aspects of life. As such he can be tapped and be magically mediated by portions. He is the metaphysical power which is sensed as really present in the worship ritual and which transports its participants into an euphoric mood. But we find little of the Pauline and Johannine description of the Holy Spirit as the personal Lord, who through the living Word guides his Church and by his indwelling transforms the Christian into the image of Christ.

This means that in our missionary communication, even of such a central topic as the concept of the Holy Spirit, something has gone fatally wrong. The church in Africa is still facing an elementary hermeneutical task. How should it be approached? I would suggest three steps:

The *first* step is to make a number of theological analyses of how the Christian key terms like God, spirit, sin, grace and redemption are understood in nativistic communities. Equally crucial is the significance attributed to the institutions of the church, the sacraments or the ministry. This could be done systematically by studying the hymns and by evaluating a great number of sermons, prayers and spontaneous witnesses which are recorded during the worship rituals.[6]

The *second* step would be to give all Christian instruction, both on the catechetical and the theological level, in constant confrontation between the authentic biblical meaning and their nativistic re-interpretation. This is very important, because the members and workers of main-line churches in Africa have also been influenced by such Christopagan concepts (Beyerhaus 1964; Häselbarth 1972:95-107).

A *third* step, finally, might be the formulation of a *Confessio Africana*. It would affirm the historic Christian faith in an African terminology. And it would simultaneously denounce the current Christopagan distortions of this faith just as e.g. the Nicene Creed affirmed the divine Sonship of Christ in refutation of the Arian heresy: *"Genitus, non factus est . . ."*

Equally important with the authenticity of our message is its *pointedness*. This is our *kerygmatic responsibility*. Evangelism in Africa should hit the existential questions, needs and anxieties which have led to the Afro-messianic misinterpretation of the Christian message. I do not mean that African Traditional Religion and biblical revelation can be harmoniously correlated in terms of hope and fulfillment. But I maintain that only such Christians can approach the members of other religious communities as preachers, teachers, doctors or counselors who have tried to identify themselves with the needs, fears and desires out of which the Afro-messianic movements have been born. And if such questions are directed to the biblical revelation, it is quite feasible that they might touch on aspects which have not fully come into the focus of our western churches yet. The decisive question which is put to our missions by the concept of a black messiah is this: Have we really proclaimed Jesus of Nazareth to the Africans in the same joyfully convincing tone as the angel did to the shepherds, "For *to you* is born this day a Savior, who is Christ, the Lord!"? If this is to be done, four important aspects of New Testament Christology (Häselbarth 1972:210-230) have to be emphasized:

Firstly, we should proclaim Christ the *conqueror,* as he is depicted in the Gospels and in the Epistle to the Colossians: the One who by the finger of God casts out evil spirits (Luke 11:20); He who "disarmed the principalities and powers, and made a public example of them, triumphing over them" (Col. 2:15). He is the answer to the African who is haunted by the fear of ghosts and witchcraft.

But *secondly,* in order to avoid making Christ the symbol of hero worship, we have to preach him as the *crucified* one. Not the magical threat of the human enemy is our real danger, but the righteous wrath of God. Only at the Cross could this wrath be overcome, and only in accepting our own cross we will find peace in the fellowship of Christ.

Here we find him, *thirdly,* as the *present* One. He does not need to be represented by a Bantu messiah. For as the Resurrected One (see Mbiti 1971:161-164) Christ is really in our midst. Such a proclamation of Christ, the invisibly present One, needs, however, to be verified by the existential witness of an African congregation, which itself has become free from the traditional fear of witchcraft and ancestral indignation.

To be free from anxiety does not imply freedom from suffering. As the African worldview does not know of a future ontologically different from the present, Africans crave for complete salvation here and now. I agree with Dr. Tippett that Christianity must "provide a vital eschatology." Such a vital eschatology can only be centered, *fourthly,* in Christ as the *returning* One. The utopic fancies of Afro-messianism are both judged and convincingly replaced by the proclamation of the coming Kingdom. Through the means of grace it appears already now and transforms Christian lives. And this Kingdom will become visible in its completion when Christ returns with great power and glory (Mt. 24:30). If this vision is proclaimed in its radiance, it will generate in the congregation the power of Christian endurance. The ability to "rejoice in our sufferings" (Rom. 5:3) has always been a most persuasive factor in the spontaneous expansion of the church.

(2) Reshaping the Liturgy

If the African church experiences a fresh encounter with the "Christ for you," she will also develop new liturgical forms to give expression to this meeting. Here the church could, indeed, learn much from the nativistic movements (Oosthuizen 1968:238-243; Berglund 1966). According to my observation, there are four elements which make the rituals of these groups so attractive to their participants:

(a) The spontaneous involvement of all members, which satisfies the African craving for rhythm and movement.

(b) The impressive symbolism of the cult in its dramatic procedure and its colorful vestments.

(c) The concrete relatedness to the individual needs. Any trouble and any subsequent relief are told to the group and shared by all members in compassion or joy.

(d) The originality of the religious songs. Their melodies, rhythmics and harmonies derive mostly from traditional Bantu music, but they are quite open for a gradual acculturation with western styles and instruments.

On account of these factors there is no meritorious boredom in these cultic meetings. Rather they are festivals of joy where nobody counts the passing hours. When in the sixties our Lutheran Church in Transvaal celebrated a number of Jubilees, these gained a tremendous popularity among the Christians. My African students told me that this was the direct reaction of Lutheran Christians to the festival of the Zion Christian Church. African Christians wanted visibly to manifest their wider community and joyfully to break the routine of the normal congregational life.

Most main-line churches are still too inhibited to introduce a radical innovation or Africanization of their liturgies. The reason is partly that they do not want to imitate the sects. But more important is that in the minds of first-generation Christians traditional melodies and dancing cannot be dissociated from paganism. Therefore, enforcing "cultural identity" on African churches is as detrimental as keeping them captive in imported western forms. It will have to be left to the spontaneity of the living faith of African Christians themselves to find those liturgical forms which give a genuine expression for their encounter with the triune God. Here the Christian youth with their new songs are already paving the way for the church of the future.

(3) Mediating Social Integration

There is still a third field where main-line churches in South Africa should heed the challenge of the Afro-messianic communities. It is their capability to establish themselves as factors of social integration. Welbourn, in his study of East African independent churches (Welbourn and Ogot 1966; Welbourn 1961:201-213), has called them "a place to feel at home." This could be stated with equal appropriateness of the messianic movements in South Africa. They do, indeed, serve as new tribes in a time of socio-political disintegration.

The misery of Southern Africa is that the principle of ethnic separation has torn to pieces a population which through history is destined to become a multi-ethnic and supra-racial society. The Afro-messianic movements have not stemmed the process of ethnic separation. On the contrary, they have wholeheartedly subscribed to it. They have become crystallizing centers of social integration in ethnic ghettos. In a way the Group Area Act and other Apartheid laws do not leave much room for an alternative option to the main-line churches either. There is, however, still plenty of room for them to begin to further fellowship in daily life among their own members. The African has an innate feeling of human solidarity. It is much closer than our western individualism to the synoptic concept of our responsibility to our neighbor or to Paul's teaching about the corporate personality of Christ's body. Here the African churches will become more African inasmuch as they become true churches in the New Testament sense. I have found tendencies within urban church choirs to bring their members into closer community and to provide even social protection for them. The special pastoral charisma of the African ministry will be to discover and to develop the *koinonia* function of the church (Beyerhaus 1964; Häselbarth 1972:95-102).

Still, a true church in South Africa can never recede into an ethnic ghetto and acquiesce with the status quo. Christ, as the Church confesses him, is no Bantu messiah, but the head of an universal body. In him there is neither Jew nor Greek, neither free man nor slave (Gal. 3:28). Therefore, the churches in South Africa are called to make manifest that Christians belong together because of a new bond of loyalty (Beyerhaus 1972:89-102). Neither the color bar nor ethnic divisions can suspend their mutual solidarity. Churches in South Africa not only have the responsibility, but they should also have the spiritual power to quench the spirit of racism. That they have not always acted accordingly is one of the main reasons why Africans asked for a native God and a black messiah. True enough, the churches are the largest social organizations in South Africa which — in different degrees — have constantly opposed the injustices of the racist legislation. But they have failed to manifest by their own *koinonia* that fellowship, which could serve as a convincing model and sign of hope for a future integrated society.

We do not know whether the chance has already passed, where all national groups involved could be convinced to agree on a political solution for South Africa's social problems. Still, even where secular agents and secular hopes fail, the churches cannot stop proclaiming the justice of God and serving as agents of reconciliation. For this is their *raison d'être*. They will be judged, not by their success, but according to their faithfulness. For it is their Judge who will make all things new (Rev. 21:4).

Notes

1. " 'Accommodation' connotes something of a denial, of a mutilation. We would, therefore, prefer to use the term *possessio*, to take into possession." (J.H. Bavinck 1964:178).

2. About the Lekganyane movement, see Schlosser (1958:181ff) and Häselbarth (1966); about Shembe, see Sundkler (1961 *passim*).

3. The adherents of Lekganyane sing "The churches of the world will finally be reigned from Morija" (Häselbarth 1966:71).

4. (W. Freytag 1961:58f) This interpretation is most consistently unfolded in Oosthuizen's book *Post-Christianity in Africa* (1968).

5. See Oosthuizen (1968 Chapter 4): "Misunderstanding of the Biblical Meaning of the Holy Spirit in the Independent Movements."

6. A good example is given by G.C. Oosthuizen (1967). Here he constructs the theology of Shembe's Nazareth Baptist Church from its official hymnbook.

CHAPTER FIVE

Formal Transformation and Faith Distortion

ALAN R. TIPPETT

IN my first chapter I considered syncretism as over against indigenous Christianity and found their common drive in a "striving for meaning," with institutions and terms that were relevant for specific historical cultural situations. Looking at syncretism anthropologically, we found that it was frequently activated and held together by any one or more of a number of identifiable forces: the persistence of cohesive clusters of ideas, an orientation to mythological thinking and belief, the demand for a therapeutic system or the notion of the living dead. Very briefly I described indigenous Christianity only enough for it to be recognizable as a viable alternative to syncretism as a "culturally relevant striving for meaning." In other words, my focus was rather on the nature of syncretism rather than on indigenous Christianity.

In this chapter which I am calling "Formal Transformation and Faith Distortion," I shall dig more deeply into the subject from the position of the indigenous church confronting syncretism, and the dynamics of the experience of the Christian fellowship group (church) in its encounter with the world and with its culture. Let me begin with an analogy.

RELIGION OR GOSPEL

I once lived near a place called Wangaratta. That is an Australian aboriginal name meaning "the meeting of the waters." For the aborigines it must have been a most exciting place as the flood waters spread out across a great swamp that teemed with wild life, and through the center two significant rivers ploughed deep courses and came together in a tempestuous meeting. As far back as the aborigines could remember it had been the same, and the meeting of the waters figured in their myths from the dreamtime. Every generation of aborigines as far back as their history went knew those streams, the meeting of the waters, the flooding, as I have known in my own day.

Let me use this as an allegory of the confluence of those two streams of intellectual endeavor known as the "history of religion" and the "history of mission," which, when they meet, create a whirlpool. No missionary who navigates these waters can escape that whirlpool. It is a timeless hazard, and every missionary must navigate it for himself, and likewise every generation of missionaries. The missionary will focus on either the universals and commonalities of religion, per se, or on the uniqueness of the gospel.

I am using the terms *religion-man* and *apostolic-man* as descriptors of missionary attitudes to cross-cultural evangelism, because I believe that most missionaries (including mission executives) do, in point of fact, navigate one of these two streams. This is manifest when they bring their respective crafts near the whirlpool. The vortex of the whirlpool, of course, is precisely the same as McGavran calls "the eye of the storm" (1972): we are dealing with the very nature of the Christian mission, bringing the pagan to his "moment of truth," helping his faith reformulation and setting him on the Christian way without destroying his cultural life style. It is in these matters that a missionary reveals whether he is a *religion-man* or an *apostolic-man*. The former may opt for some form of coexistence between Christianity and the non-Christian faiths — say, a kind of non-persuasive dialog — or he may prefer the notion that Christ is already there as a Presence and all we need to do is to be there and to be faithful, leaving everything else to him. Or he may even settle for some kind of syncretism in the hope that the second or third generation, with more Christian education behind them, will be more truly Christian. On the other hand, the *apostolic-man,* operating on the traditional definition of mission in terms of the Great Commission and other utterances of our Lord, will call for a definite and demonstrated change of faith — a conversion experience. In one sense, the recent debates about the definition of mission are beside the point: down through history these two categories may be found, and they have continuously demonstrated the disagreement, both inside and outside the church.

The notion of the whirlpool has something ominous about it. It rather suggests the possibility of being sucked in and destroyed. In my studies on *power encounter*, I have used a model for demonstrating the nature of the conversion process and have stressed a number of these danger points. In that process the ocular demonstration of an animist's faith-change is followed by his incorporation into the fellowship group; or if enough persons are involved at the same time, a young church is planted (1967a).[1] In this chapter I want to focus on that point of time in the process and take a look at the whirlpool caused by the meeting of the waters.

To do this I shall have to distinguish between *formal cultural transformation* and *faith distortion*. The former is a qualitative change within continuing cultural forms due to the acceptance of the Christian faith. The latter is a compromise of the core of the Christian faith for personal, economic or religio-universalistic advantages. The former leads to a new set of values without seriously disrupting the cultural life style. The latter leads, via syncretism perhaps, to another kind of paganism. Once the Jerusalem Council agreed that Greeks could become Christians without first becoming Jews (Acts 15), this problem arose, but it was a risk that the church had to take if it was to evangelize the world — on the human level it was the same kind of risk which God took in creating man in his own image and which Christ took with the incarnation and the cross.[2]

To show the continuity of this problem through Christian history, I shall now discuss the concepts of formal cultural transformation and faith distortion as Irenaeus encountered them in his congregation of Celts at Lyons in the second century. Subsequent to this I shall come down to modern times and try to show the similarities between the two periods of history. To return to my sustained metaphor — the meeting of the waters and the whirlpool are always there, and the dangers for our navigation are the same as those faced by Paul in the first century and Irenaeus in the second.

A SECOND-CENTURY ENCOUNTER: IRENAEUS AND THE GNOSTICS

Irenaeus has gone down in history as a Christian apologist and writer. His writing is significant as a contribution to ecclesiology, theology, church history and biblical criticism. Yet to leave the name of Irenaeus there is to miss the whole point of his life and work. Irenaeus was no armchair theologian. He was a pastor of the church *in a precise situation*. The purpose of his writing was to strengthen his flock in the belief in one God and in their faith in the redemption of man through Christ, the Son of God alone. His claim to our consideration is not that he was an early Christian scholar, but that in the cultural complex of a second century Christian community he found the forces of gnosticism impinging on and penetrating his pastorate, upsetting his young converts. Irenaeus is a concerned pastor in a precise situation. *Against Heresies* is not a theologico-philosophical treatise but the reflection of a dynamic situation and the struggles of a shepherd caring for his flock.

The gnosticism of both Valentinus and Marcion invaded his pastorate and ramified through the life and thought of his parishioners. He was dealing with a practical, not a philosophical matter, which threatened the faith of his people. *Against Heresies* does not stand as a theological thesis per se. It is merely the contemporary and culturally relevant means he chose to handle a practical problem. The important thing is not that Irenaeus wrote such a work in five books, but that he confronted a threatening situation in the church. That threat was to basic Christian doctrines — the incarnation, the resurrection, the sacraments, the Person and work of Christ among them.

The fact that he explored critical and exegetical method and thereby established an approach to Christian scholarship which became a tradition, is, for the moment, beside the point. He was not to see the course of church history in the centuries that followed. He was dealing with a threat within the church at his own point of time in history — as first John, and then Ignatius, in whose tradition he stood, had done before him. The fact that *Against Heresies* was received by the church at large suggests, not so much its brilliance, but the fact that the situation he was combating was widespread and not confined to his pastorate. Thus his writing became a bridge between the Johannine/Ignatian tradition before him and the work of the later apologists. No doubt, in the long-time purposes of God, this was good and important for "the church through time," but the real significance of this work is *within a cultural complex at a specific point of time in history,* and if that speaks to us at all it surely says that as God's servants and stewards we are concerned with dynamic confrontations in the life and culture of our own day, and with the mental, technological and spiritual equipment we have at our disposal.

Against Heresies begins with a brief description of the situation in which certain men "by skillful language" are introducing "impious views" which the "hearers cannot always distinguish from the truth," because they are "decked out in attractive dress." The argument of Irenaeus stands on the restatement of a biblical creedal statement and the claim that the Christian faith remains firm as one cohesive thing, even across the barriers of geography, culture and language.

Against this straightforward faith statement he outlines the views of several patterns of gnosticism, themselves by no means one. The gnostics used the names Father, Son and Holy Spirit, and other Christian terms, but attributed non-Christian meanings to them. Thus, for example, "the Holy Spirit was produced by the Truth [identified as one of the second Dyad, offspring of Ineffable and Silence, in the first Ogdoad] to inspect and fructify the Aeons, entering into them invisibly, through whom the Aeons produced the plants of truth" (I. 11). Again, the Logos is one with Zoe, Anthropos and Ecclesia, as coming from the Tetrad of the first and second Dyads. And again, Christ was conceived by the Mother, who was outside the Pleroma, with a shadow. Christ cast off the shadow and returned to the

Pleroma, leaving the Mother with the shadow outside. Thus they assembled all manner of strange notions and peddled them by giving them biblical names and, therefore, biblical status.

Had it not been for apologists like Irenaeus, the gnostics might well have taken over the church and made it merely another form of paganism by faith distortion.

How could the church ever have been tempted to accept such doctrine? We ask this question every time a nativistic prophet leads a breakaway from a modern mission field church. Let me put up a few feasible reasons for the success of the gnostics that occur to me as I read *Against Heresies,* and put myself back into that second situation.

1. The written Word was not then in the hands of every believer, as it is today. Their knowledge of Scripture depended on what their leaders read or expounded. Therefore, they had no personal criteria for judging a heresy.

2. There were many formal similarities between gnosticism and Christianity. Gnostics met regularly for congregational worship, used preaching from a supposedly sacred book on which they had commentaries, and they sang hymns.

3. They struggled with similar ideas — the redemption from evil and reunion with the Supernatural, for instance.

4. They engaged in missionary programs to win people to their faith.

5. They used similar terminology in pressing their theological ideas, and appropriated, not only scriptural names, but episodes for allegorical reinterpretation: the baptism of Christ, the request of the mother of the sons of Zebedee, the experience of Eve and Mary, and so forth. The young Christians recognized these as biblical.

Thus was Irenaeus much exercised because his Christian flock was unable to discriminate clearly what was the truth, because it was skillfully presented and "decked out in attractive dress." Apparently the second century saw Greek nativistic movements, which claimed to be genuine reinterpretations of Christian Scriptures. This has very close similarities with the Hauhau Movement of the Maori Wars, the John Frum Movement of the New Hebrides or other nativistic movements in Oceania and Africa.[3]

THE CONTINUITY OF ENCOUNTER

In my allegory of the meeting of the waters and the whirlpool, I made the point that each generation in its turn passes by this way. This pressure on young Christians for faith distortion is ever with us. Every Christian community with a sense of mission must inevitably come into encounter with non-Christian faiths. Sometimes it is another faith that just enters the scene like the Hare Krishna in Los Angeles today, or the Soka Gakkai, each of them using Christian missionary and witness techniques on the streets and from door to door,[4] and like the followers of Valentinus who worried Irenaeus, with carefully honed emotional jargon and attractive trimmings. We cannot escape this kind of engagement — not unless we shut ourselves off from the world in isolation, which, unhappily, some churches have done, and for which they must some day surely give answer to him who sent them into the world as he was sent into the world.

If we suppose that the cultural structures themselves are amoral, there are only two feasible directions for young converts and new congregations to move. First, using the structural and formal similarities of the religions — prayer, worship, art, music, liturgy, etc. — as stepping stones, the church may strive to win them for Christ, what Bavinck calls *possessio* (1964:178-179)[5] and the ethnolinguists call *transformation* (Kraft 1973b:237-248), to transform the cultural forms by making them Christocentric. Formal cultural transformation is thus a *faith reformulation*.

Second, over against this is the possibility of *faith distortion*, which is often the easy way out. One accepts the presence of gnosticism (or paganism or animism) on the basis of formal similarities regardless of the faith content. This may be an unintentional acceptance — maybe a mere resignation to coexistence or rationalization about it. It may be accepted in the hope that with time and Christian education the faith will come. In any case it is bound to lead to syncretism and eventually to another form of paganism. In the case of Irenaeus, he recognized the subtlety of using biblical incidents and the names of the three Persons and the Trinity as "validation" for a spurious doctrine. He accused the gnostics of using the name of Christ "as a kind of decoy," misguiding the people and "spreading their evil poison of the Serpent, the prince of apostasy" (I. 27:4).

The apostle Paul had felt the same dangers in the first generation church, and dealt with it firmly in his letters, which, like *Against Heresies,* are not merely literary documents but products of dynamic situations: "Ye cannot drink the cup of the Lord and the cup of devils" (I. Cor. 10:21), he asserts. And yet Paul drew on many of the cultural forms and values of the Greek colonial world, enough to serve as a data base for a textbook in anthropology.[6] Nevertheless, the one thing on which neither Paul nor Irenaeus would budge one inch was the nature and work of God, the Father, Son and Holy Spirit, and the way of salvation they opened to the believer. And, of course, they had the authority of Jesus for this (Jn. 14:6).

Thus, in our own day, Visser't Hooft resists the notion of Christianity as a "species of the genus religion," just one other expression of the universal religion. He argues that Christianity is an "adequate and definitive revelation of God in history," that classifying Christianity as one expression of "a general phenomenon called religion is to set it in a framework which is foreign to its nature" (1963:94-95).[7] This, of course, is just what the *religion-missionary* does when he permits coexistence or syncretism in the hope that Christian education will correct the matter in a genration or so, or when he allows Christ to be regarded as on a par with the Indian holy people,[8] for example. Christ can break into a cross-cultural situation and possess or transform a social structure, an institutional complex or a language, but *the transformed form must be Christian:* there must be no tampering with the Persons of the Trinity or the saving work of God for mankind; the basic core of the gospel, the supracultural, must stand. Formal cultural transformation by all means, but faith distortion, certainly not. There is no place in Christian mission for any theological Walt Whitman:

> I respect Assyria, China, Teutonia and the Hebrews,
> I adopt each theory, myth, god and demi-god,
> I see that the old accounts, bibles, genealogies,
>   are true, without exception.

or again:

> Thee in thy all-supplying, all-enclosing worship—
>   thee in no single bible saviour, merely,
> Thy saviours, countless, latent within thyself,
>   thy bibles incessant within thyself,
>   equal to any, divine as any, . . .[9]

Despite its cultural dissimilarities, our day is not very different from the day of the Christian conflict with gnosticism. Many of our would-be policy makers are indeed "gnostics". They would engage in faith distortion by removing Christ's place as only Savior and the biblical emphasis of persuasion for decision in Christian witness to the nations. They compromise with the religions by seeking a universal religion, which supposedly finds Christ or the Spirit in all the religions. These are the "gnostics" within our ranks. Out in the streets the missionaries of the religions buttonhole people with enticing words of self-realization, calling on Christians in their homes, striving for a faith distortion. Our worship patterns are borrowed and people sing, "Buddha loves me, this I know." Our theological terminology is used to their ends and the meanings are manipulated. Christ and the Spirit are sweet and beautiful names that "become decoys," offering instead a "bitter poison from the prince of apostasy." One has to ask if we are with Irenaeus in Lyons or in the Christian West. The only difference is that all our lives we have had the written word of God in our hands, and therefore surely we are more responsible for the preservation of the faith.

Manifestly we are dealing with an aspect of the Christian encounter with the world that runs through history, and will continue to do so as long as we are called to Christian mission. If this be so, then maybe we should take a hard look at a few cases of formal cultural transformation and faith distortion, so that we may understand it better as we meet them in cross-cultural mission today. We are not hard pressed for examples.

CROSS-CULTURAL ENCOUNTERS

The case of the Chamula Indian, who supposed himself to be a Christian, we have already discussed at length. The supposedly Christian features of his faith touched on the Virgin Mary, the symbol of the cross, the trinitarian formula and the patronage of the saints, all appropriated somewhat magically. His attitude to the spirits of the dead, his communion with his ancestors, worship of the sun, his totemistic and shamanic beliefs and practices were all thoroughly animistic. The festival performances and mythical worldview were syncretistic. His anchor in Christianity was rooted in the names of the Godhead, the saints, biblical characters and events, all wrenched from their true context. What purported to be the life of our Lord — the nativity, flight into Egypt, death on the cross, etc. — was interwoven with sun and moon worship, animistic *pukujes* and *chulels*, demons on the mountains, a Maya myth of the cornfield, a legend of biting flies (equated with the Jews) and so on. The Virgin Mary was confused with a local fertility goddess and also with the moon divinity. The trinitarian formula was a magical chant. The Father was beyond the reach and knowledge of man in the place of the dead. The Son of God was equated with the sun, who goes to visit the absent Father by night and returns for the day. The moon was his mother.

Each time I dip into Irenaeus's *Against Heresies* and consider the gnosticism that troubled him, I am reminded of Juan, the Christopagan Chamula. The similarities between the two syncretisms are remarkable, and the fallacies on which the respective faith formulations were accepted are identical. The distortion is due to the acceptance of biblical characters, places, names and events as truth, purely for their own name's sake; the words being biblical but the myths pinned onto them being quite false. [10]

This is why the post-conversion instruction is so important when new believers are being incorporated into the Christian fellowship group. It also shows why the Christian pastor or teacher must be quite clear in his own mind about the difference between the transformation of forms and the faith formulation which goes with it. Let me develop this a little by comparing formal transformation and faith distortion, first, in the field of indigenous art and crafts, and then in the rhythms of a people whose social regulations are preserved by oral tradition; art and rhythm being mechanisms of communication.

(1) Formal Transformation and Faith Distortion in Art

A converted Navaho Indian woman, an expert rug maker by pre-Christian profession, who had always hitherto depicted such things as the activity of the corn spirits in the rug design, now worked out a Christian design based on symbols like the cross and Scripture references. She presented the rug to the church for use in the worship service — a most appropriate gift. In another nearby congregation, the church is ornamented with Navaho paintings. They feature the corn but not the corn spirits. They rather point to the Lord of the harvest. In the case of the rug, the materials, the Navaho vegetable dyes and the technology are indigenous. In the painting, although the paint medium is introduced, the style of indigenous sand painting is preserved. In both cases the skills and psychological satisfactions are all preserved both for the craftsmen and the audience, which knows and understands the meaning of these forms of communication. They recognize that the message and not the form has changed. This formal cultural transformation speaks to them to the effect that Christ is glorified and not the corn spirits.

By way of contrast, let me comment on a beautiful book I received the other day — an anthropologist's delight. It is a well-written account of the origin myths of a community of Australian aborigines, hitherto nomadic but now practising transhumance, with their central location under missionary patronage. The book is beautifully illustrated from a series of panels painted with the indigenous pigments in native style by aboriginal artists. These panels depict the spirit people and fauna of the tribal origin stories. I am certainly pleased that this tremendously interesting folklore is to be preserved both in art and narrative. However, I would expect it to be done in a museum or a culture center. One is certainly surprised to find the panels arranged as a background to the communion table in a Christian church, not because aboriginal art should not be there — I believe it should — but because the display is *a record of what they are supposed to have left behind them.* It will undoubtedly force the converts who worship in that church to so dwell on the dreamtime that their worship will be a coexistence and probably in time highly syncretistic — for *the panel and the altar cross symbolize two incompatible belief systems.* Over against the empty Christian cross which symbolizes the death and resurrection of our Lord, the Christian hymn books in the pews and the lectern with the Bible on it (i.e., the pull towards the gospel) is set the record of spirits with an eschatology and origin of the dreamtime, the totemism, the ritual bag, the animism of Thunderman, the totemic tree of life linking earth with the spirit world, and its totemic animal messengers going to and from between the two with communications (i.e., the pull towards the ritual song cycles and Australian totemism).

The two represent quite different theologies and confront the congregation with two different focal points for today's and tomorrow's religion. The placing of the two conflicting views before the congregation at every worship service is bound to be confusing. In an historical culture center, the presentation might have been preserved with historical respect and treasured as tradition, but it is not the kind of thing to put before young converts when they enter the place where they specifically want to worship the Lord. In that church they must find the supports they need for a religion which will stand by them today and tomorrow. For the Australian aborigine this is a day of acculturation. It is anthropologically unsound to build in the archaic features of totemism, which will only let them down in more ways than one. More important still, if they have really become Christian, they need a worldview that is relevantly Christian. One is surprised that the missionary invitation to the aboriginal artists should have been in terms of "whatever they would like to paint" and not in terms of using their art forms to paint something Christian. This suggests a "religion-attitude" rather than an apostolic one. In that it has set a "bone of contention" before the young converts, it is regrettable. In that it fails to provide for the problems of today and tomorrow, it is again regrettable. In that it fails to present the Christ in a Christian church it is, in my opinion, misguided and irresponsible and will be seen as such even by anthropologists who rejoice that the folklore is preserved. It was the anthropologist Malinowski who pointed out what a missionary was bound to be and do if he was to be true to himself (1965:xv).[11] What I can only speculate on is why it was put there. Was it an attempt to make a western church building more indigenous? Was it to reduce the culture shock of rapid culture change by letting the converts see that the missionary was not anti-cultural? Was it to help the converts retain their sense of ethnic entity? Was it to impress upon the aboriginal converts that it was their church, not that of the westerners? Was it the "religion-attitude" which claimed that we should look at totemism and find Christ already there? Many of these would have been valid reasons for setting an aboriginal panel there in the central place in that church. But the fault lies in the fact that it is a totemistic panel, a belief system which by profession they have left. Anthropologically it does not relate to their current profession. Theologically there is nothing Christocentric about it. Both anthropologically and theologically it offers nothing for today or tomorrow in a rapidly changing world: it offers nothing but a conflict of values. Furthermore, the fact that the aboriginal artists elected, with the approval of the people, to depict the dreamtime as the subject for the panel, shows something sad or disillusioning about the depth of their conversion and their need for Christian instruction.

For a non-literate people like this, with whom symbolic communication is by art instead of letters, it is essential for their art to be won for the purpose of communicating the Christian faith and ethic. For semi-nomadic people like this, the notion of the journey is a key image for the preservation of their faith and the establishment of ethical and procedural reference points in the traditions of the people. This is one reason for the tremendous value of *Pilgrim's Progress* in so many societies for reinforcing and applying biblical values.[12] Furthermore, it is narrative in form. In the light of this, what can be done to correct the problem panel in the church, short of removing it and offending the tribes concerned?

Anthropologically and historically it is incomplete. It could be completed in the same art style so that the last panel depicts the conversion of the people to Christianity. This would bring it into line with their present belief. A Christocentric panel as the end of the journey would change a faith distortion to a formal transformation, and remove the perilous dichotomy of the panel over against the altar cross. As things are at present this dichotomy can lead only to unnecessary conflict, a phony coexistence or syncretism. If the panels show the journey from totemism to Christ, there is harmony in the belief system and considerable teaching value, as there was when Ratu Cakobau, the cannibal Fijian, had the killing stone at Bau transformed into a baptismal font and set it before the congregation as "a reminder of the greatness of their salvation."

To build in the conflict between totemism and Christianity, for whatever motivation, is to misunderstand the whole nature and function of these cultural art forms and tribal story-telling. These things are never static. The whole idea is that they represent the ongoing process of tribal history. The events of the journey depict the characters who have molded history and the significant innovations at their historic points of time. They tell the living how things came to be as they are. Therefore, if the art and story-telling techniques are to be genuinely preserved, the total art or story complex must tell the Christian congregation how they came to be what they now are. Thus the most recent panel will show the foreigners bringing the good news, the people accepting it, the discovery of the Bible from which they read at worship, the building of their church — all in the same artistic medium. Thus would the art and narrative show the people how they became what they currently are. Unless something like this is added, the totemic panel will not be credible in a Christian church, or else it will injure the Christianity by faith distortion. The road is perilous but it has to be followed if the church is to be indigenous, and if the passage from animism to Christianity is to be meaningful and smooth. The history of schism, syncretism and nativistic movements in the church shows how long we have taken to learn the lessons of the whirlpool at the meeting of the waters.

*(2) Formal Transformation and Faith Distortion
    in Rhythmic Transmission*

Much of what I have said of the aboriginal panel series of paintings may also be said of oral traditions — stories, songs, dirges and rhythmic history. The people are brought along the road to their present state. If that is a state of Christian experience, at least for the first generation of Christians, that must be reflected in their songs and sagas. What happens fifty years thereafter is the business of the church of fifty years after — and that is a different matter, which we are not discussing at the moment.

The question of what is to be done with pagan dances and chants when a people becomes Christian has long been a bone of contention among missionaries and missionary supporters, but it is a foreign and western problem. The fear of syncretism has led many missionaries to reject the dance and chant as a communication form, lest the people continue to cling to their pagan associations, but the argument is not rational. The fallacy of the reasoning is that all these media of rhythmic transmission are bundled together under one judgment of the form rather than the content. Would it be reasonable, for example, to deny ourselves the use of language itself because it can be used for communicating profanity?

Yet many missionary supporters have advocated this with dances and chants among their converts, equating a native dance with the sex associations of its western analog. Many anthropologists have grouped all missionaries under the condemnatory generalization for prohibiting and destroying these art forms. The charge is not fair. Where it has been true, the converts have usually felt a cultural void, social needs have been unmet and sooner or later there have been reactions. But all missionaries have not been like this.

The British missionaries in Fiji, for example, prohibited certain dances, like the *wate* and *dele*, which were associated with victorious return from war and sexual abuse of the bodies of the victims, followed by cannibal festivities. They demanded that their converts reject any dances or entertainments which were vulgar and sexy, but they did not prohibit the dance and chant per se. In this way they taught their converts to discriminate between appropriate and inappropriate dances and songs. Dances were retained for social entertainment, even for church festivals. The people still preserved and dramatized their sagas. They composed new chants to cover their unfolding history in Christian times. They commemorated their church building instead of pagan temples. They created dirges in their bereavements; in their lighter moments, opened the door to satire and hilarity. I have seen all these dances and have the accompanying chants of many of them. One of them covers the history of a century of the expansion of the church in their islands. With their own peculiar cultural rhythmic media they did exactly what we in the West have done with radio, television and the printed book — used them for communicating the gospel. Indeed, one of the most dramatic dances I have ever seen was an old Fijian war dance resurrected for a precise instructional purpose, years after the acceptance of Christianity. It ended with a declaration of the coming of the gospel at the climax of the dance, whereupon every dancer gave a shout (an honorific act) and broke his beautifully carved spear across his knee. A white man in the audience bewailed this destruction of native artifacts. What he failed to realize was the dramatic symbolism of this act in the chant and dance, which the Fijian spectators understood full well: the gospel had broken the spear. The dance was the talk of the countryside for weeks. This was a true indigenous creation in the best form of oral tradition. It brought the audience out of the past and left them in the present. It demonstrated that Christianity did not destroy the indigenous creativity in chant and dance, and distinguished again between "formal transformation" and "faith distortion" — for in this case, however old the transformed form, the new faith formulation was no faith distortion: its meaning was truly Christian.

Another feature of the transmission of faith and ideas through rhythm is the chant, which, in many societies whose traditions are orally transmitted, was used in pre-Christian times for both educational and liturgical purposes. An indigenous church in such a society would be one which retained the form, transforming it with a new faith formulation. It will be no surprise, then seeing I have been speaking of the dance in Fiji, to find beside it the educational and liturgical use of chanting. The old Fijian pre-Christian chant has been sanctified and made holy unto the Lord. [13] In the traditional manner, led by the matrons in the village congregations, for over a century, the Psalms of David and the lyrical and descriptive passages of Scripture have been chanted both before and as part of the regular church worship service. Here the story of the creation, the building of the temple of Solomon, the glory of the New Jerusalem, the Ten Commandments, the Beatitudes and David's lament over Absalom (to name but a few of many I have heard) have been features of Fijian worship.

This was a learning experience, but it was far more. It was a communal participation in worship, which was thoroughly Fijian in form and thoroughly scriptural. Originally the *form* was used over the bodies of the slain, as the triumphant villagers lauded the exploits of their fighting men before a cannibal feast, and at the time of the presentations at the pagan temple. But by the gospel it was *transformed* and found appropriate for use in transmitting a new and better message from Scripture and catechism.

Events in the life of the village church were also commemorated through chants. This preserved the creativity of the village poets and made the church a center of village life. In the same way, songs of farewell and dirges in memory of those who had died in the faith were composed and chanted.

For a century now in Fiji, the ongoing operation of the life of each village community has been stimulated by these transformed indigenous forms and patterns, and the strength of the church today is partly due to them. A secular anthropologist working in Fiji described this Church as "a Fijian-orientated institution . . . guided by a spirit of tolerance. . . ." (Belshaw 1964:14).

THE RISK TO FAITH

To this point we have been considering the experience of the Christian fellowship group in its encounter with the world and the culture to which it belongs. We understand that the church has to maintain its life and witness in the world, with a message which is transmissible in the cultural forms that are comprehensible in that familiar world. Yet there is always a danger of becoming so accommodated to that world that it is no longer recognizably Christian. I have spoken of the *risk to faith* which comes with involvement in the world. Here is our paradox. Here we could well be sucked into the vortex at the "meeting of the waters." Yet our Lord pointed out to his disciples that this was the inevitable risk in the Christian mission, when he prayed for them whom he left *in the world*, but not *of the world* (John 17:14b, 18).

Encounters there had to be, but encounters need not necessarily bring about syncretism or faith distortion. Syncretism is not the only kind of faith-reformulation. Cultural forms may be transformed. How this can happen I have tried to demonstrate with examples of forms of art and rhythmic mechanisms. It might have been done in other areas of culture also, but the point is clearly made. The notion of consecrating, or dedicating or sanctifying a cultural artifact or institution unto the Lord is not uncommon in Scripture. Where Scripture is iconoclastic, it is the faith-formulation and not the cultural form that is under attack. Elijah's encounter on Mt. Carmel was an attack on the worship of Baal and its pagan associations, not an attack on the idea of sacrifice.[14]

Despite the great social differences between the world of Elijah and that of the New Testament, the basic principle of the divine word spoken and demonstrated to man through man is the same. The notion of salvation certainly developed through Scripture history, but the human problem is still the encounter between the *religion-man* and the *apostolic-man*. In his work, *No Other Name*, Visser't Hooft demonstrates numerous New Testament forms of the same conflict. There was the case of Simon Magus, where the issue was the incompatibility of the service of God and the exploitation of divine gifts for self-glorification. There was the disturbance in Ephesus, where folk believed their social stability depended on a harmony between the gods, and where the notion of the uniqueness of a revelation in Christ alone had disturbing consequences. There was the letter to Colosse, where folk in the young Christian communion were faced with elemental spirits and cosmological speculations, which Paul dealt with by a dogmatic statement of the exclusiveness of Christ, who was certainly not trying to establish another mystery religion. And then there was Pergamos, the center of great gods and powerful cults, to whom the word was decisive: no compromise with other gods (Visser't Hooft 1963:56-62).

Faith formulation may be developing or distorting. Developing faith has to be related to formal transformation. If the form is not transformed, the faith will be foreign and distorted and its meaning confused. This builds up problems for the next generation. Any form of religio-social change involves some degree of encounter, and this certainly applies to the Christian mission as it brings the gospel to the non-Christian world. The only tenable and reasonable base for Christian mission, as Kraemer pointed out, is the "apostolic attitude." With him also, while requiring a respectful and humble approach to the non-Christian religions, and refraining from too critical a mind against their infusion with Christian values, and recognizing the religious possibilities in the spiritual unity of mankind (the voices of religion-man), I endorse his italicized qualification of these approaches: *"provided they are kept in their place."* He goes on:

> If they usurp the place of the apostolic motive, which is the alone valid and tenable one, they transform the Christian Church into a goodwill agency for the diffusion of refined and cultural idealism, which has lost all intrinsic relation with the central apostolic consciousness that we are to be witnesses to God and His revelational dealing with man and the world (1938:293).

If the gospel is to be communicated to the non-Christian world, as our Lord instructed, the risk of faith (the risk of the emergence of syncretistic communions) is always a dangerous possibility. But that is no reason why the Christian mission should not continue as he directed unto "the end of the age." My own missionary and research experience suggests that there is a strong correlation between the Christopagan in Christian mission and the religion-man attitude of the missionary, and as a corollary, little correlation between Christopaganism and the apostolic-man attitude.

On the other hand, I am not suggesting the apostolic-man has no lessons to learn. Here again, my experience as an anthropologist is that he is rather in danger of the unjustifiable destruction of cultural ingredients and of planting a foreign church.

The common misunderstanding in both these errors relates to the problem of meaning. In one the meaning is not Christian. In the other it is not culturally relevant. And in my opinion, one is as sad a distortion of faith as the other. The greatest methodological issue faced by the Christian mission in our day is *how to carry out the Great Commission in a multi-cultural world, with a gospel that is both truly Christian in content and culturally significant in form.* I hope that when we interact with each other in the final presentations of this colloquium we can come to grips with that problem.

Notes

1. The dynamics of the cross-cultural conversion experience was presented by the writer to the annual meeting of the American Scientific Affiliation in 1967, and discussed. The paper was circulated in a multigraphed form as a "Research in Progress Paper." Subsequently a smaller additional paper developed the topic further. The reader may also refer to the 1973 edition of *Verdict Theology in Missionary Theory*, pp. 122-127, and for further discussion on the concept of power encounter, see *Solomon Islands Christianity* (1967b:100-110).

2. The conference at Jerusalem, stimulated by certain Pharisees who had become Christian and insisted on the forms laid down by the Law of Moses being applied to Gentile Converts (Acts 15:1), determined that the Gentiles should be Christians in their own way, being merely warned of the dangers of idolatry, religous prostitution and heathen sacrifices (vv. 19-20), which might well lead to syncretism. This was a significant step, not only because it gave a Greek Christian the right to remain a Greek, but also because it recognized the element of risk, the risk to faith, as it were.

3. Hauhauism and its offshoots have been discussed at greater length in *People Movements of Southern Polynesia*, in a study of the obstructive factors which cut across the Maori people movements into Christianity (Tippett 1971:59-73, 181, and fns. 93-106, pp. 246-248). The notion of the people movement and nativistic movement as a positive/negative polarity is discussed in the same book, pp. 214-216. For further factual information on Hauhauism, see Babbage's book on the subject and for the John Frum Movement, see the writings of the French anthropologist, Jean Guiart.

4. The Hare Krishna have headquarters in forty major cities of the U.S.A. In the 1960's Soka Gakkai was claiming growth of 35,000 a year, and another Japanese sect was winning 2,000 converts a month, only 5% of them Japanese.

5. Bavinck says, "The Christian life does not accommodate or adapt itself to heathen forms of life, but it takes the latter in possession and thereby makes them new" (1964:178-179).

6. He draws his imagery from the social configurations of military life, architecture, agriculture and athletics, to name a few of the more important. To take athletics, for example, one might refer to V.C. Pfitzner's *Paul and the Agon Motif* (1967), a major scholarly work. It also receives good coverage in

Howson's *Metaphors of St. Paul* (1872:65-91). It also has a place in many works on biblical customs, e.g., Chapter 31, in F.H. Wright's *Manners & Customs of Bible Lands* (1953). The same may be done for the other configurations mentioned. But the point made here is that although Paul was not ignorant of the world scene in which the Christian encounter was taking place, and was living in the world and not an isolationist, and was talking to farmers, athletes and townsmen in real life situations; he was, nevertheless, quite intolerant of syncretism in their Christian faith.

7. In differentiating the world religions from the world of revelation, Jean Danielou says, "The worst misunderstanding of Christianity or of Judaism is to make them religions among other religions — the very error of syncretism" (1964:17-18).

8. This is the attitude, for instance, of the members of the Navaho peyote-eating cult when they seek a corporate religious experience "in the Peyote Spirit, rather than in Christ, for Christ is but the culture hero of the white man."

9. The first lines cited come from "Birds of Passage," and the second from "Thou Mother with Thy Equal Brood." These are typical of Whitman's pantheism, of which many other passages might have been cited, for example:

> My faith is the greatest of faiths and the least of faiths,
> Enclosing worship ancient and modern and all between ancient and modern,
> Believing I shall come again upon the earth after 5000 years,
> Waiting responses from oracles, honoring the gods, saluting the sun,
> Making a fetish of the first rock or stump, powwowing with sticks in the circle of obis,
> Dancing yet through the streets in a phallic procession, rapt and austere in the woods a gymnosophist,
> Drinking mead from the skull-cup, to Shastas and Vedas admirant, minding the Koran,
> Walking the teokallis, spotted with gore from the stone and knife, beating the serpent-skin drum,
> Accepting the Gospels, accepting him that was crucified, knowing assuredly that he is divine, . . ."
> (Poem 43 in "Song of Myself")

Apparently it does not occur to Whitman that many of these religious patterns are incompatible. His pantheism can be no more than an abstraction. Such syncretism is impossible if one accepts the Gospels as John indicates ("Leaves of Grass," 319, 176, 60).

10. Another form of the same fallacy I have met in the Solomon Islands and in the United States, where people calling themselves Jehovah's Witnesses exploit the same persuasive device. They cite Scripture, one passage after another, each time getting a nod of approval from the listener, in spite of the fact that they are quite unrelated and all extracted from their context. Thus the bare fact that Scripture was cited elicits a belief in a non-scriptural position.

11. He says of the missionary, "He would not be true to his vocation if he ever agreed to act on the principle that Christianity is as 'any other form of cult.' As a matter of fact, his brief is to regard . . . Christianity as entirely different, the only true religion to be implanted. . . ." (1965:xv — originally published 1938).

12. Possibly no Christian book has been more influential in the spread of Christian values than *Pilgrim's Progress,* which was translated into scores of languages during the last century. It had its cross-cultural appeal, not only in the notion of the pilgrimage, but also in its literary form and the use of the "name with a meaning," a common device in preliterate societies.

13. In the same way the original collection of Christian Fijian hymns, created by John Hunt and R.B. Lyth, were composed as Fijian lyrics, even with Fijian euphonistic particles. It was a later (and more Victorian) generation which made them rhyme and organized the parts to fit sheet music. The *Te Deum* was used in Fijian whenever some sinner "bowed the knee" before God, the whole congregation bursting spontaneously into the praise. For an evaluation of Hunt's mastery of Fijian hymnody, see Nettleton's *John Hunt* (n/d:84).

14. The scriptural notion of sacrifice is itself a good example of faith-reformulation and formal transformation. The forebears of Israel, who came over the desert, practised human sacrifice, until the Lord brought Abraham to Mt. Moriah, in an experience of crisis or encounter, leading eventually to his provision of a lamb as a functional substitute. Thereafter, Israel passed through the phase of animal sacrifice as developed in the Law of Moses. This continued throughout the Old Testament times and is terminated in the beginning of the Christian era, with our Lord's encounter with the forces of human sin on the cross at Calvary. This is spoken of as "a better sacrifice" because, among other things, it is an eternal one. So the faith-formulation grows or is reformulated, passing from Semite, to Hebrew, to Christian faith, and the form of the salvation motif is transformed by a new faith content. Incidentally, converts to Christianity, coming out of a society which practices human sacrifices, need an early translation of the Letter to the Hebrews to help them in that journey of faith.

CHAPTER SIX

Possessio and Syncretism in Biblical Perspective

PETER BEYERHAUS

THE scope of our deliberations in this symposium seems to be conveniently pinned to one specific missiological issue: Which anthropological adjustments should be made when presenting the gospel to the peoples of different cultures without running into the risk of distorting Christianity? But the question of the rights and limits of missionary adaption is also a theological issue, which brings us in touch with the drama of salvation history. We would not do justice to our topic if we were to take the word "possessio" only as a new technical term of missionary strategy. First of all, we have to reflect back to the basic act of him who takes into possession that which by eternal right is already his sole property.

In the messianic Psalm 2 (v.8), God speaks to his Anointed One: "Ask of me, and I will make the nations your heritage, and the ends of the earth your possession." What is mission? God the Father puts his creation in the power of the Holy Spirit under the dominion of his Son, who on account of his universal act of redemption, has been installed as its sovereign ruler (Isa. 53:12; Dan. 7:14; Mt. 28:18; I Cor. 15:22-25). But this rightful taking into possession is not a harmonious process: it is the continuation of that war which began with the original rebellion in the invisible world and which will be concluded only when even death, the last enemy, is destroyed (I Cor. 15:25). It is against this cosmic background that we have to consider our issue of the "possessio-syncretism axis."

We can, therefore, distinguish between *three stages of possessio*:

In the *first stage* God invades this occupied world of nations and establishes bridgeheads of his sovereignty. He does so by a chain of specific elections. Partly they belong to the history of biblical revelation, partly to the history of Christian missions. Here the whole emphasis lies on demonstrating the uniqueness of God's Godhead, and in guarding it against the insidious counterattacks of the present demonic usurper of the world.

In the *second stage* these bridgeheads of elected communities become the basis of operation for a progressive reconquest of the whole ethnic and cultural territory which they represent. Here the principle of doctrinal exclusiveness of the missionary message is complemented by a strategy of a sifting inclusiveness: The distorted elements of the first creation are reclaimed for the Kingdom of Christ.

The *third stage*, finally, lies beyond this present age. Here the Devil, the prince of this world, will completely be removed and the kingdoms of the world will totally have become the kingdom of the Lord and his Christ (Rev. 11:5).

In missiology we are only concerned with the first two stages of *possessio*. We may distinguish them as *exclusive* and *comprehensive possessio*. If they are seen against syncretism as the other end of the axis, a tripartition of our discussion becomes logical. We have to speak firstly about the principles of biblical identity, secondly about the danger of its syncretistic falsification, and finally we have to outline a missionary strategy of translation which is aware of both.

EXCLUSIVE POSSESSIO: ESTABLISHING BRIDGEHEADS OF GOD'S SOVEREIGNTY

Within the entire world of human religion, the faith of the Bible appears as a unique phenomenon by the emphasis it puts on its exclusiveness. The Judeo-Christian religion is, as far as its convictions are concerned, the most intolerant of all religions — a feature which, to some degree, was inherited from it also by Islam. This exclusiveness consists in the fact that the cosmic redemption proceeds by a series of elections, which are bound together by a chain of continuity. God has chosen specific times, places and persons to reveal himself, a specific way to save the world, a specific people to be the bearer of his plan of salvation, specific means to bring redemption to the world, and above all, a specific human genealogy in which the central mystery of our faith, the birth of the divine Redeemer, God's own incarnation, should take place.

This must not be, as it so many times has been, understood as the expression of a primitive tribal religion. Rather it introduces us to the unique concept of a sovereign God who cannot be disposed of by the religious manipulation of man, but who himself establishes contact with mankind and determines its destiny by binding it to the mysterious ways of his contingent self-disclosure.

The central concept of Old Testament religion, therefore, is the *covenant* between Yahweh and his elected people. The story of the Old Testament is the account of one single drama: Yahweh struggles to insure the validity of his covenant with Israel by demanding her undiverted loyalty and by demonstrating his own faithfulness to his promises connected with this covenant.

A very peculiar feature in the image of God, therefore, is what G. von Rad (1963:216-225) calls the "holy jealousy" of God Yahweh. He is tremendously concerned about the respect for his majestic position and the exclusiveness of Israel's loyalty to him. But jealousy is only the anthropomorphic expression of God's holiness, which finally is to be adored by all mankind.

This finds another expression in the special weight carried by the First Commandment. It is not only the fountain of all other commandments, but at the same time the substance of the central creed of Israel, the "Shma Israel," and the main key to understand her historical tragedy.

The negative consequence of the particular character of Israel as elected people is the derogatory and sometimes even hostile attitude to the other, not elected, nations, the "goyim", and her strict separation from them.

Still Israel does not understand herself as a secluded ghetto, removed from the history of the rest of the world. Rather she regards herself as the center of the world. Her history appears finally as the clue to the outcome of world history. The idea is especially emphasized in the messianic announcements of the prophets and in the tradition of the significance of Mount Zion as the navel of the earth.

This constitutes the Old Testament's particular centripetal concept of the Gentiles' salvation (Blauw 1962:34). It is no mission in the literal sense. For the barrier of the historic confinement of God's favors will not be crossed by Israel going out to evangelize the nations. Rather the nations will come themselves to Zion, feeling irresistibly attracted by the manifestation of God's glory in the rule of his Messiah as an offer of renewal to the whole earth (Isa. 2; 9:2-7; 11:1-10).

By such terms the Old Testament uncompromisingly maintains its basic affirmation: the redemptive transformation of the world will remain the prerogative of the sovereign God reclaiming his creation. Autonomous human movements within the sphere of religion, politics or technology will play no constructive part in this process. The kingdom of God will be built on the ruins of the empires (Dan. 7).

Coming to the New Testament, we should first of all notice its close connection with the basic assumptions and the general outlook of the Old Testament. It is simply wrong to state the relationship between the two Testaments in terms of particularism versus universalism. The New Testament emphatically remains in the continuity of the particular history of revelation and election centered on the people of Israel. It remains Israelo-centric, even where history passes through an epoch of rejection of the physical Israel (Rom. 9-11).

The real progression of the New Testament does not lie in the introduction of new foundations, ideas and values. It consists firstly in the kerygmatic affirmation that the Old Testament prophecies have been fulfilled, and secondly in the interpretation of the peculiar, unexpected way in which they have been or still will be fulfilled.

What is constitutive for the New Testament is that Jesus of Nazareth is the expected Messiah promised by the Old Testament prophets, not a new religious ideal, but a new reality. This is what H. Kraemer (1938:62ff) referred to by his term "biblical realism." But Jesus was a Messiah rather different from the expectations of the contemporary Jews. And the way in which he brought redemption to his people, as victim on a cross, was neither anticipated not understood by them. The reason was that the different aspects of the revelation, contained in the various prophetical writings, had never been grasped fully by the Jewish readers.

Jesus Christ is not only the fulfillment of the Old Testament Scriptures; he gives also their authentic interpretation. He does so partly during his earthly days, partly through a special revelation by the Holy Spirit — another newly entered biblical reality — after his ascension. Therefore, the apostolic *kerygma* and *didache* about Christ and his work receive an importance for the salvation of men which is secondary only to his person, although inseparable from him. Paul regards the integrity of his gosspel as indispensable to salvation (Gal. 1:6-9). This presupposes, of course, that the early church was convinced both of the authenticity and the essential oneness of her belief. The historic-critical approach to the Bible has led to the theory of a pluralism of didactic types within the New Testament itself. Each should be representative of a different understanding of Christology, soteriology, pneumatology and eschatology, and, therefore, of a different ecclesiastic tradition (Käsemann 1964:262-267). Such an idea was inconceivable to the apostles.

Doctrinal disunity would have been equal to the disunity of the church herself, a monstrous thought! For the church is nothing less than the new Israel, the people of the New Covenant. As Christ's body, she stands in an even closer relationship to God than the Israel of the Old Covenant. For through Christ, the Christians have already received the Spirit of life, and only here could he be received. "In Christ" is an ecclesiological term (Richardson 1961:249-252). *Hoi exoi*, the people still outside, are those who are "separate from Christ, strangers to the community of Israel, outside God's covenant and the promise that goes with them. Their world is a world without hope and without God" (Eph. 2:11-12). Therefore, the church has to fulfill that priestly ministry to the nations to which Israel once had been called (Ex. 19:4-6; I Peter 2:9-10).

This brings us to the New Testament concept of Mission. There is both a difference and a continuity to the Old Testament understanding. The act of redemption has removed the historic barriers between Israel and the Gentiles. Therefore, apostolic messengers are sent to the ends of the earth to proclaim the gospel of the Kingdom to the nations. Yet this new *centrifugal* dimension does not substitute for but complements the classical *centripetal* (Blauw 1962:66; Kvist 1957:124-134) concept: The gospel preached to the Gentiles is an invitation to become aspirants of the Kingdom of God by joining the Church of Christ. The people of God, it is true, is no longer tied to a specific geographical realm, the country of Israel. But it is still an elected community of people who have responded to a special calling, the *ekklesia*. They have passed from the realm of Satan to the realm of Jesus Christ and expect his second coming. The church is not equal with the Christianized nation, because the church is not the Kingdom yet. It rather constitutes the bridgehead of the coming Kingdom over the whole nation. Therefore, the church is not established by developing or revolutionizing the former ethnic structures, although these might be used pedagogically as "Bridges of God" (McGavran 1955). The constituting principle is a crossing of the border: through personal belief, repentance and baptism, individuals are incorporated into a totally new community — the chosen race, God's own people (I Peter 2:9). They live as strangers in the *diaspora*, having their true citizenship no longer on earth but in the Kingdom of Heaven to come (Phil. 3:20).

All this means that social entities, cultural values and former religious systems can only be a later concern to Christian missions. In biblical perspective "possessio" has a *personal* connotation. Mission, as the continuation of Christ's redemptive work, wants to take into possession living men. Scripture, in its teaching about the divine concern for the Gentile world, never refers directly to cultural values, religious ideas or technological achievements, except twice in an eschatological context (Isa. 60:10; Rev. 21:24). God addresses his vocation to each person, calls him by his name and brings him into an intimate fellowship with himself. Therefore, we are left in a certain aporia, when we expect direct biblical answers to the question of possessio in terms of cultural adaptation. The Bible is almost silent about our theme.[1] Primarily it is concerned with the personal allegiance of people, based on a change of mind, a metaphysical liberation and a spiritual regeneration.

This change of allegiance is nothing less than a divine miracle. It can neither be accomplished by the methodical skill of the missionary nor by the free decision of the convert. The whole initiative lies with the sending God. The means by which he accomplishes the new birth and the plantation of the new church is the preaching of the eternal gospel. It carries with it the power for salvation to everyone who has faith, to the Jew first and also to the Greek (Rom. 1:16), and, therefore, also to the Indian Brahmin or the Russian Marxist.

This biblical truth must be affirmed today, especially in view of a rapidly spreading missiological heresy. It is cherished in ecumenical circles and presently goes together with the new concept of *dialog*. Here it is stated that the content of the gospel and the nature of salvation are neither known by the Christian messengers beforehand, nor determined by a fixed type of doctrine. Rather they are to be discovered in the *situation* in which the dialog takes place (Hollenweger 1973:10-11). Here Christ speaks through the non-Christian to the Christian partner, no less (rather more!) than vice versa (Bangkok Assembly 1973:78-79).

The theological rationale for such a concept is sought in four propositions. The *first* is that the character of the Christian gospel itself is situational and pluralistic. The *second* is that God himself — this means the forces at work in the historical process — works towards universal salvation irrespective of whether the Christian church understands it or not.[2] This goes together, *thirdly*, with the idea of history as a principle of continued revelation in situations.[3] And there is *fourthly* the idea of the cosmic Christ, working anonymously among the "living faiths" of other peoples as well as in Christianity.[4] Such views lack any solid exegetical support in Scripture. They open the doors of Christianity widely towards the entrance of syncretism.

Christian mission, although it needs courage to maintain this today, is basically a one-way traffic. It originates in the sovereign self-disclosure of the biblical God. It is carried out by ambassadors elected in Christ's stead. It goes into a world which lives in a state of ignorance and demonic captivity. It carries a message which no heart of man conceived (I Cor. 2:9). It establishes elected communities as bridgeheads of God's coming Kingdom.

I am, of course, aware of the fact that in the past this one-way road very often has been misused to export western cultural imperialism. The goal of the work of the American Board among the red Indians, e.g., was "to make them English in language, civilized in their habits and Christian in their religion" (Anderson 1875:61)! But painful as this historical insight is, the remedy is not to encourage all types of fashionable theologies which substitute Marxist or Afro-pagan ideas for western paternalism. Church renewal for mission can only be accomplished by a new concern for and an uncompromising loyalty to the authentic gospel.

FACING THE SYNCRETISTIC COUNTERATTACK

(1) Syncretism as Religious Phenomenon

The word "syncretism" does not occur in the Bible. But the reality of syncretism was an ever-present phenomenon throughout the history of Israel and Christianity. The semantic origin of the term is given most convincingly by Plutarch (Kraemer 1959:385). He related that the rivaling Greek tribes of the island of Crete were usually involved in minor warfare against each other. But as soon as they were attacked by a common enemy from outside, they agreed to form a military alliance. Since then the word syncretism carries a note of an opportunistic fraternization without a deeper conviction.

Among missiologists, none has dealt more with the theological problem of syncretism than the late Hendrick Kraemer (1938; 1959:396ff; 1960; 1962). He ingeniously distinguishes between spontaneous primitive syncretism as a popular religious tendency, and conscious, philosophical construction of syncretism (1959:384-394). The latter may be attempted either by religious thinkers or by political rulers. Both forms are to be found in biblical times as well. We shall see, however, that in order to understand the real nature of "Christian" syncretism or Christopaganism, we have to dig at a deeper level still. Let us start by giving a working definition:

> We understand syncretism as the unconscious tendency or the conscious attempt to undermine the uniqueness of a specific religion by equating its elements with those of other belief systems.

In this understanding, syncretism is not just the simultaneous practice of two unrelated religions, which might be motivated either by external pressure or inner anxiety. Neither should it be confused with the *adoption* of formal elements of other religions into Christianity for missionary reasons. Syncretism equates heterogenous religious elements and thereby changes their original meaning without admitting such change.

(2) The Battle Against Syncretism in the Old Testament

The whole history of Israel as described in the Old Testament is a gigantic fight for the validity of the First Commandment. The attacks against the Yahweh faith came from two directions, from inside and from outside.

The first threatening of Israel's belief started as soon as the people had settled in the country of Canaan. The Isralites had received their revelation during their nomadic existence in the desert. Now they were met by the Phoenician-Canaanite fertility cult, which was so persuasively fitted to the needs of an agricultural society. In the Old Testament we find a three-fold answer to this challenge: segregation, eradication and adaptation.

In the early writings we find continuous warnings not to have any social contact with the Canaanites, or even the injunction either to kill or to enslave them (e.g. Deut. 20:16-18). This frightening expression of intolerance must be understood as a harsh but necessary preventive measure. For the imminent danger was that the divine mission of Israel, as God's elected instrument for universal shalom, was swallowed up by the temptations of the heathen religion. The second measure was the destruction of the sacred places of the Canaanite cult and harsh prohibitions against indulging in any such practice. The third reply was the attempt to overcome the Baal religion by way of "possessio". Certain Canaanite assumptions, practices and places (especially Zion!) were incorporated into the religion of Yahweh and subdued to his authority.

None of these methods was entirely successful. The danger to the faith of Israel persisted in two ways: on the one hand the cult of Baal and Ashera on the hill tops and in the groves continued secretly. Together with this went the secondary religion, the practice of magic and spiritism, which lends itself so readily to combination with any of the higher religions. On the other hand there was the even greater danger that the process of adaptation go out of control. Instead of reinterpreting the elements of Baalism in the light of the Yahweh revelation, Israel's religion became Canaanized. Yahweh assumes the feature of Baal! Analogous to the plerophorous manifestation of nature forces the images of Baal and Ashera oscillated in an immense number of different local appearances. The same process now occurred to the concept of Yahweh. As O. Proksch, German Old Testament scholar, comments: "Yahweh himself, the God of Israel, seemed no longer to be the one only Yahweh (according to the 'shma Ishrael'), but he became multiplied into the Baalim of the country" (von Rad 1969:II:25; Proksch 1950:215).

The threat of religious disintegration became even more acute after the 8th and 7th centuries B.C.. Now the country was drawn into the imperialistic struggle of the ancient oriental powers of Assur and Babylon. Israel faced foreign religiosity not only in the archaic forms of the indigenous nature cult, but in the more refined ways of worship of the official state cults. The foreign conquerors tried to demonstrate their authority over Israel by introducing altars of their god (e.g. II Kings 16:13). The new religiosity fascinated the minds of the Jews. Voluntarily they sacrificed on their roofs to the host of heaven (Jer. 19:15). The women of Jerusalem participated in the cultic weeping over the mythical death of the spring god Tammuz. Thus Yahweh was downgraded to become one deity among others in the oriental pantheon.

In those dark hours in the history of Israel the entire people seemed to have committed apostasy or become given to syncretism. How then did the miracle happen that as the outcome of the struggle the Yahweh religion finally emerged in a thoroughly purified form? How could the Jews become the first really monotheistic people in the whole history of religion?

Several forces joined in the battle for the maintenance, survival, and restoration of the genuine faith: There were those exemplary kings like David, Hezekiah, and Josiah, who took their vocation as messianic representatives of their covenant people very seriously. They established or reformed the

Yahweh cult as the only tolerated state religion. The deuteronomistic reform centralized the sacrificial cult exclusively in the temple of Jerusalem. After the exile Nehemiah and Ezra consolidated the Jewish community socially and religiously. In their zeal for purification they went to the extent of separating ethnically mixed marriages. Of greater spiritual importance was Ezra's canonization of the Pentateuch as the sole standard of reference in religious and social life.

But all this would have had little effect without a corresponding inner revival. The religious conscience of Israel as the elected people with its specific corresponding promises and obligations had to be stirred up. This function was exercised by a series of outstanding men whose ministry was as unique in the phenomenology of religion as the faith of Israel as such: the prophets.

What was the proper function of the prophets, in all the difference of their personalities, historic horizons, and theological emphases? It was to remind their people of its specific calling and to enable it to understand and accept its historic destiny within the framework of this unique vocation. Three main features are common to their mission and message:

Firstly they were deeply moved by the obligatory character of Israel's ancient holy traditions. They contrasted the pure beginning of the people's history, its election, and its experience of God's miraculous acts of salvation with the present accommodation to the religion and morals of the heathen.Passionately they call for a decision: "How long will you go limping with two different opinions? If Yahweh is God, follow him; but if Baal, follow him!" (I Kings 18:21). Never has syncretism been denounced more sharply than in these words of Elijah, the prototype of prophetism in Israel.

The *second* characteristic of the prophetic message is that is applies the will of God as clearly known from the Torah to the actual situation. This corrects our modernist misunderstanding that prophetism means to discover the unknown will of God in the situation! Israel's task is not to seek pragmatical answers like forming alliances with neighboring heathen nations to solve the present crisis. Isaiah and Jeremiah adamantly insist that faithfulness must prevail over the temptation to political opportunism: "If you will not believe, surely you will not be established" (Isa. 7:9). This is literally the opposite to syncretism!

The *third* main feature of the prophetic message is the eschatological vision. The prophets interpreted the political catastrophe as the divine punishment for Israel's syncretistic apostasy. This meant that history by no means had gone out of Yahweh's control. He both has the power and the intention to change its course again in favor of his people. In the final days God will remember his promises to Israel and renew his covenant with her. Zion will become the highest mountain on earth, and God will be really present in his holy city to establish messianic shalom over his people and from there over all nations.

Thus in the prophetic message past, present, and future were bound together by the continuity of the specific history of election, revelation, and salvation of Yahweh with his chosen people. Thereby the unmistakable identity of Israel's faith was safeguarded against any syncretistic desintegration.

(3) Syncretism Unmasked in the New Testament

When the message of Jesus Christ as the Savior of all mankind was proclaimed for the first time in the Hellenistic-Roman world, the danger of being swallowed up by other religions was even greater than in Old Testament times. With the reign of Alexander the Great, a tremendous syncretistic process had been introduced into the Near Orient and the Mediterranean world. Visser't Hooft refers to it as the second historical wave of syncretism (1965:16-24). He calls it "the most powerful and comprehensive blending and combination of different religions which ever has taken place in history."

Many religions of most different origins and characters participated in this religious process (Lietzmann 1932:158-183): the ancient religions of Egypt, Persia and Syria; the two pantheons of the Greeks and Romans; the emperor worship which had been established by Alexander the Great as an ecumenical ideology of salvation; the universal popular religion of animism; the Dionysian and oriental mysteries; the Greek-Roman philosophies of Stoicism and Neoplatonism; the esthetic poetry of Horace and Virgil; Judaism with its different sects; and finally the newly emerging gnosis.

It was a thoroughly religious age. But it was a religiosity which was detrimental to the maintenance of any clear doctrinal profile. How would Christianity as a profoundly missionary faith be able to preserve its unique tenets on which its universal claims were based? Liberals like Gunkel and Harnack maintain that Christianity became the victorious religion of the Roman Empire by being transformed into a syncretistic religion (von Harnack 1906:I:262). But this thesis is neither logical nor can it be proved by a proper comparative religious analysis. Real syncretism never grants the victory to any particular religion.

The early encounter between the gospel and the contemporary religiosity are indicated in several New Testament writings. Visser't Hooft discusses a number of these early occurrences (1965:57-64). The temptation to syncretize the Christian faith came from different sources: Judaism changed the liberty of the gospel into a legalistic system. Dionysian enthusiasm perverted this liberty into an orgiastic libertinism. The cosmic speculation in Asia Minor introduced the elementary spirits of the universe (stoicheia tou kosmou) as intermediary forces between God and man. Magicians like Simon desired the charismatic aspect of the Holy Spirit as dynamic means to reinforce their mediumistic abilities. In the Book of Revelation the first encounter with compulsive emperor worship is hinted at. Not all of those interfaith encounters described in the New Testament were syncretistic temptations in the proper sense. Some cases were open intrusions of clearly competitive religions, acting either by enticement or by force.

Still, the New Testament indicates instances of a real syncretization of the Christian faith. The clearest evidence is found in the first Epistle of John. It is written at a relatively late stage of the New Testament period. Here the process of syncretistic assimilation has already become so refined that it could penetrate deeply into the heart of the Christian doctrine. We know from the post-apostolic period that this was accomplished most successfully by gnosticism. Indeed, the heretics against which the epistle polemicized bear the features of gnostic charismatics. They claim for their teaching a divine authority by speaking in the *ekstasis* of the Spirit. Therefore, their fellow Christians hesitated to question their truthfulness. But John recognizes that their Christology and soteriology are as incompatible with the genuine Christian faith as their behavior violates Christian ethics. Four observations about the way in which this apostle of Christ deals with the emergence of syncretism appear most relevant to our theme:

(a) John, like Jesus, identifies the falseness of these prophets by their unethical behavior: their lack of genuine Christian love. It originates from their pseudo-spiritual arrogance and leads to strife and hatred in the brotherhood and even to open indulgence in sin (2:4-6).

(b) John encouragingly points out to his readers that they possess an inner equipment by which they themselves can cope with the seducers. It is the *anointing of the Holy Spirit* (2:27). It constitutes the inner fellowship between the believer and God the Father and his Son Jesus Christ. Therefore, their faith is no mere intellectual agreement to a doctrinal proposition. It is a loving communion leading to a degree of certainty which, if it is cultivated properly and illuminated by insight, can never be shaken by any sophisticated argumentation. The spiritual intuition and Christian common sense *(sensus Christianorum)* of the ordinary congregation are the most powerful ally in the struggle of the church's watchmen against its constant syncretistic temptation.

(c) Still, true spirituality is no mere feeling. Its authenticity is to be verified by objective doctrinal criteria. The most important of them are plain enough to be used by all believers, and usually they suffice. In the case debated in John's epistle — as in almost any case of syncretism — the person of Christ is the chief target of the heretical attack. He is not plainly discarded. Obviously the heretics had their own Christology. Probably it was the gnostic myth of a transcendental savior figure who appears to the souls of men and reveals to them the way back to their heavenly origin. Typically enough John, like all other New Testament authors, pays no attention to the speculative ideas of the heretics. He does not engage in dialog with them. He does not expect a more comprehensive understanding of Christ by listening to his speaking through the testimony of his partners about their living faith. Nothing is important to him but the devastating consequence of their teachings to the genuine Christian belief. The syncretistic Christology of the gnostics implies the denial that Christ is the Son of God who has come into the world in the human person of the historical Jesus. Here the central Christian belief, the mystery of incarnation as unfolded and defended in all writings of John, is at stake. In fact this early gnostic controversy introduces a Christological battle which soon will engage the whole ancient church, until it is settled dogmatically in Nicea and Chalcedon. These two ecumenical councils laid foundations which have proved to be and always will be indispensable for combating syncretism: the doctrines of the divine Trinity and of the two natures of Jesus Christ.[5]

(d) Still something more remains to be discovered about the real issue at stake in pseudo-Christian syncretism. This is its metaphysical dimension: "Test the spirits to see whether they are of God!" (I John 4:1). This does not happen on the intellectual level alone. John does not act like a scholar of comparative religion. He does not consider the gnostic aberrations as an interesting intermingling of foreign religious or philosophical ideas which in the historical situation is quite normal. Instead he treats it as a conscious attack planned and directed by a demonic enemy. The conflict displayed in the congregations of his readers is already the foreshadowing of a future apocalyptic drama: the emergence of Antichrist. According to general Christian convictions ("as you have heard" I John 2:18), this person will come at the close of the present age shortly before the *parousia* of Christ (cf. II Thess. 2:3-12). In the power of Satan he will usurp the place of God, making himself the object of worship. When John speaks of a plurality of antichrists he does not refute the expectation of the one single Antichrist. On the contrary, the present antichrists are imbued with the spirit of the coming Antichrist (4:3). The gnostic heretics are antichrists because essentially they are already now doing the same thing on a smaller scale as the final Antichrist will do in a universal dimension: they deprive Christ of his central place in the life and faith of his church. Syncretism in the light of John's first epistle is the constant sublime anticipation of the final battle between Christ and Antichrist. For the church this is a matter of life and death. At stake is nothing less but our belonging to Christ, the reality of our experienced redemption and the reliability of the promise of eternal life when "we shall be like him, for we shall see him as he is" (I John 3:2).

COMPREHENSIVE POSSESSIO: TAKING CAPTIVE TO OBEY CHRIST
(II Cor. 10:5)

Syncretism is Satan's constant attempt by way of theological camouflage to intrude into the exclusive relationship between the biblical God and his elected people. But this does not place the biblical faith in a permanently defensive position. On the contrary, there is no more aggressive, conquering force in the world than the gospel that proclaims Jesus as Christ and Lord.

(1) The Theological Implications of Possessio

The term "possessio" could be used as a valid synonym for the missionary task as such. For it is the apostolic commission "to bring about obedience to the faith for the sake of his name among all the nations," i.e., all those "who are called to belong to Jesus Christ" (Rom. 1:5-6). If we understand "possessio" in this context, we discover a dramatic notion in it.

The Latin word can signify both the fact of ownership and the act of acquisition. This distinction is meaningful to our topic. Mission is the process by which the original owner, God, regains that which by eternal right is already his property. Thus the converts are God's possession in a double sense.

The doctrine of creation, on the one hand, introduces a rather comprehensive note to the concept of possessio. Man does not only consist of his immortal soul, but also of his body. He subsists in a cultural and social involvement which was willed by the Creator. And in this total natural existence even fallen man remains in a basic relatedness to God. God bestows his fatherly mercies on him. He reveals his eternal power and deity through the things that he has made (Rom. 1:19-20). Man expresses his relatedness to God by way of religion (Acts 17:22-28). All this cannot be left out of account in the act of missionary possessio.

On the other hand, the same world which on account of its

creation is the property of God lies also under the dominion of God's adversary, the devil. There is, in fact, a whole demonic structure which has imposed itself on the world, the *stoicheia tou kosmou*. They affect every aspect of man's life. They control his transpersonal relations in society, culture and religion. Therefore, man lives in a state of estrangement from God and of captivity which distorts his way of perceiving, thinking and acting (I Cor. 12:2). The Christian missionary has to consider that the task of taking into God's possession is antagonized by the state of demonic possession which characterizes fallen man and his world (Eph. 6:10-18).

The ancient church was conscious of this dramatic nature of mission. The admission into the fellowship of Christ by baptism was, therefore, preceded by an act of exorcism. The converts had to renounce Satan and all his ways and works, and thereafter submit themselves to the living God (Acts 26:18; I Thess. 1:9). Having become "ransomed by the precious blood of Christ" (I Peter 1:18-19), they now had become truly God's possession in a second sense.

Now it should be noted that an analogous procedure was followed when the conceptual world of the Gentiles was Christianized. Mission implies translation. When the biblical message is transmitted into the realm of a different culture, this culture necessarily will have to provide the material elements in which it will be embodied.

Some theologians regard this transculturating process in the history of the biblical faith as the consequent syncretization of the Jewish-Christian religion. Hermann Gunkel has stated that the Christianity of Paul and John is a syncretistic religion (1903:88). His proposition has been renewed by W. Pannenberg (1967). He whole-heartedly accepts such a syncretizing process by revaluating its traditional theological verdict. He considers it as the way in which the history of religion finally leads to the unification of mankind in one religious culture. Pannenberg justifies his position by claiming that religious accumulation was the way in which the Yahweh religion assimilated the Canaanite cults, and Christianity assimilated the Hellenistic mystery religions. Thus they emerged victoriously as the integrated religions of their times.

But such a view presents the history of biblical religion as a snowball system which is contrary to what really happened. The bearers of the biblical faith were extremely conscientious about its uniqueness and incompatibility with the basic assumptions of other religions. There was no possibility of plainly equating biblical concepts with non-biblical ones, because the latter lacked the authenticity of God's historic self-disclosure. And there was still less a possibility to enlarge the biblical message by non-biblical elements which were not unfoldings of what God really had said and given to Israel in his historic election and deeds of salvation. In fact the Epistle to the Hebrews regards the history of revelation as concluded with Christ (Heb. 1:1-2). The ancient church dogmatized this conclusion of revelation by fixing the New Testament canon and by developing the creed as the standard of its correct interpretation. In fact, the canon and the creed become the church's two main weapons against accumulating and transmutating syncretism.

(2) The Three Steps of Biblical Adaptation

In the history of the biblical faith there was, indeed, a certain amount of assimilation of elements from the cultural and religious environment. But this was practised in a very peculiar way. It was a possessio which led to an affirmation rather than to a loss of spiritual identity. This was achieved by three decisive steps: *selection, rejection, reinterpretation.*

(a) *Selection.* The first observation which strikes us in the study of biblical "possessio" is the extremely cautious, self-conscious and discriminating way in which it proceeded. As to its form, the biblical faith expresses itself in the categories, symbols, ideas and devotional practices of human religion in general. It can, therefore, be studied within the framework of comparative religion. Whenever the trans-cultural borders were crossed, the phenomena of indigenous religion provided the material to be adapted for the missionary translation. But not all concepts and terms within the religious world were found equally compatible with the biblical revelation. Some lent themselves readily; others appeared ambivalent; still others were totally disagreeable to the basic thrust of the creed of Israel and the church. It can be shown that both in the Old Testament and New Testament a careful selection was practised, in which only such elements were adapted as could be integrated into the continuity of the prophetic and messianic tradition. For example, in the Old Testament the faith in Yahweh led to the adoption of titles like "King" and predications given to El, Baal and other oriental high gods which undergirded the belief in the supreme power of Yahweh. This was done in the conviction that only Yahweh was entitled to such majestic dignity, and that the honor taken by the other gods was in fact a usurpation. Yahweh reclaims the right and adoration which is due to him alone. At the same time other concepts, which went together with the worship of those gods, were experienced as extremely repulsive to the holy nature of the God of Israel. Here their matrimony with goddesses could be mentioned. We also can refer to the practice of human sacrifice or sacred prostitution. We know that occasionally some of these things were adopted by the Israelites. But this led always to a furious reaction of the prophets as the watchmen of the genuine and pure adoration of Yahweh and to the final elimination of the offending features.

The same selective procedure was followed in the New Testament. When the apostolic church crossed the border from the Hebrew to the Hellenistic world (Riesenfeld 1969), the proclamation of Jesus Christ attracted a whole number of religious and philosophical concepts, like the popular divine titles Kurios, Soter and Son of God, or the stoic idea of the Logos as the rational principle of the cosmic structure. Still, in none of these cases was a completely new or even heterogenous element added to the Christian faith. For all of these titles were already found in the Septuagint as divine attributes of Yahweh or of the Messiah. The concept of Logos was developed in the Chokma literature and could be found in the Proverbs and Wisdom of Solomon. Thus the selective possessio of oriental and hellenistic concepts did not lead into syncretism. Instead it achieved a progressive invigoration, unfolding and clarification of the potentialities which were already inherent in the genuine tenets of the biblical creed.

That such selection was possible at all shows that, on account of general revelation, non-Christian religion may contain some foreshadowings of that divine reality which is brought authentically in God's historic self-revelation to Israel. But the realm in which general revelation can be traced is an ambiguous field. Therefore, the first step of possessio, selection, is always followed by an antithetical one:

(b) *Rejection.* No part of creation remained unaffected by the original rebellion. Here is a basic distinction between the Thomistic worldview and the Reformed one. The former describes the effect of the fall in terms of deprivation, the latter in terms of distortion. Therefore, Roman Catholic missions often are less inhibited than evangelicals in their accommodation to non-Christian practices like ancestral worship.

The biblical procedure is clearly determined by its dualistic view of salvation history as a warfare between the kingdoms of God and Satan. Therefore, possessio is always accompanied by a conscious rejection, a rejection in a double way.

Firstly, the discriminatory principle of selection implies a preliminary ruling out of all elements in heathen culture which are incompatible with biblical faith.

Secondly, rejection is also practised within the procedure of adaptation. It is the purification of the adapted material from those elements which have defiled and distorted the original beauty of creation and man's sincere response to general revelation. Whenever Christian missions by way of translation and indigenization take into usage native concepts and practices, they have to guard these adopted elements against their interpretation in the light of their former conception. This is done already in the first kerygmatic approach to heathen listeners (cf. Acts 17:29-30), and it is followed by catechetical instruction. The apostolic exhortation to the converts, therefore, always points out their former state of ignorance and perversion. Sometimes it refers to the analogy of their religious concepts and experiences now and in the past. In this case the complete contrast between the former influence and fruits of the Holy Spirit is pointed out (I Cor. 12:2; Eph. 2:11-12). The spiritual communion experienced at the Lord's Table has, indeed, an analogy in the heathen sacrificial meals. But far from justifying their continuation, this analogy serves as the strongest argument for their rejection: "What pagans sacrifice, they offer to demons and not to God. I do not want you to be partners with demons" (I Cor. 10:20-21; II Cor. 6:16).

The neglect of this principle is the greatest menace in the present encounter between ecumenical Christianity and non-Christian religion: its quest is a wider human community on the basis of merging the various spiritual experiences in the name of Christ. But the metaphysical dualism in the spiritual world is not seen any more. There is an embracing without rejection. The act of possessio becomes mutual.[6] But since the Holy Spirit refuses to coexist with the spirit of Satan, such interfaith experiences will lead to the occult possession of the initiating Christian partner.

(c) *Reinterpretation*. The step of exorcistic rejection cannot be the final one. Otherwise it leaves a vacuum which eventually will be filled by the old usurper again (Luke 11:24-26). Possessio becomes complete only through the third step, reinterpretation and rededication. It means a complete change of propriety, function and direction of the pre-Christian concepts, practices and goals. The titles of divine dignity, the existential experience of trans-personal realities in fear and hope, as well as the ritual symbolism of the other religions were regarded as shells. Having been evaccuated and purified, they were filled with the new reality of God's grace in Jesus Christ and the Holy Spirit. Visser't Hooft gives a good example in pointing out the reinterpreting change of the term "metamorphosis" (1965:75). In the hellenistic mysteries it meant a physical penetration of the initiand by the nature of the God through a magical ritual. Paul adopts this concept — which is one of a few religious words with no semantic correspondence in the Old Testament — and fills it with an unmistakably new Christian significance. It now means that the convert through his repentance, regeneration and faith in Christ changes his mind into conformity with the mind of his Lord (Rom. 12:2). This means that the place which through a mystico-magical union formerly was occupied by the mystery deity is now occupied by Christ. But he is a partner of a totally different nature, and so is the nature of the spiritual communion.

The same change by way of reinterpretation could later be practised by the ancient and medieval church also in connection with visible cultic means. Harnack sees in this the "complete development of Christianity into a syncretistic religion" (von

Harnack 1906:I:262). Many evangelicals will be inclined to agree with him on this point. Still, I am not sure that Harnack was wholly right. For such possessio of sacred rites, rituals, symbols and instruments was done by way of changing their possessing authority and spiritual function. And it was done deliberately to exhibit the victory of Christ over the demonic idols. We may think of the apostolic fight which in the power of Christ led to the disarmament and servitude of the principalities and powers (Eph. 6:10-17). In Old Testament times the tempting power of booty taken from heathen enemies was so great that it had to be totally destroyed (I Sam. 15:3). The New Testament demonstrates the superiority of the power of Christ by turning the rebellious arguments of gnostic philosophy into weapons against the validity of the heathen cult (II Cor. 10:5).

Such possessio by way of reinterpretation and rededication is, of course, full of risk. The answer to the question whether it is legitimate and will be successful depends on three conditions:

The first is the painstaking execution of the first two steps of selection and rejection.

The second is the spiritual power of the missionary church to refill the adopted elements with a genuine Christian meaning which really will convince and capture the minds of the young native Christians.

The third condition for a successful reinterpretation is the spiritual condition of the converts themselves. Here the well-known argument between the weak and the strong (I Cor. 8-9 and Romans 14-15) becomes most relevant to our theme. If the young Christians are still *weak*, i.e., tempted and scared by the associations of their former heathen existence, extreme restraint will be imperative for the missionary. If they are *strong*, i.e., if they have outgrown their former motivations, bolder experiments may be ventured, although only with their consent, or better by their initiative.

This third consideration leads to the conclusion that the proper time of large-scale adoption is not the first generation of converts. Nor is it such a later generation which is spiritually starved and engulfed by a violent antichristian environment and is in danger of relapsing into heathenism. For such "adaptation" will simply condone the real desire to secure one's existence by compromising with the nationalistic renaissance of heathenism. Here, indeed, the insight gained in the struggle of the Reformation becomes valid: *in statu confessionis nihil est adiaphoron.* Indigenization must never become a euphemistic term for a badly concealed apostasy.

The acceptable time for vigorous possessio will be when an indigenous church has grown in biblical insight and spiritual maturity and aggressively challenges its environment for Christ, the Pantocrator. Then progressive adaptation will be a symbolic anticipation of that eschatological state, when creation will have been set free from its present satanic corruption and the kings of the earth will bring their national treasures as a holy tribute into the City of God (Isa. 60:11; Rev. 21:24).

Notes

1. Missiologists frequently quote as their standard key passage in this connection I Cor. 9:19-22. Here Paul refers to his apostolic condescencion to become a slave to all men. He does not, however, refer to cultural and ethnical distinctions, but to differences in religious position and spiritual insight. He does not say "I have made myself a Jew to the Jews, a Greek to the Greeks," as this verse is misquoted frequently. Instead he refers to the different obligation to the Mosaic Law of those who formerly were within the Old Covenant and those who were outside of it.

2. Drafts for Sections Uppsala 68:29: "Certainly renewal does not depend on our understanding or misunderstanding of what God is doing in His Son."

3. Ibid.:10: ". . . some Christians look upon the processes of secular history as furnishing new divine revelations which the churches must accept."

4. Khodre (1972:141; IRM 55, 1966:201): ". . . we believe that Christ has more of His truth to reveal to us, as we seek to understand His work among men in their different Asian cultures, their different religions and in their involvement in the contemporary Asian revolution."

5. Walter Hollenweger (1973:21f.) in his recent book on evangelism pleads that exactly these two doctrines are dispensable when translating the gospel into an Indian context!

6. Cf. the following quotation from the Bangkok statement on dialog in Bangkok Assembly 1973:79: "A desire to share and a readiness to let others share with us should inspire our witness to Christ rather than a desire to win a theological argument."

CHAPTER SEVEN

Missiological Observations

J.C. HOEKENDIJK

INTRODUCTION

(1) THIS chapter is supposed to deal with some of the basic concepts of Dr. Tippett's frame of reference. Conveners of our symposium suggested the rubric: "Historical (or Philosophical) Principles which (might) Apply." This is too ambiguous an assignment. Look around and consult the pertinent literature, and everybody will notice that there is too much *history* and too little *philosophy* for arriving at a reasonable balance. And *principles* seem to be out altogether. They smack of supracultural, non-historical and, therefore, *always* valid entities, akin to the principalities and powers from which we are, hopefully, released. Whatever we imagine of our present world *(imago mundi* is a solid, certified, orthodox term in theology), we know that the world is an event (Von Rad speaking about the Old Testament) or an historical process (in current missiology).[1] An historical principle seems to be a *contradictio in adiecto;* the two words do not fit together.

(2) For these and other reasons, I ventured to change the title to "Missiological Observations." A change in wording, of course, does not help to solve problems. Perhaps issues can be more easily identified, however, when we look at them within their authentic context.

To argue the case:

The term "missiology" is too young (1915) to be generally acceptable. Volumes have been filled with arguments pro and con this neologism.[2] Everybody remembers that through the 1940's up to the late 1960's, Protestants rejected this "Roman" innovation. They were far more happy with their "own" nomenclature, "science of missions" (1832?) with the whole parade of "supporting sciences" (Myklebust 1955:76; 1957:128). As in other aspects of the history of missions, this term question seems to be, now, a matter of the past. In the last few decades, Protestant-sponsored missiological societies have arrived on the scene. Everybody is invited to be informed by the new international review, *Missiology* (1973).

With Dr. Beyerhaus, I would agree that missiology can only be thought of as "an empirico-theological discipline" and that, therefore, its *modus operandi* has to be inductive (Beyerhaus 1956:20ff). An important decision. In old times, theology was mostly conceived of in terms of a science of conclusions (Thomas Aquinas); now we are challenged to experiment in history.

Consequently, all possible guidelines are "situation variable." Or, to borrow a phrase from current science vocabulary, tentative formulae for doing things authentically, without pre-defined dogmata and fixed denominational positions.

GENERAL EXPLORATION

(1) Our common agenda is about the question: "How does Reality happen to people?" To be sure, we need some qualifications later on. But as a starter: "How does Reality open up, become disclosed, no longer hidden and, therefore, truth (*a-letheia*)?"

When this Truth-event happens to *us* we can celebrate this "revelation" in a variety of ways: stories, confession, kerygmata, worship, etc. I presume that this is what people mean when they speak of *Realgeschichte*, history as it touches us.[3]

But how to relate the *Realgeschichte* of others? The more we are removed from the dis-closing event, the more likely we will use our stereotypes, our orthodoxies, our collection of isms. In other words, the more the real story is bound to become a paragraph of *Ideengeschichte*, a history of ideas.

The gospel, as it becomes truth, cannot be verified. We have to rely upon hearsay, a good biblical term: *akoe* fame, report, rumor. In his incomparable narrative-kerygmatic style, Luke makes this clear: the resurrection story begins with "the rumor of angels" reported by women to the board of apostles (!) and they decide: "this is an idle tale, sheer imagination, nonsense" (Lk. 24:11).

One example, now often referred to in the literature, might serve as an example: Mark 5:1-20. Commentators tell us that this is a folktale current among the heathen, now used as a folktale about Jesus of Nazareth, the exorcist. A heathen demoniac: strong, wild, confused; he had made himself a home where no human being is supposed to live, "among the tombs." With the arrival of Jesus on the scene, Reality begins to happen to this outcast, and he raises the question of all questions, *"What* is this thing *(ti)* between you and me?" An act of healing, that is what. And Jesus asks: *"Who* are you? What is your name?" "No name, (people call me) Legion, 6000. There are so many of us," everyman, nobody. At the end of the pericope the man is sent from the area of death to where people live: "the Ten-Town-Area" to preach *(kerussein)* how God had happened to him in the *historia Jesu.* It does not seem correct to surmise that this story argues the beginning of Gentile mission, as we hear so often.

(2) To get somewhat closer to our own present situations, we might look at the *Real-/Ideen-geschichte* tension in the so-called "Christendom" complex. The case has often been argued that missiology proper could only begin when and where the *corpus christianum* syndrome was no longer taken for granted (Beyreuther, Margull, etc.). In our rhetoric we will all accept that this fantastic synthesis of faith-civilization-power is an "archeological fiction" (Neill) now, but we continue to live under the shadow of this construct. We had better try to analyze it.

There are *who* and *what* questions involved. *Who* are the participants in God's mission, or *who* do they think they are?

And as mission always involves (at least) two parties, *who* do the missionary agents suppose the "others" are? Only after proper identification of the "sending" and the "receiving" end (in old missiology people did not hesitate to use misnomers such as "missionary subject," "missionary object") can we describe *what* kind of interaction is conceivable ("What is there between you and me?"). That is: what is it the participants in God's mission intend to do and what response do they hope for?

We may represent what has often happened as follows:

A. CHURCH——————— evangelization——————————HEATHEN
   +   +   (conversion)   +
B. CULTURE———————civilization———————BARBARIANS
   +   + (cultural assimilation)   +
C. EMPIRE———————conquest/pacification——————ENEMIES
   =   = (submission/death)
Total: CHRISTENDOM——Christianization—————— PAGANS
                                        (transition into Christendom)

Several comments need to be made about this diagram:

(a) At the outset the "sending party" clearly understood itself to be the church. The apostolic church, that is the church *doing* what the apostles were called to do. The others were identified as "all human groupings" *(panta ta ethne);* the whole world (Mk. 14:9); the whole creation (Mk. 16:15); etc.: humankind in all its diverse organizations. One could make comity arrangements, like sending Peter to the Jews and Paul to the Gentiles (Gal. 2:7), but this was no more than a division of labor for evangelism among the non-Christians.

The intended interaction might be summarized as evangelization. Paul could describe the apostolate in the one word: gospel/gospelling (Roloff 1965:23ff); that is, to represent the gospel in word and deed. The hoped-for response is conversion in both biblical nuances of: turning away *(epistrephein)* from the dominion of Jewish law and heathen idolatry, *and* a change of heart and mind *(metanoia).* [4]

(b) As the church became more and more "hellenized", that is began to accept and use Greek-Hellenistic concepts to bring home the good news in such a way that Greek-Hellenists might understand the message ("becoming to the Greeks as a Greek, to win them over"; I Cor. 9:19ff), it also adopted the Greek worldview: that is, the church operated on the assumption that there were, mainly, two categories — the civilized (Greeks, of course) and the barbarians. These barbarians were often depicted as non- or sub-human creatures.

Famous, even on medieval maps, were the *skiapodes:* deformed beings with extremely large feet *(podes)* which they could use as an umbrella against the burning sun, so that they could sit in the shadow *(skia)*. Apparently Christians were sometimes identified with these monsters. Tertullian writes (II), "we are not skiapodes. We are (really) human."

This Greek distinction is already documented in Scripture: e.g. "I am under obligation (to preach the gospel) both to Greeks and barbarians" (Rom. 1:14, etc.). For a long time to come, "educated" Christians did not hesitate to call Abraham and other saints in Israel "barbarians". Even the *thenach (th*orah-*ne*biim-*ch*okmah; everybody who has been involved in the Jewish-Christian dialog knows that this is the word used to refer to the Old Testament) is sometimes referred to as "barbarian Scripture."

In this cultural milieu the interaction of the church with the others tends to become evangelization *plus* (or understood as) enculturation/humanization. The response hoped for is now conversion *plus* (or understood as) cultural assimilation, proselytism: become what we are.

(c) In the course of the 4th century the existing complex (church plus culture) became more and more romanized. I would think that there is general agreement on this point now. Ideas of "baptizing" or "christianizing" the Roman Empire are erroneous. The others were defined as (heathen, plus barbarians, plus) enemies. The interaction (including the motifs of previous stages) is conceived in terms of conquest (or, euphemistically, pacification). The others are supposed to surrender or, *in extremis,* to die.

I suggest that the sum of:

Church+Culture+Empire is CHRISTENDOM;
Non-Christians+Barbarians+Enemies is PAGANS;
Evangelization+Civilization/Humanization+Pacification is

CHRISTIANIZATION;
Conversion + Cultural Assimilation + Submission is
TRANSITION INTO CHRISTENDOM.

In case one might think that this schema is a bookish construct *(Ideengeschichte)*, let me just give a couple of references to document my hypothesis. The first one is a text around A.D. 800.

> When the Lord King Charles [Charlemagne] had happily reigned for four years [in Christendom, 772], the Saxon people were still savage [barbarians!] and most hostile [enemy!] in every way and wholly given over to heathen [gentile!] practices [the three keywords in one single phrase]. So King Charles brought together a great army [soldiers and priests] with the intention to cause this people to take upon them . . . the mild and gentle yoke of Christ. When the king came thither he[!] converted the greater part of this people to the faith of Christ by sword [current expression: to preach with an iron tongue], by persuasion, or through gifts (Addison 1936:149).

This is only one typical instance. There is ample evidence of similar enterprises recorded in the same terms of reference. The delicate analysis of the many prayers *contra paganos* by Tellenbach elucidates this Christendom posture.[5]

It would be too easy and irresponsible to suggest that this little vignette of the "dark ages" (Neill) is simply part of the past. We are beyond that, as people "come of age." We use different nomenclature. But whatever our rhetoric is, as "missionary agents," our sisters and brothers at the "receiving end," most of the time, still look at us in the framework of this outdated Christendom complex. In Muslim countries we are still "crusaders" (Kraemer 1938:275 passim).

(3) This very rough sketch of an old, perhaps not completely antiquated, model is merely inserted here to raise some questions. For instance, if the assumption is correct that missiology proper only emerged in a post-Christendom situation, we have at least to ask: "Why?" More existential is the issue, whether we can dissociate ourselves from this sorry prehistory. And, one step further, is it possible at all to communicate the *Realgeschichte* of, e.g. Mark 5 without *ideengeschichtliche* terms of reference? Basically, is it possible to transmit *(traditio)* the gospel without adding extraneous motifs? Is there a "pure gospel," not scandalized by the gospellers?

I would think that the answers to all these questions are obvious. Walter Freytag has reminded us, time and time again, that a "witness" cannot dissociate her/himself from the life-context.[6] Even with the purest intentions they will witness out of their enculturation. It would seem to me (and I discussed this with Freytag many times) that this has to do with the mystery of the incarnation: God, graciously, assumed flesh *(assumptio carnis)*, and missions are nothing, unless they are set to let this happen again, in other cultures and in other parts of the globe. Not to question the uniqueness of the Christ-event (Heb. 1:1f), but to carry on the *messianic ministration*, hopefully, to let God assume the flesh (always historically indexed and culturally defined) again and again.

SPECIFIC COMMENTS ON THE SUGGESTED "AXIS"

A generally acceptable frame of reference, as suggested by Dr. Tippett in his basic paper, is hard to come by. Partly, I assume, because all the terms have been used in so many different situations that it is hard, if not impossible, to arrive at universally acceptable "definitions". Partly, I guess, because our capsule-formulae have often been used in such a sloppy way that precise meanings have become blurred.

Allow me to try and go through the list:

Accommodation has been used to explain the mystery of the Trinity *(Handbuch theologischer Grundbegriffe* 1962:I:25f). To oversimplify, God arrives *(ad-)* to be Emmanuel *(cum-)* with, identified with, the styles *(modes)* of human life. The word opens a window on the whole plan of God. This is *one* window and I would not dare to ignore the overtones and associations, to make accommodation, merely, a keyword of missionary technique.

Adaptation is, as far as I know, simply another risky adventure to verbalize the same mystery in another linguistic field. I think that we have agreed, by now, that adaptation is the French version of accommodation (Ohm 1962:695ff).

The phenomenon of *syncretism* has perhaps been more analyzed in recent history than any other of our symbol words. Without going into detail, syncretism was originally a political term: banding together all the different Cretan groups against a common enemy. Later connotations ("to mix different gods," *theokrasis,* etc.) are fallacies.[7] More than anyone else, I guess, Kraemer has been fascinated, even obsessed, with the history of the attempts to transculturate the gospel into other milieus.

He distinguishes two types of syncretism: on the one hand, "spontaneous primitive syncretism." This we cannot avoid. Every translation of the Bible belongs in this rubric. And on the other hand, "thoroughgoing syncretism," accepting that there are many different routes to come nearer to God. It really does not matter: you take the high road and I'll take the low road, and both of us will arrive. This he rejected on the basis of the uniqueness of the Christ-event.

With the term *Christopagans* I really do not know what to do. We are all Christopagans or Pagano-Christians. The language issue is basic here. Any person who uses the King James Version ("thee/thou") or any kind of modern versions of the Bible, confesses that he/she is a Christopagan. Language is more than a matter of words.

Bavinck's term *possessio* I have never been able to understand. He wrote, of course, in a tradition of scholarly research in which people had no difficulty to speak of "Christian imperialism" (early church). To take possession of what? Is not the good news the message that God-in-Christ already possesses the whole of creation? What does it mean, pragmatically, that through missionaries, Christ becomes the possessor of a melody (worship) or a language (Bible translation)?

Our fellow Christians in Indonesia and the Netherlands have suggested on various occasions, that the better word would be *usus.*[8] As Christ, the *pantokrator,* is in full control of all aspects of our life anyway, let us use what is useable. And let us chance, living within his reign, more functional modes of expression, celebration and so forth.

To conclude: the different aspects/stages are too neat to be true.

SOME QUESTIONS

(1) There is, it seems to me, no need to bring up all the painful queiries about the "crisis of mission" once again. Some have clear answers. Others have skeptical suspicions. We are, I assume, in neither case, discussing the *missio Dei* (Rosin n.d.). That is a gift and we are called to be stewards of the gift.

(2) The various debates in the early months of 1974 on the "internationalization" of missionary work force us to look at the problems within a differently defined world context: like economic, political and religious ecology.[9] Whatever one intends to do, honestly, is colored by the context. And this is a post-Christendom milieu in which people of all different brands intermingle, ignoring their religious labels (or using their religious identities as unconvincingly as a powerless decoration).

(3) In many parts of the world the whole unfortunate polarization of salvation vs. humanization seems to be *passé*. And the carefully defined distinctions in the *axis* appear to the antiquated.

> If the world were a global village of 100 people, 70 of them would be illiterate. . . . Over 50 would be suffering from malnutrition. . . . Only 6 of them would be Americans. These 6 would have the world's income. . . . How would they live "in peace" with their neighbors? (*Grapevine* 1974).

In this oppressor-oppressed scheme, only by miracle would the Word come through. The point I am trying to make is that it is not a recent event to politicize the missionary enterprise. That happened long before we were born. But it happens again in a different setting. And the same question is asked: hold on to the accepted status quo, with its pseudo-theological rationale, or recognize that we are doing the same thing all over again?

(4) The *axis*, which I admire (as stated before), seems to me disincarnate. *Ideengeschichte.* Perfect for angels. As human beings we are far more involved in sociopolitical realities. As Max Warren is fond of saying, "to sit (*sessio*, not *possessio*) where people sit" (Ez. 3:15) and, without labels, let God happen.[10]

Notes

1. (Reutti 1972:15 passim). Out of the many reviews of this book, I would like to single out the lengthy discussion of Dr. W. Aldenfels, S.J., in *Priester und Mission* (1973:4:201-217).

2. A. Mulders (1962:139ff) summarizes the discussion up to 1962.

3. R.G. Smith (1966:86): "History may be summarily described as: what happens to you."

4. M. Green (1970, ch. 6: "Conversion"). For a quite different view see P. Aubin (1962).

5. Tellenbach, Bibliography in *Evang. Kirchen Lexicon*, Vol. 4, p. 843.

6. A summary of Freytag's bibliography is given in G.H. Anderson, *Bibliography of the Theology of Missions in the Twentieth Century.* A fuller account is in the "Freytag Festschrift," *Basileia* (1959:503ff).

7. Kraemer's contributions to a clarification of the issues have been investigated in the theses of Hallencreutz (1966) and Brisbois (1972:7-97), the latter an unpublished French thesis. For a discussion of this whole issue in the ecumenical movement, see Schmidt (1966).

8. To quote only two out of many titles, see Abineno's dissertation on indigenization of worship (1956) and Koper's dissertation on missionary Bible translation (1956).

9. "Mission in an International Age," *Grapevine* (JSAC; Feb. 1974).

10. Max Warren has, of course, been one of the most significant contributors to current missiology (see Anderson's *Bibliography*). His *Theology of Attention* (1971) demythologizes, I would think, all pompous pontifications about "fixed positions."

CHAPTER EIGHT

Variations in Adjustments

DONALD A. MC GAVRAN

IN my first chapter I emphasized the biblical base from which all adjustments must be made. I pointed out that the "faith once for all delivered to the church" was non-negotiable. As Christianity spreads from culture to culture, it must remain Christianity. It must bring men into living contact with Jesus Christ and incorporate them in his church.

This chapter stresses the other side of the picture and falls into two halves. In the first, I emphasize the great variation which embodied Christianity has always manifested and allowed, and discuss four missiological aspects of the resulting tension between faithfulness to the pure gospel and incarnating it in new cultures.

WIDE VARIATION ACCEPTABLE

If, as Christianity spreads onto new ground it preserves intact the pure biblical faith, almost any degree of adjustment may occur with full churchly approval. I illustrate this with the marriage ceremony. We shall see how a very wide degree of variation has been tolerated and indeed encouraged in orthodox Christian denominations.

(1) Tremendous Variations in Early Wedding Ceremonies

We do not know how marriages were solemnized among Jewish Christians in the years A.D. 30 to 50 or among Gentile Christians in Ephesus, Corinth, Alexandria and Rome during the years 50 to 100. It might be possible to piece together references in the Jewish and pagan writings of those days and archeological evidences, and thus compose a picture of some validity. Some indications are available in the Bible as to wedding customs. Copious quantities of fermented wine were part of the wedding feast at Cana — but this is scarcely a unique Christian characteristic.

Each of the many peoples who made up the Roman Empire certainly had its own way of creating a new family. Arrangements by parents, employment of go-betweens, family considerations, consultation of the stars, wise men and omens as to the auspicious day, traditional garb for groom, bride and attendants, the payment of dowry, the legal transaction whereby man and women were united (walking around a sacred fire, joining hands, giving and receiving gifts, repeating formulae, etc.) the part played by the priest, and the worship offered to the gods — some of those and other elements in different proportions went into each form of marriage.

For example, Proctor and Frere in their authoritative *A New History of the Book of Common Prayer* say

> According to the old customs of Rome in heathen times a sacrifice accompanied the legal transaction of marriage: when Christian Matrimony began, the Christian Sacrifice of the Eucharist with a solemn benediction took the place of the heathen rites, but otherwise the old transactions went on and continue down to the present time (608).

Again, speaking of marriage rites and ceremonies in England in 1549, they say that the bride was covered with the veil "which, according to Roman custom even in pagan times, was the symbol of her marriage" (618).

Let us focus attention on the kinds of wedding ceremonies used as the various peoples of the ancient world gradually became Christian. The first great people movement (A.D. 30-35) was out of the Hebrews living in Jerusalem and Judea. The Christians out of that movement beyond doubt married by the pre-Christian Jewish rituals.

The second movement (A.D. 36, let us say) was out of the Samaritans. When "all Samaria" turned to the Lord, we may be sure that marriages in the next month were solemnized according to the formulae used by the Samaritans in the months before their baptism. Christian Samaritans in the succeeding decades used the form of wedding ceremony to which they were accustomed.

The third discipling (A.D. 50-75) was a rather loose people movement out of the synagogue communities around the Great Sea. It seems reasonable to suppose that both Jews by race and proselytes, after they became Christian, continued to marry their children by the Jewish rites common in the synagogues of the Dispersion, adding possibly a reading of suitable sections of Paul's letters as the spirit moved them.

In the fourth great discipling (A.D. 75-250), house churches by the thousand were formed in the conglomerate communities of many kinds of Gentiles which composed the great cities of the ancient world. These Gentile Christians were less likely to use the synagogue form of marriage, even though it may have had prestige as "the Christian way." The strict Christian sexual code and the intense consciousness of Christians that "we are Christ's people" must have given their wedding solemnity and weight. Paul's high ideals for husband and wife voiced in Ephesians 5 likely formed a part of developing rituals. However, when full allowance is made for "an emerging Christian marriage ceremony," we must concede that for a very long time very varied ceremonies must have been common because of the very varied Christian groups.

Then came the period from about A.D. 250 to 1000. During these years, both the eastern and the western churches slowly developed a "Christian wedding ceremony" in Greek and Latin. The vows were brought over from the old synagogue wedding forms. The giving of rings, an old pagan Roman custom, became common among the affluent. Passages of the New Testament pertaining to marriage were read. Gradually appropriate prayers were written, copied by hand and circulated. The fixed forms of marriage which the Church of Rome prescribed came into common use about the seventh century. Before that (and to some degree after that), each bishop in his own diocese developed and used his own form.

During the Dark Ages (with migrations of tribes, the sacking of Rome, the stamping out of North African Christianity,

Moslem capture of Spain, raids and rapine, invasions and counter invasions, Viking plunderings, Charlemagne's conquests and unceasing warfare between petty principalities), how widely the slowly forming "Christian wedding ceremony" was in fact used is an open question. Liturgies had to be copied by hand and were in Latin.

That the festivities and extra-liturgical but legal activities were according to local tribal custom seems specially likely when we remember that during this period scores of people movements to Christ swept in whole tribes. A Berber people movement occurred in Libya between 288 and 300. The Armenians moved to Christian faith about 310. Led by Ulfilas, the Goths south of the Danube became Christians between 350 and 380. The tribes of Ireland became Christian around 450 and — to pass over scores of other peoples — those of Iceland around A.D. 1000. As each became Christian, it continued for decades to marry its youth according to its own rituals, with some "Christian form of marriage" gradually spreading from the upper ranks of society downward and from monasteries outward.

Thoroughness of discipling varied from tribe to tribe. In some, a few Christian outposts waged a centuries-long battle for survival. In others, the whole tribe became Christian and soon even remote villages — by royal order — built churches and put themselves under the direction of the clergy or monks who worked under the protection of the king and were often sent by him. It takes little imagination to perceive that together with a slowly increasing use of the "Christian ceremony," *hundreds of thousands of weddings must have been solemnized in the old tribal ways.*

A modern illustration helps us see the situation. In Pakistan in the very solid church (a community of about 100,000) planted by the United Presbyterians between 1880 and 1940, as late as 1920 most marriages in the villages were celebrated by pre-Christian rites. Steady pressure by the missionaries and the clergy had failed to offset the new Christians' preference for the old Hindu rites, "our way of getting properly married."

This brief review of the institution of marriage over the first thousand years of the expansion of Christianity shows the church accepting many different forms of marriage. Freedom to employ any was permitted — sometimes no doubt reluctantly by a helpless church, but often because the local customs, with a prayer and a blessing by a priest or monk, appeared adequate to the church. The natural compact which is the essence of marriage was non-liturgical. In it, use of local customs must have been universal (Proctor and Frere:608). The question "is a given ceremony to be accepted as Christian" seems to have been answered in the affirmative, not because it was like any generally accepted Christian form in force in the early church, but because those using the ceremony were in fact Christians, the Scriptures used was the Bible and the deity invoked was the Triune God.

(2) Eurican Patterns

Attend a wedding in North America today, and observe how heavily dependent it is on forms of marriage hammered out by the church in Europe during the days of chivalry. The families gather in the church dressed in all their finery. The bride is preceded by flower girls (as were the kings and nobles) strewing flowers along the carpeted way. When the bride enters, all stand — for she is the daughter of the powerful noble who rules the land. The bride is attended by bridesmaids and the groom by his best man. The bride is given away by her father according to a set formula, vows are exchanged which rest on biblical principles but have no models in the Bible, golden rings are placed on fingers, the priest-minister pronounces the pair man and wife and they march out of the church in procession to the strains of high music. In this framework, hymns, prayers and biblical passages are, of course, inserted.

All this is Christian *adjustment to the high feudal culture of the Middle Ages.* Most of these elements were not available to Christians during the first fifty years of the church. Nor does it seem likely that they were commonly used in Christian marriages out among the newly converted tribes for the first thousand years of Christian history. As Christianity again enters a time when many new peoples from many cultures are flooding into the church, the experience of the church during that early period of great growth will be instructive, both positively and negatively. Adjustments on a grand scale will be made again, but the mistakes of the first thousand years need not be repeated.

Dr. Bernard Ramm, writing on "Divorce and the Lord's Command" speaks pertinently to the issue, calling adjustments "improvisations":

> The New Testament does not intend to contain an exhaustive ethic on any matter. It is a partial, limited, but sufficient revelation of the mind of God. . . . Its burden is to set out the great salvation of God. Therefore many topics are treated only in passing. . . . There is not a single line in the New Testament about a marriage ceremony or a funeral, yet we participate in these rituals as if they were lifted out of the New Testament itself. They are all improvisations. The materials about ordination in the New Testament are so slim that any ordination service is largely improvised . . . In the territory of ethics where many new practices have come into existence since biblical times, the Church [has to improvise]. . . . Where the Church is responsible to speak or act and the New Testament is silent it can do none else than improvise.
>
> We work with [improvise within] the spirit of revelation as well as the letter. We attempt to postulate what the New Testament would say if it were to speak on the subject. We . . . improvise in harmony with that which is specifically revealed. We do not sanction any improvisation but that which seems in keeping with the whole tenor of the original divine revelation (1973:20).

Of particular importance is his affirmation that we make adjustments (improvisations) within the spirit as well as the letter of revelation. If this is done adjustments are correctly made.

If this review of the development of wedding ceremonies, which are at once Christian and culturally agreeable, has been accurate, it would appear that, as the Christian faith expands around the globe, provided they are used by good Christians, we can regard hundreds of different wedding ceremonies as biblically permissible. They will join what the pre-Christian peoples used to suitable biblical admonitions and Christian prayers, and will reflect the biblical ideal that in marriage God joins man and woman for life.

(3) A Global Ceremony?

In this missionary process it would be stupid to think that we stand today where the church stood in — let us say — the year 288. Then there was no commonly used wedding ceremony. None had been prescribed in either the Old or the New Testament, so Christians were free to do what seemed best to them. One single Christian form of wedding ceremony did not exist. The Roman Catholic form only gradually appeared, reaching its apex in the thirteenth century.

The common wedding ceremony of the church in the Middle Ages was a skillful adjustment which joined the best of several cultures to Christian ideals. It was a noble ceremony and has spread on its own merits throughout the globe. It exalts Christ, honors womanhood, sees marriage in the light of eternity, as well as providing a notable day in the lives of the persons concerned.

The grubby little ceremony which I shall soon describe taking place in a village hut is culturally relevant, but unlikely to displace the color, pomp and drama of the global ceremony. The missionary may advocate the culturally relevant ceremony, but the people will reject it. Villagers in the first generation may accept it, but when their youth go off to school in the big towns, they will opt for marriage according to the prestigeful, impressive worldwide ceremony.

Nevertheless, acceptance by the new Christians in the villages in the first generation is important and the grubby little ceremony may in time be made glorious and may continue on for several generation. It may even add elements to the worldwide ceremony, thus enriching the global church. The process I have described here in terms of a wedding ceremonial may be applied equally well to other components of culture. The important thing is that as the pure Christian faith spreads, it pours itself into whatever cultural mold it finds. Becoming a Christian should never be a process by which the convert automatically denies everything in his cultural heritage.

Let us now apply this principle to marriage in a caste in India from which large groups are declaring for Christ. In the days and months following baptism, marriages long contemplated take place. With what ceremonies will they be solemnized? I suggest that it will be entirely proper that following age old custom in that caste, the bride's *saree* be tied to the groom's *dhoti* and the pair walk seven times around the central pole which holds up the roof, chanting a wedding song. This will employ tunes and rhythms currently in use, but from it the names of the gods, vulgar references to sex and other sub-Christian elements (if any) will have been eliminated. The ceremony will use suitable verses from the Bible. Prayers in Christ's name will be offered. There is nothing to compel Indian Christians to use the global form worked out by Europeans during the days of chivalry. There is nothing to prevent it either. Since the ceremony by which Christians are joined together is not described in the Bible, Christians are free to use any ceremony they please. Provided that those forming the wedding ceremony are Christian and make their adjustment as Bible obeying disciples of Christ, almost any degree of adjustment is legitimate.

I have argued that when a church acts from a position of strength, holding intact its obedience to the Lord and its faithfulness to the great central teachings of the Bible, it can make startling change in customs, rituals and beliefs. Changes may be made for many reasons — to fit changed circumstances, because of new apprehensions of biblical truth, under pressure from government or hostile neighbors — but the church continues strong, biblical and Christian.

FOUR MISSIOLOGICAL CONSIDERATIONS

Adjustments to environment and circumstances are commonplace. In greater or less measure, denominations and congregations make them all the time. Christians studying the changing conditions of their day, new sciences, new organizations of men, new ways of regarding language or society, new dimensions of brotherhood or justice, propose new adjustments in ecclesiology, polity, liturgy or theology. Sometimes the church judges their proposals to be what Christians who are *in Christ* and faithful to the revelation of God can do. Sometimes the churches judge their proposals unwise or even heretical. The church lives in constant tension in regard to these matters. A battle of persuasion and counter persuasion rages at this point.

(1) Missiology Concerns Advance on New Ground

All these commonplace adaptations in well-established

churches are the business of theology, ecclesiology, liturgy and polity. None is directly the business of missiology. Missiology is not concerned with what well-established congregations or denominations do, whether they be old or young. Missiology is the science which deals with the propagation of the gospel on new ground. Two hundred years of universal usage has established that the missionary is one who is *sent* by the Lord and his church across culture barriers onto new ground to proclaim Christ as God and Savior and, in the power of the Holy Spirit, to persuade men to become his disciples and responsible members of his church. Missiology, therefore, includes everything which has to do with proclaiming Christ on new ground and multiplying his churches there. Adjustments to changing conditons which well-established churches make are no business of missiology. But when adjustments to other systems of belief are judged to make the proclamation of Christ more convincing, the persuasion of men more enduring or the multiplication of sound churches more extensive, then such adjustments are an important business of missiology. One may say that when the *church* makes the adjustments, the process is indirectly a concern of missiology. Only when the *missionary* — of whatever color or race — rightfully plays a part in making the adjustments, is the process directly a part of missiology.

(2) How to Present Christ Effectively – The Easy Questions

The missiological question, therefore, is what the missionary faces as he studies the culture to whose adherents he is proclaiming the gospel. How can he evangelize so that Christ may be most truly seen and most sincerely loved? Obviously the missionary must be there, must be present not only physically but as a sympathetic friend. He should speak the language fluently, know the customs and appreciate the values. He should spend time with those to whom he seeks to communicate Christ and appear to them as one who is "for us." At the same time he must appear as an ambassador, an emissary of the Lord, one announcing a new way. He ought to arouse curiosity and command respect. He has something important to say which, he claims, "you, my friends, do not know."

In addition to these elementary characteristics of the missionary, he must study the culture and discover which of its components help and which prevent its adherents from understanding and accepting Christ. The apostle Paul was continually searching the Old Testament Scriptures to find passages which pointed to Jesus as the Messiah. Opening the scroll to Isaiah 53, for example, he would say, "This passage points directly to Jesus of Nazareth. It can point to no other. He alone was wounded for our transgressions. On him alone fell the chastisement which we had earned." In a similar way, the Christian evangelist to the Hindu turns to the passage in the Hindu Scriptures which speaks of a coming sinless *Avatar,* and says, "The sinless incarnation you expect has come. His name is Jesus Christ. Him I proclaim. On him rest your faith."

All cultures and religions have in them apprehensions of the divine, understandings of reality, beliefs concerning gods and men, which when properly used help non-Christians understand the gospel. These points of contact are numerous.

Hendrik Kraemer, however, following Barth, maintained adamantly that there are no points of contact. To assume that the truths and beauties of other religions were anything more than the discoveries of men, Kraemer held, was the essence of syncretism. God had made but one authoritative revelation of himself, in Christ. There was no other. There was, therefore, "no point of contact." What Kraemer meant was that these apprehensions of the divine had not been revealed by God to those other cultures, and, hence, could not be considered revelation on which the Christian message could build (1938:130-140). Kraemer was quite ready to grant, however, that the missionary could make use of any illustrations he wanted. They had a validity as great as the missionary himself — no more.

Kraemer's point is well taken today. The adjustments which are being made and will be made as Christianity spreads among the multitudinous cultures and subcultures of the world must not be as between "how we understand God" and "how you understand God," but rather between "how on the one hand God has chosen in Jesus Christ and the Bible to reveal himself and his plans for men" and "how on the other, mortal fallible men of all races including the Caucasian have thought about God."

As we pursue the question of effectiveness, we must go a step further. As we present Christ to those who have never heard of Jesus of Nazareth, and men of the new Religion and culture seek Christ and desire to become his disciples, *what changes* in *our* embodied Christianity ought we to make so that (while remaining truly Christianity) it becomes *their* embodied Christianity? Many common-sense changes will, of course, be made. Worship will be in their language. Hymns of praise will be sung according to their tunes. Worshipers will dress in ways which, in that culture, are appropriate to divine worship. Styles of architecture will be used in church buildings which induce in Christians of that culture feelings that they are in a holy place. Leaders, from among the new converts, will be chosen and trained and installed as soon as possible. In short, every cultural hint that ours is a foreign religion should be erased. Changes in such adiaphora can be proposed and carried through by missionaries without qualms. Article XXIV of the basic Anglican Statement of Faith reads:

> It is not necessary that Traditions and Ceremonies be in all places one or utterly like; for at all times they have been diverse, and may be changed according to the diversities of countries, times and men's manners. . . . Every National Church hath authority to ordain, change and abolish Ceremonies or Rites of the Church ordained only by man's authority, so that all things be done to edifying.

Article XXIV was written to defend changes which the Church of England was making in Roman Catholic ritual; but it is equally true regarding changes in embodied Christianity, which missionaries institute and churches modify in Kerala, Korea, Kinshasa or Quito. These are, however, the easiest and most elementary of adaptations with which we shall deal as we consider the syncretism-adjustment axis.

(3) The Difficult Questions

The difficult questions lie ahead. Many adjustments which would make acceptance of Christian faith less difficult and more natural seem to necessitate changes in essential parts of the Christian revelation, allow the worship of other gods, sanction the use of other scriptures, assign devotion to other mediators or saviors, or add elements to the Christian religion by which it ceases to be solely allegiance to Jesus Christ according to the Bible.

A classic instance is that presented by Robert de Nobili around A.D. 1600. De Nobili was an aristocrat, related to two popes, and highly educated. Arriving as a missionary in India, he soon judged correctly that the caste system placed tremendous power in the hands of the Brahmins. He believed that if India was to accept Christ, a way would have to be opened for the Brahmins to become Christians without infringing their high social status. He probably reasoned that as the nobility of Europe were Christians, while considering themselves enormously superior to the peasantry, so the Brahmins could and should retain their exalted status while becoming disciples of Jesus Christ. After years studying the situation, and learning the language thoroughly and living according to the Brahmin code, he proposed that Brahmins should be accepted as Christians while they retained the sacred thread, grew the distinctive tuft of hair on the head (*kudumi*), applied sandalwood paste to their bodies in ceremonial fashion and bathed at stated times during the day with appropriate ceremonies and recitations.

The Portuguese had arrived in India about a hundred years before, had taken Goa and were influential all up and down the west coast of India. Jesuit missionaries had travelled all over India and had received great favors at the court of the Emperor Akbar. The Roman Church had captured half of the ancient Syrian Church in what is now Kerala, and on both the east and west coast had received low caste converts into the Roman Catholic Church. De Nobili was proposing a new and controversial adjustment. Was it syncretism? Could these four brahminical practices be brought into the church without making the church sub-Christian? De Nobili said yes. Other Roman Catholic thinkers in India said no. The matter was referred to Rome. Ships with letters left India, sailed around Africa, through the straights of Gibraltar and on the Rome, to and fro for many years carrying on a great debate concerning the adjustment-syncretism axis. Pope Gregory XV issued the Apostolic Constitution *Romana Sedia* and sent the following ruling to India, as quoted by Cronin:

Taking pity on human weakness, till further deliberation by us and the Apostolic See, we grant by the present letters, in virtue of Apostolic authority, to the Brahmins and other gentiles who have been and will be converted to the Faith, permission to take and wear the thread and grow the kudumi as distinctive signs of their social status, nobility, and of other offices; we allow them to use sandalwood paste as an ornament and ablutions for the cleanliness of the body; provided however that, to remove all superstition and all alleged causes for scandal, they observe the following regulations and conditions:

They must not receive the thread and the kudumi in the temples of idols, nor, as it is alleged to have been done, from a minister of idols, whom they call *yogi* or by some other name, nor from a preacher of their law or priest whom they call *bottou* or otherwise, nor from any other infidel whoever he may be, but let them receive these insignia from a Catholic priest, who will bless them, reciting pious prayers approved by the Ordinary for the whole diocese; and before receiving the above insignia let them make a profession of faith in the hands of the same priest. However, when giving the thread, the priest, to remove all secret idolatrous significance which might be attached to that ceremony, will avoid holding the upper end of the thread with the thumb of the right hand and the lower end with the left hand and raising the right hand, as we are told is the custom. Moreover those who are to receive the thread will no longer go to the priest of the pagoda, if that custom existed, to be initiated there.

Cronin comments:

The thread of three strands was to recall the Holy Trinity; it was not to be held in the hand during prayer; threads already received during the intitiation ceremony were to be destroyed and replaced with new ones blessed in honour of the Trinity. All prayers or mantras associated with the thread and tuft were forbidden. There was no insinuation that Nobili had tolerated such superstitious practices; the cautionary phrases were merely included as a safeguard (Cronin 1959:229-230).

Observe how carefully the Apostolic See defined the issue. The four components of the Brahminical culture were to be allowed, but under strict conditions which made certain that they brought with them no allegiance to the Hindu religious system, to other gods, other holy places and other religious leaders. Some thinkers, enthusiastically advocating that all cultures be counted equal and any suspicion of European imperialism be quenched, during the last fifty years have frequently proposed loosely defined adjustments entailing mixed loyalties and leading not to the straight gate and narrow road, but to the broad way and many roads. Rome's wise policy in contrast was framed after careful scholarly study. In these days when national churches are defining adjustments, such scholarly study needs to be done by them.

A seminary in America during the year 1972, working on a similar contemporary problem, conducted a conference on "Alternate Life Styles and New Communities." The conference concluded that alternate life styles are equally valid. Men living according to each may become Christian. Its conclusion is ambiguous. Certainly men of any life style may become Christian, but only if they are willing to submit the components of their culture to Christ and change such as he may require. "People following any life style may become Christian" is true only if one quickly adds "and change some elements of their life style to accord with the revelation of his will for men which God has given in the Bible and through his Son."

The difference between scholarly and shoddy thinking is precisely the balance maintained between appreciation of other cultures and submission to the authority of the Christian religion. The four elements of the Brahman life style and social status may be retained, said the Apostolic See, provided the convert understands that they are in no way related to other gods and other religious loyalties.

(4) Humanist Adjustments Beg the Question

What is legitimate adjustment and what is illegitimate syncretism cannot be decided correctly from a humanist point of view. The humanist has already decided that religion is only a reflection of man's felt needs. Humanists say, "If the men concerned are satisfied, the custom is good." The Christian, on the contrary, holds that whether men's felt needs are satisfied or not, the custom is good only if it accords with God's will. The point is important, for during the tremendous swing to humanism during the last hundred years, some Christians have adopted humanist definitions of religion, while still counting themselves "good Christians." When these talk about adjustments which should and should not be made, they have really written off any real revelation.

Sociology of religion deals with phenomenology. It takes the phenomena as they are and avoids the question of ultimate truth. "Men of culture A believe this way. Men of culture B believe that way. Each claims that its beliefs are revealed by God and are the absolute truth. The social scientist should place himself above both and deal with each religion as a reflection of the questions and needs of men." Once this posture has been taken, however, it becomes mandatory to consider one custom as good as another. The only standard is whether it meets the felt needs of the people. "Those who practice it like it, don't they?" Here again, *if* the custom concerned has no biblical implications, one can readily grant that one custom is as good as another. If, to clean his teeth, a man likes a *neem* stick better than a tooth brush, he should certainly use it. The Bible says nothing about either. But in that small percentage of cultural components which contravene biblical faith, or may do so under some circumstances, the case is otherwise. Here the church will want to take a firm biblical position.

The Christian may use the sociology of religion as a convenient tool. It is one good way to study and understand the complexities of the religions. But the Christian presses on through phenomenological understandings to the truth. He maintains that it is easy to distinguish matters in which there is obviously no ultimate truth, where the options are clearly matters of taste, from those in which commands of God are involved and ultimate truth is concerned. In making adjustments, the Christian cleaves to what is required by the Bible and makes whatever changes in the culture are necessary to bring it into conformity with the will of God.

As missiologists advocate adjustments which they believe will help seekers from other cultures understand the Savior better and help the new churches serve their neighbors better, they make a clear distinction between empirical, embodied Christianity and the essential gospel revealed by God. They hold that revealed truth must not be changed. To borrow a metaphor from St. Paul, we may say that the missionary is free to change the shape of the earthen vessel so that it may be more acceptable to men of another culture. He is not free in any way to change the treasure which the vessel carries. That must be transmitted intact. The missionary, as he disciples *ta ethne*, will find earthen vessels of shapes quite different from his. He will accept these gladly, provided the treasure rests comfortably in them.

CHAPTER NINE

The Meaning of Meaning

ALAN R. TIPPETT

HOW does one react to a set of presentations such as we have
had over the last two days? The subject of this symposium might
well have led us into some strong disagreements in any of three
or four areas, but on the whole there has been more agreement
than disagreement. The points of disagreement are present, but
they have been latent rather than manifest.

One could argue, for example, on what is really the business of
missiology,[1] or how we define culture,[2] or on the point of time
when large-scale cultural adoptions should be made,[3] and I am
methodologically unhappy about the model of an axis-ladder,
with Christians on different steps in their ascent[4] which, in spite
of its possible utility, has too many problematical
presuppositions. I dislike the statistical use of the notion of a
global village.[5] I question the exegesis of Mark 5 in Dr.
Hoekendijk's second presentation,[6] and I have reservations
about how far we can use his schema of Christianization.[7] In any
of these we could get into long (and perhaps profitable)
arguments, but they would take us far afield from the subject
before us. Therefore, I intend to let these points pass, by merely
indicating my reservations, and in this presentation I shall direct
my response to my colleagues in a symbiotic rather than a
reactive form (see ch. 1).

In the opening presentation, I pointed out that the whole program of cross-cultural communication of the gospel was caught up in the basic *problem of meaning,* of how a supracultural gospel could be communicated and manifested in meaningful cultural forms. All the papers of my colleagues demonstrate the truth of this *fundamentality of the problem of meaning.* Therefore, rather than debating a few points of disagreement (profitable as that might be), I shall try to draw together in terms of my own discipline what I believe is a basic ingredient of all our presentations.

MEANING — A FUNDAMENTAL PROBLEM

Let me recapitulate briefly some of the issues raised by my colleagues which sprang from the problem of meaning, although they did not always articulate it as such. Let me take them one by one.

(1) *Dr. McGavran* took up the question of "the pure faith delivered to the saints," and tried to identify its essential ingredients, laying down criteria for validating the message to be communicated to the nations. Taking two phrases of mine, "a pure faith" and "an essential gospel," and presuming that we participants were more or less of one mind in this, he pointed out that for many people there was "enormous confusion," and he devoted half of his first paper to defining the phrase "a pure faith." Thus he identified this basic issue as a problem of meaning.

Then he went on to deal with secularism, deism and Arianism. Although I have some difficulty in pinning down just what he means by secularism,[8] and although I cannot accept the notion of "deist culture,"[9] nevertheless, he manifestly is struggling again with the whole problem of meaning — the meaning of the gospel and the false trails which lead into syncretism.

In the case of de Nobili and the Brahmins, and the test of whether this was syncretism or *possessio,* the answer he received from Rome provided a criterion for meaning. It was not a direct "yes" or "no", but depended on whether the "sacred thread" or "tuft of hair" had Hindu significance, or whether it brought honor to Christ — not Christ as one person of the supposedly all-incorporating Hindu pantheon, but Christ, the only way to the Father. Here again we have the problem of meaning. And this time the focus is on the form (the thread and tuft of hair), rather than the message, but the implication is that the form itself may have a meaning for those who set it in a different frame of reference from the missionary. A similar point arose when McGavran discussed the Christian Christmas festival as a functional substitute for the festival of the winter solstice. The common issue between these two cases is whether the form is given a new and Christian meaning or retains its pagan significance. The meaning makes all the difference in the world — the difference between possessio and syncretism.

Again he speaks of "morphological fundamentalism" — attributing radical new meanings to old words, semantic shifting, to adjust to some cultural or philosophical change, and passing it off as if no change had taken place; we are once again involved in a problem of meaning which, among other things, bears on mission policy and promotion. Likewise, in his discussion of the rejection of "traditional Christianity (creed, cultus, organization and customs)" for the sake of philosopher-theologians who want "a radically new form of Christianity," we have a striving for meaning on the part of the armchair missionary theologians.

We have before us a wide range of cases of the problem of meaning — wide enough for me to say that there may be peculiar problems of meaning at every level — that of the missionary supporter and the policy maker, that of the observer and critic in the street, that of the missionary himself as communicator or advocate, and that of the listening audience, either of practising Christians or of potential converts. At every one of these levels we are confronted with some aspect of the problem of meaning.

(2) When *Dr. Beyerhaus* discussed the separation of mission churches and Afro-messianic movements, he pressed that this was at base a theological problem. His approach to the subject was itself surely an attempt to discover meaning. We placed ourselves in the position of the advocates of the African movements in order to pose the right questions to western missions. Then we made ourselves critics of the answers we

received. It was, I think, an illuminating exercise, and did indeed point up the theological character of the problem — but it was a problem of meaning even so.

Dr. Beyerhaus pinpointed a number of significant things: the failure of converts to realize that the incarnation of Jesus Christ was an historic fact, the failure to appreciate New Testament eschatology, the failure to develop a relevant pneumatology, the failure to achieve a biblical view of the psychosomatic unity of man or to arrive at a true koinonia in the disrupted society. When we confront the penetrating nature of these shortcomings, we begin to ask how missionary communication could possibly be so far off its basic goals; clearly somewhere there was tragic misunderstanding. And we are back again to the problem of meaning, as Beyerhaus cited Freytag: "The gospel heard is different from the gospel preached." The Spirit is equated with African *life force,* but this never becomes the personal Holy Spirit, and this, Beyerhaus rightly points out, is "a hermeneutical task."

In responding to this, I believe that the existence of African concepts like life force (cf. *mana* in Melanesia) gave the African a capacity for receiving the gospel. The gospel was potentially credible (Tippett 1972:133-139). The goal of mission is manifestly to get beyond the notion of life force to the Person of the Holy Spirit, and I agree this is a hermeneutical task, but it is bigger than hermeneutics. Here the problem of meaning has to get beyond conceptualization to an experience for which we have no words — either in the language of the advocate or the receiver of the message. Perhaps Paul would have called it "the mystery." This, of course, is the work of the Holy Spirit himself, and it is at this point that conversion to Christ differs from all other kinds of conversion.

When people in a messianic movement "bypass the crucified Lord" through "seeking a national hero," or confuse the "notion of civilization" with the "coming Kingdom of peace," we are dealing with problems of meaning at the acceptor's end of the process of evangelism. This raises the allied question of motivation — why people become Christian. When people, especially large groups of people, become Christian from wrong motives, or with wrong expectations, they automatically give a wrong meaning to the message and eventually are disillusioned. This is one of the causes of nativistic breakaways.

Dr. Beyerhaus has confronted this kind of syncretistic response to the gospel with a better alternative — namely, a striving for possessio. His important discussion on the threefold concept of "selection", "rejection" and "reinterpretation" aims not only at eliminating the heathen elements, but at fulfilling "the adopted elements with genuine Christian meaning"; thus the preservation of cultural forms is not syncretistic, for "by structured catechetical instruction" they are "filled with the new reality of God's grace." Clearly also Beyerhaus' theological concern is a striving for meaning.

(3) *Dr. Hoekendijk* confined his first presentation to an historical survey of Indonesian data. But here we saw that at each historical period and in each pattern of Christian mission, the problems discussed could all be reduced to matters of meaning. In a few sentences let me nominate a few of his ideas which tie up with this dimension of meaning:

(a) People movements, to be fully meaningful, have to be seen in their sociopolitical contexts.

(b) The missionary is never a speaker only; his whole life is part of the kerygmatic event.

(c) What is said is not always what is heard.

(d) The question is raised of whether syncretism may not indicate the "undetected beginnings of an indigenous theology."

(e) Xavier saw one of his major problems as the task of translating "the mysteries of faith into language one does not understand."

(f) There are cases of pre-Christian mythology being used to bring Christology close to the heart of the people, like the Javanese messianic expectation of "the liberating Lord of Justice."

There is the use of traditional *adat* for theological developments. Dr. Hoekendijk just mentioned these in passing, but a moment's consideration reveals that they all raise the question of meaning. The same applies in his second presentation, especially his discussion on terminology. However, in my response I want to go beyond the meaning of our own terms to the meaning of meaning itself. I feel free to do this because strategist, theologian, historian and anthropologist have all, in a sense, reduced the issue of syncretism to the problem of meaning.

MEANING — A PASSIVE QUALITY OF CULTURAL ELEMENTS

I now propose to analyse this problem of meaning a little more deeply and theoretically in an anthropological manner. The missionary, or evangelist, or communicator (I usually employ Barnett's term *advocate* because we are involved in an innovative or decision-making process that seeks a response of acceptance [Barnett 1953]), has the task of advocating the acceptance of the gospel. He is striving to communicate something which is supracultural, but which he only knows in a cultural form, to people whose cultural forms and worldview are different from his own. We have been confronted with the truth that frequently our missionary effort ends up with syncretism, or a new form of animism or polytheism, and if the new Christian community is really Christian, its form of Christianity is often unrecognizable by western Christians who cannot see beyond their own worldview and cultural trimmings. In my first presentation, I tried to distinguish between the two: "syncretism and indigenous Christianity." The data presented by my colleagues also have indicated that we are indeed confronted with these two kinds of community as the result of missionary activity. The humiliating question then is: *how does so much sincere Christian missionary activity end up as syncretism rather than as indigenous Christianity?* (I am not talking about that kind of missionary activity which ends up with a small, enclosed, static, foreign congregation and a western Christian worldview. That is another problem altogether.)

There are several ways in which we might approach our present problem. Hitherto, our papers, for instance, have analyzed it from different angles — theologically, strategically, historically and culturally — but in each of these areas we come up with the same finding, namely, we have on our hands a problem of meaning. I now wish to probe the theoretical base of that problem a little more deeply and ask another question: *for the missionary advocate, what is the meaning of meaning?*

(1) The Integration of Passive Qualities

Cultural elements (including say, a Christian hymn or prayer, a rite, a translation of the Bible or even a cultural institution like a congregational group) according to the anthropologist Linton (1936:402-404), have four related qualities, two of them dynamic, namely *function* and *use*, and two passive, namely *form* and *meaning*. In this theoretical unit I am concerned with the passive qualities of the cultural elements of the cross-cultural Christian mission. What I want to say may be applied to cultural artifacts (like, say, a symbolically carved lectern, or a composed liturgy), or a craftwork design for an altar cloth, or an institution like a communion service, or the process of evangelism itself, or an organization (like an operating indigenous church). To ascertain whether or not we are studying a syncretistic or truly Christian cultural element, be it at the level of an artifact, a craft, an institution or an organization, we have to probe the passive level and consider form and meaning.

Now, on the strength of the variety of data in our present discussion, I wish to go a step beyond Linton's theory. The distinction between form and meaning is not always clear-cut. The form will also have a meaning. It may have a different meaning to advocate and acceptor, especially if they have different worldviews. The same form may have different meanings to the same audience in different situations. Linton's categories are only abstractions. In reality they cannot be segregated. The categorization is merely a mental exercise to help us identify the ingredients of the passive quality of cultural elements.

But I think there is good reason to add a third ingredient, which we may tentatively call the *value*. There is some determinative factor interwoven with both the form and meaning. It also influences the dynamic factors of function and use, but it is itself passive and subjective. It conditions the very orientation which strives for meaning or gives meaning. It covers the principles of an institution, the criteria of an experimental process and the belief behind an act of worship. It has to be distinguished from meaning because it is largely the cause of the meaning. Change the belief system and you will change the meaning of the form.

Sometimes the value system is articulated in a precise form, as for example, in a code of law, or a policy statement or a creed. Sometimes it is implied in the cultural idiom of the language, for example when we say that some action is "not playing the game," or is "hitting below the belt." This quality of value in the cross-cultural institution of evangelism surfaces into visibility as the gospel message, which may be considered in terms of "unarticulated belief," or as a concrete form in "the revealed but written word of God." Two of my colleagues have argued, correctly I believe, that one reason why we run into syncretism is by departing from, or manipulating, the message. We can say this when we focus on the value aspect, which conditions the meaning.

Whether we are communicating a gospel for acceptance in the program of outreach into the world (Jn. 17:18), or in the interpretation of Scripture for growth in grace in the program of the inner life of the fellowship group (I Pet. 5:1-11), we need to examine "the passive qualities of value, meaning and form," as *an integrated system,* to ascertain whether the program be syncretistic or really Christian. I think this theory, which is itself derived from a data base of concrete missionary and anthropological research, should help us at least to ask the right questions of the syncretist.

The theory may be conceptualized in a diagram which suggests the integrated qualities of evangelistic and educative thrust by means of a rope-like linkage communicating the gospel cross-culturally from advocate to acceptor.

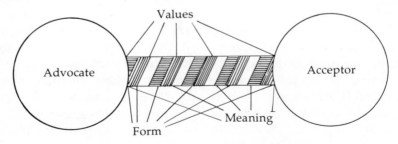

Passive Qualities of a Cultural Element

Let me demonstrate the basics of this theory from the researches of Melville Herskovits, an anthropologist who studied religion at both ends of the slave trade. He worked in Dahomey and Nigeria, on the one hand, and in Cuba, Haiti and Brazil, on the other. In spite of the Iberian overlay and supposed Christianization in the New World, and in spite of the fact that people called themselves Catholic and Christian, the form, value and meaning of many cultural features were Yoruba and Dahomean. Herskovits listed about sixty Catholic saints in the New World, which when investigated could be identified as Dahomean and Nigerian deities — some 30 of which he identified by name. Although the worshipers professed to be Catholics and were led by priests who used normal Catholic procedures, nevertheless, the deities were African and the ceremonialism (forms) and ideology (value) were Dahomean and Yoruba — the meaning was mainly African. One could classify the syncretism of form, value and meaning. The general religious frame of reference being handed down from one generation to another is African, and enquiry of a Catholic saint will bring descriptions of African deities for a response. These syncretizations have developed independently in each locality — Brazil, Cuba and Haiti.

If we look at the two ends of the process, we see that although Catholic missionaries advocated their own form of the faith, the acceptors themselves really determined the meaning to ascribe to the forms. Thus enquiries of Christians — devotees of the Christian St. George in Rio, for example — were given the description of the African Ogun, and St. Anthony and St. Peter in Haiti are identified with Legba, the Dahomean trickster. Thus it is the acceptor of the new religion who ascribes the new meaning. This is also seen in the symbolism of Dahomean and Yoruba mythology and worship of the elements. It all holds together as an integrated system, and survives from one generation to another. It may be that the slave lost his freedom in political and social life, but his religion survived as the "governor" of his society (Wallace 1966:4) and that religion was African (Herskovits 1937:635-643) — the religion of the acceptor, not the advocate.

(2) *The Advocate and Acceptor Ends of the Process*

Let us take a deeper look at that way of studying our problem. We may use the same diagram if we include the "advocate" and "acceptor" as the two ends of the process. Both the advocate and acceptor impinge themselves on the process, firstly because they influence the passive qualities, and secondly, because they may have quite different worldviews. We bring out the cross-cultural element by depicting the two ends of the process. Thus either the advocate or the acceptor may be responsible for the ultimate syncretism, the former by transmitting his own worldview with the message, or the latter by misinterpreting the message in terms of his pre-Christian worldview.

I was once present in a gathering when a young Meso-American Indian from a syncretistic Catholic background was making his public profession of faith before an evangelical congregation. When he handed over his "fetish", as the custom was in that place, I was surprised to find that his fetish was a cross, and I assumed it was a formal expression of conversion from Catholicism to evangelicalism. I later made some enquiries and discovered that it was not regarded as a Christian cross at all, for there always had been a pre-Christian cross in the symbolism of that tribe. This fetish tied him with the ancient traditions before the Spanish entered the New World. There was no Christian symbolism about it. Certainly it was not a physical reminder of the great event of salvation history — the death of our Lord. For this young man, and for his co-religionists in general, it was a magical object with its own inherent power and the shrine of a spirit. After a real confrontation with Christ, the young man felt he had to make a disclaimer of the fetish, as part of his public confession of faith.

The problem here goes back to an earlier generation when the Spanish first "converted" these New World Indians, and the latter accepted the symbol of the cross as a recognized and approved motif in their supposed Catholic Christian faith. The point I am raising here is that for those early Catholic missionaries, the cross had a precise meaning, with a whole set of associated ideas. For the Meso-American "convert", it had a completely different set of mental associations derived from the pagan pre-Chrstian religion. Each religion used the physical form of the cross, but the matrices of belief constructs within which the cross was used were entirely different. To the observer these people were *manifestly* Catholic using a Catholic cross, but in point of fact, the *latent* belief (which was transmitted to succeeding generations) came from the Indian complex, not the Spanish one. Here is a good example of the point made by Barnett (1953:338), that innovations or newly accepted ideas derive their meaning *from the acceptor*, not the advocate.

In the case I have just described, we had a religious symbol which was common to two different religious systems, but even where there is no common formal element, the form of Christianity adopted may be conditioned or interpreted by entirely secular factors from the pre-Christian cultural system of the acceptors of the new faith. The gospel advocate should be familiar, not only with the religion of the people to whom he goes, but with their whole worldview. There is no such thing as bringing men to Christ in a cultural vacuum. The missionary who imposes his western Christianity on his converts (focus on the advocate end) and fails to educate himself on the religion and worldview of the people to whom he goes (focus on the acceptor end), is bound to plant a syncretistic church because his lack of perception of cross-cultural, social and psychological needs which the gospel has to speak to will be misunderstood. That is once again the problem of meaning, and one good reason why every missionary should have anthropological training and understand the worldview of the people to whom he takes the gospel.

WORLDVIEW AND CULTURAL COHESION

Somewhere in this discussion on the problem of meaning we must bear down on the matter of worldview and cultural cohesion, in particular its significance for the communicator of the gospel, when the advocate and acceptor do not share the same worldview.

(1) The Worldview: Dynamic Cultural Themes in Equilibrium

The worldview of a people in one respect may seem an extremely complex pattern, but we should remember that its multitudinous features are not of equal value (a trap for researchers who work out scales of variables for measurement). Usually we find a limited number of strong themes which determine a worldview. In anthropology we call these the *dynamic themes of culture* (Opler 1946:198-206). They stand out as the marks of normalcy in any given society. They indicate the group feelings of the people. They show how a society meets its felt needs. They reinforce the moral values. They maintain social equilibrium. If greatly disturbed, both individuals and society begin to manifest psychological stress. What is most important to us today is that they condition the nature of *acceptable* cultural change — including religious change. If we consider evangelization in terms of "directed change" that has to be advocated and accepted, we will understand how important it is for the cross-cultural advocate to appreciate the dynamic themes of the culture pattern and organization of the society to which he takes the gospel.

Normally themes manifest themselves through certain key persons, operating within key institutions, recognizing and using key customs and key artifacts which have symbolic values. Thus it would surely be wise for the evangelist or advocate to recognize these significant persons and things. Malinowski was struggling with this when he said:

> When moving with savages through any natural milieu — sailing on the sea, walking on a beach or through the jungle, or glancing across the starlit sky — I was often impressed by their tendency to isolate a few objects important to them, and to treat the rest as mere background.

and again:

> Out of an undifferentiated background, the practical Weltanschauung of primitive man isolates a category of persons. . . . (1927:331,332).

The worldview of the community where the advocate hopes to win men for Christ must be understood — the key institutions, and people and values. These are the "givens" of missionary work. These are the frame of reference within which the gospel has to be made credible and acceptable, and the advocate must adapt himself to it. Although the advocate may not be himself *of that world,* nevertheless, he must minister *in that world* (Jn. 17:18). He strives to win that world for Christ. To be sure, this will bring changes, but all societies have their regular mechanism for change, and this should not mean the disintegration of the society or even its leadership patterns.

In my study of Fijian history for over thirty years, I have been constantly reminded how the really great indigenous leaders of the early Fijian Church (men like Epenisa Cakobau,[10] Ilaitia Varani,[11] Ra Esekaia,[12] and Josua Mateinaniu[13]), all men of tremendous Christian experience and initiative, were previously great leaders in their paganism — chiefs, warriors, heralds, priests, craftsmen, and all of them cannibals. One of the great things about the Fijian mission was that, confronted with the tremendous task of eliminating cannibalism, widow-strangling, patricide, infanticide and human sacrifice (all tied up conceptually and ceremonially with the value system), the missionaries and their indigenous evangelists (who were the spearhead of the thrust) were able to win these people without dismembering the society. They won the social organization and the leadership; they preserved a great deal of the custom and utilized it in the church, and they captured the natural capacity of the Fijian language for the expansion and the development of a Fijian Christian theology. The society itself continued and experienced a new birth. I do not wonder, then, that compared with some other parts of the Pacific which I have visited and know well, Fiji has been remarkably spared of nativistic movements. Those which have occurred have been due to local stress situations of a different character, more aimed at the colonial government than at the church and based on local factionalism.

(2) The Meaning of Demoralization

On the other hand, as Herskovits pointed out, there is a relationship between the meaning of a body of custom and the integration of the culture, and too much of a disturbance leads to *demoralization* (1951:633).

This demoralization may be collective or individual. Collective demoralization leads to a situation propitious for the emergence of a charismatic leader. It is amazing how in the study of cargo cults, one finds that the charismatic figure, who captures the stress situation and creates the movement, turns out to be an ex-policeman, an ex-schoolmaster or an ex-catechist, who could not get beyond the first rung of the ladder of the foreign structure to which he had attached himself, because the foreign officials under whom he worked did not recognize his capacity for leadership through their use of western criteria and educational requirements for advance. Here is a beautiful (or tragic) example of the incompatibility of worldviews — again a problem of meaning. It opens up a whole area of missionary dynamics in which we are abysmally ignorant and which calls for research.

The same applies on the level of the individual whose worldview is shattered by acculturation, and who gropes in vain for satisfactions from outside his own world. Here is demoralization on the personal level, and here again the "solution" is syncretistic.

Dr. Harold Turner has given us an account of a young West African who had truly searched the world for religious satisfaction and had ended up as a corresponding member of religious organizations in England, America and India. To all of them he had contributed funds through the post, either to gain merit thereby, or to protect himself from possible physical ailments. His bookshelf showed him to be an avid reader of both Protestant and Catholic literature in addition to that of Jehovah's Witnesses, Islam, Theosophy, Yoga, magical arts and healing manuals. One volume on the Psalms indicated how to use Psa. 119:169-176, for example, as a charm to accompany the dropping of onion juice into the right ear for curing a boil. His sacred paraphernalia lay on a little shrine and included crucifixes, a plaster figure of St. Anthony, a bottle of water, some candles; a Bible and a box of contraceptives lay nearby. This form of multiple syncretism does not just demonstrate tragically how far astray a man can go in his search for peace, but it also asks us the question how he had gone so far without being found by an advocate of the gospel, who could have spoken to his seeking soul (Turner 1960:189-194).

Individuals of this experimental or searching type quite often end up in leadership roles in nativistic movements. Anthony Wallace has shown that these movements begin with the experience of some individual, who first faces stress situations and then becomes innovative (1956:264-281). Along the same lines, the psychologist, Sherif, demonstrated that an individual, confronted with an unstable situation and finding a solution, might well create thereby, consciously or unconsciously, a new norm for a group facing a similar stress situation (1936: ch. 6). Sherif's research has been brought into anthropology by Barnett (1953:116-117) and is applicable to people movements to Christ as well as to nativistic movements away from him (Tippett 1971:210-220). This is another dimension of the problem of meaning in missiology crying out for deeper research. Until we know more about the dynamics of these movements, we will still fall short in our handling of them.

(3) Subliminal Striving for Meaning

I have argued that the worldview of a people provides a conceptual structure which holds a society together as a cohesive unit. To throw this conceptual structure into disequilibrium is to rob life of meaning. But always there is a "subliminal striving for meaning," as Barnett describes it (1953:117ff.), and this is why people are often innovative in times of stress. However, they will not accept new advocated ideas unless these can be integrated into their universe of experience. They are drawn into what Barnett calls "the matrix of the known."[14] Only thus can the new ideas have significance, and therefore unless the would-be acceptor can ascribe meaning to an innovation, he will not accept it. It is the would-be acceptor "striving to complete the gestalt" (ibid.: 434-435).[15]

The need for fitting a sensation (which for us in mission includes the step of faith) into a framework of known experience, may well distort the data presented by the advocate, and thus the individual to whom the advocate is witnessing may color it by his own interpretation, because he is ignorant of the worldview of the advocate. This is a human characteristic. Westerners do it as much as the Maya Indian of my first presentation. Let me for a moment reverse the advocate/acceptor roles. Barnett records a case of an American Indian myth, spoken of as "The War of the Ghosts," which was relayed to a number of white Americans, and passed on among the latter over a period of some months. Each white American rephrased it slightly, mainly at the points of the mythology and the concept of the supernatural in the original Indian story, but even perfectly innocuous elements were changed — for example, canoes became boats — and point by point the story was unconsciously modified to suit the western frame of reference. In the end, it was absolutely unrecognizable.

In his study of the Shakers, Barnett again demonstrates the process of striving for meaning — the meaningless is given meaning, the unstructured is given structure (Barnett 1953:120). Barnett says a thing has meaning only when "understood in terms of its mental associates." This meaning may be fantastic by another standard, yet it may be ascribed by the acceptor because it provides a rationale for acceptance (ibid.:335). This explains why a message preached in all sincerity by the Christian advocate with one worldview to an acceptor with another worldview, can be completely distorted by the acceptor and end up as a syncretistic or heretical theology (ibid.:338).[16] Many of the misinterpretations of Juan, the Maya Indian I described in my first presentation, were due to this factor. Many of the contemporary New Guinea cargo cults have emerged because the now disillusioned converts originally misinterpreted and distorted the Christian gospel message, confusing Christianity with western civilization, and the acquisition of wealth and status with white power. The older missionaries often took conversion at its face value. Today, because of the insights and tools we have acquired through a more developed study of man, and because of the responsibility which increases with the growth of knowledge, it behooves us to pay better attention to post-baptismal instruction.

Now, before I pass on from this discussion of the significance of worldview for the problem of meaning, let me pinpoint again three things I have been trying to say: (a) What Dr. Hoekendijk called "the kerygmatic event" must take place within the framework of the worldview of the people to whom we go with the gospel. This is why we have to study a people's cultural world and operate in their language. (b) It is not our task to destroy their worldview, but to bring Christ into it. If we destroy it, they will suffer from cultural voids (Tippett 1963:60-70), from normlessness (Yinger 1964:158-173), from anomie (Durkheim 1951:258; Giddens 1972:15, 173-174), which history shows may well lead to depopulation because the zest has gone out of life

(Rivers 1922:84-113). (c) When people accept the gospel they make it fit their worldview and interpret it — as the acceptor and not the advocate is the innovator— and "the gospel" in any society means just what the acceptor (not the advocate) makes it mean. This is why the program of Christian nurture and education must be continuous. Conversion is not a goal, but rather a doorway into the fellowship of believers.

APPROXIMATE AND DYNAMIC EQUIVALENCE

Once a missionary realizes that to witness cross-culturally he must step outside his own world into a completely different one, to come into encounter with people who have a different worldview and to engage with them within that frame of reference, and in a language of which they are the experts and he is the learner, he realizes the burden of the stewardship the Lord has entrusted to him. The question now comes to him with force — can I communicate the gospel to these people meaningfully? Can I divest the gospel with which I am familiar of the cultural trimmings I know I have given it, so that the written word may be incarnated in their cultural forms and the living Word in their hearts? This is the risk of the Christian mission. There is little comfort in knowing that if I fail there may be a syncretistic church there tomorrow.

With some fear and trembling then, I turn to the problem of meaning at the level of actual communication in the field situation.

(1) Getting Beyond Approximate Equivalence

Although Bronislaw Malinowski could not have done his research in the Trobriands without the help of the missionaries, and especially their linguistic work on which he built, nevertheless, he pointed out a shortcoming of their translation and preaching which often led to misunderstanding. He called it the problem of *approximate equivalence.* He argued that "All the words which describe the native social order, all the expressions referring to native beliefs, to specific customs, ceremonies and magical rites are absent from the English" (1927:299-300). He argued that these words were peculiar to them and acquired their meanings from the life and tradition of the people, that the language was rooted in reality and was meaningful only within what he called its *"context of situation."*

If Malinowski is correct and the gospel has to be preached in the language of the hearers, can it ever be preached then without a pagan meaning being ascribed to it?

I must confess that I know nothing so futile as a missionary trying to communicate the gospel to people in a language they do not know. I had a most disillusioning experience of this in a Navaho hogan, and it convinced me that the missionary must use the language of the people. But how does one discuss, say, the Fatherhood of God with a matrilineal people where the father role differs from the biblical one? Where does one find words for such concepts as prayer and worship, and the moral qualitites, and the terms for God himself and the Holy Spirit? One has to find these words within the language and vocabulary of the pagan religious life itself: which is another reason which commits the missionary to a sincere effort to understand that pagan religion, so that he can lead people from pagan prayer to Christian prayer, or from a pagan idea of God to a Christian one.

Yet I am satisfied that it can be done with time and patience. However, it is not merely a matter of finding an accurate word for each concept. Neither is it entirely a matter of translation. These are never more than approximate equivalents. One has to understand the context of the situation and feel something of its nature and atmosphere. Approximate equivalence of vocabulary is not good enough. This is only the way to misunderstanding and to syncretism.

The capacity to place oneself in another religious worldview has to operate in two directions: first backward into Judeo-Graeco-Roman contexts from which the divine message comes, and then forward by looking into the context of the pagan society to which the biblical message is to be transmitted. I have struggled with this two-dimensional cross-cultural adjustment in an attempt to short-circuit my own ethnocentric perception of the gospel, and worked out my own methods on the mission field.

I decided never to translate an English sermon into Fijian. I put myself in the Fijian context and spoke extempore until, after many years, I believe I began to think in Fijian. For three years, I served as the official keeper of the Fijian Synod daily journal and discovered that when it had to be translated back into English it assumed a vernacular character my normal English never had. I have at home a number of old missionary reports of Fijian testimonies, and I believe I can tell in a moment whether the writers were recording them themselves or translating Fijian documents. When I learned to forget translation and interact in Fijian, I got much better responses.

Sometimes I wanted to communicate a biblical idea, say, a Pauline concept or phrase. In this case I would try to go direct from the Scripture to Fijian. I might have to take the congregation for a "guided tour" round Corinth or Ephesus, but not until I felt that the cultural situation was clear would I dare use the key phrase. Then, afterwards as we ate our meal together and they talked over the sermon (a humiliating custom they have), I would know if I had got through with the biblical meaning. I know no other way of cross-cultural communication of biblical truths but by narrative reconstruction of the cultural contextual situation in which the key word, or phrase, was first spoken. In any case, the Fijians love to hear how other people live, and have different values from them, and why. Then often, when they had the situation clear, they would tell me how to say it in a single phrase of their own that was not in the dictionary. I have thus accumulated some four or five hundred Fijian situational phrases not in the dictionary because they are idiomatic and not literal.

Let us remember then that the theological terminology of Scripture is already a vocabulary of divine ideas in cultural garments. We should not need to be reminded of this since the day of Adolf Deissmann.[17] Every theological word we have came originally from a cultural context — redemption, adoption, reconciliation, sanctification, atonement, and so on ad infinitum. And the glory of God is that his purpose for mankind in the "notion of redemption," for example, was capable of enshrinement in a concept from pagan Rome, which happened to have an institution of slavery figuring prominently in its worldview. The essentiality of incarnation is as true for the written word as it was for the living Word. When God spoke to human beings, he used no universal Esperanto, but he spoke in their own language.

(2) Dynamic Equivalence

The battle for dynamic equivalence is won or lost in the initial program of translation or preaching. The first two missionaries in Fiji quarrelled about this subject. One wanted a perfect literal translation of Scripture. He was a skilled linguist, quickly mastered the grammar and built a good vocabulary, but at best his work was a case of approximate equivalence. He saw words without their contexts, even though his translations were literally accurate. His companion studied the Scripture passage he wanted to communicate and wrote a paraphrase of it as he would tell the story, as if to a Sunday School class. He wrote it out and gave copies of it to the first preachers he trained to read. They studied it, asked questions about it and went forth into the pagan villages and "dialogued" the Scripture narrative, as if they were communicating something that had happened on the forest path along which they had come. This second man never gave the Fijians a translated book of the Bible, but the first villages to accept the gospel in Melanesian Fiji were those where his paraphrases were discussed. And these people got the heart of the gospel.

Many years have gone since then. Fiji has a strong indigenous ministry now. Something of this free expression of the gospel remains. I found it thrilling to listen to Fijian preaching, though sometimes the exegesis brought me up with a jolt. I recall a preacher who had done missionary service in North Australia in a totemic aboriginal community which still practised the cultic rituals in which the religious symbolism, tribal loyalties and their notion of spiritual unity with the totem were stressed. He had witnessed their elaborate preparations for one of their totemic dances as they marked their bodies with the totemic symbols. After a long and graphic description of this, he led into a discussion of Paul's bearing in his body the marks of the Lord Jesus — a rather daring analogy. His name, strangely enough, was Paul. He carried his hearers along with him in a description of a worldview so different from their own. Then I asked myself — was his interpretation of the *stigmata* so very far from the original? Where did Paul get that figure of speech anyway — from a pagan brand on the body of a slave, or a Roman soldier pledging his loyalty to his captain, or an offender taking refuge in a pagan temple to escape his just penalty by becoming a slave of the deity of that temple? Whichever meaning Paul had in his mind, the term came from a pagan cultural context, but he used it as a symbolic expression of loyalty and identification with his Lord.

I heard another Fijian preach on treasure in earthen vessels. He did not know Greek, but the Fijian word for vessel has a multitude of meanings in different contexts — a pot, a ship, an envelope or an object possessed by a spirit. The sermon was a normal one for a Fijian audience though a biblical scholar might have found the exegesis strange. In any case the congregation was with him and, I believe, strengthened in the faith.

A third Fijian sermon I might mention discussed the atonement. First, the preacher reminded the congregation of the nature of a Fijian ritual of atonement and enumerated the various offences which could be rectified by such an offering. From this he proceeded in the true style of the typology of the Epistle to the Hebrews to demonstrate how the atonement of Christ was a superior, universal and eternal work of grace, more perfect in every degree than the Fijian type.

Each of these presentations came from a non-western and non-biblical worldview. Each preacher, in a way, took the risk of syncretism. Yet those sermons were all essentially Christian, characterized not by approximate, but by dynamic equivalence. They were all preached to the glory of God, and the goal in each case was to bring the congregation to a deeper experience of Christ. They were all well-received, and even I, a stranger, felt I was at worship. They all utilized concepts and feelings which would have been difficult to translate back into English. They were indigenous sermons, but they were thoroughly Christian. There wasn't a touch of syncretism in any of them. The problem of meaning had been solved.

In those parts of the world where good indigenous churches have emerged, this is quite normal and has a long-standing history. But mostly the reporting of it to the West has been confined to missionary deputation tale-telling. It has never been seriously studied in the theory of mission as a subject for phenomenological research. One of the new features of post-colonial missiology is the recognition of this dimension of indigeneity and the development of the research area of *ethnotheology* (Kraft 1973a:109-126), and under this head a sub-area of *dynamic equivalence* (Kraft 1973b:226-249; 1973c:39 ff.). We may expect to hear more of this in the next decade or so. It arises from a feeling of our need to solve the problem of meaning in preaching and translation.

CONCLUSION

To conclude the last of my contributions to this symposium, I ask myself what our encounter here at Milligan College has to say to Christian mission as we enter the last quarter century of this millenium.

Although there are many ways in which we are already speaking of "a new era of mission," we all know that the day of *colonial missions* is dead, and that *post-colonial mission* has to operate within an entirely different set of "givens". We seem to have overcome the pessimism of the sixties and the notion that "the day of missions is dead." It is still an active business, as Stephen Neill has pointed out (1970:1),[18] and we have no directive from the Lord that the Greek Commission is defunct. Already new contours are taking shape, both for *missiology* as the field of research and theory, and for *mission* as the applied activity of that theory in the world. The *idea of mission* (Warneck's phrase), is nothing new, but both the opportunities and the techniques for it have changed out of all recognition. And perhaps it is at this point where I suppose that, as the anthropologist of this symposium, I would be expected to speak.

The problem of syncretism is not a new one. The New Testament church confronted it, as the growing church in every age through history has also done so. However, although it is the same problem, we have certain advantages in our day for dealing with it and, therefore, an even greater responsibility. We recall how William Carey (1792) in his day argued that the researches of the navigators and explorers, the new charts and techniques of navigation, the knowledge of languages spoken by newly discovered people who knew nothing of the gospel, all gave a new dimension to the meaning of the Great Commission for the church of his day — and thus began a new era of mission.

In our day many new ways and means of research have opened up to us. We have new disciplines on which we could be drawing for the training of missionaries. We have historical research over a long period of history, which is full of lessons to be learned. And surely of him who has received much, much is expected.

Therefore, at the level of the individual missionaries, we must recognize that there is no longer any excuse for the home church sending out missionaries without adequate training, and in the light of our discussion on syncretism, that availability of knowledge and techniques certainly includes anthropology — social anthropology, applied anthropology, cultural dynamics, cross-cultural communication and "primitive" religion, as a minimum — and perhaps also a refresher course to up-date them on each furlough.

At the level of academia, there is a desperate need for more intensive missiological research on both syncretism and indigenous Christianity, in the assembly and classification of data, in theory and in application. The contemporary people movements to Christ, and cargo cults away from him, demonstrate the dynamism of our times. For every case of a well-handled people movement one could counter with a badly-handled one. And how to handle a cargo cult is something in which both the field missionaries and home boards are equally out of their depth. In many ways, the animistic world is "turning over" today on a scale quite unprecedented in history, and when I speak of the animist world, I am not confining myself to forest tribes, but include the great religions of Asia and the streets of the great American cities. We live in a syncretistic world, and we know next to nothing about its phenomenological character and how to deal with it. A cultural gulf lies between us and the people to whom we have been sent.

The research of the kind I am asking for must come *from inside the missionary movement itself.* Most of the exciting research has been done by anthropologists, frequently agnostic scholars, who think these things can be studied objectively; or from comparative religionists, mostly armchair scholars who have never confronted the phenomena in the flesh. These human sciences will take us so far, but will not lead us to the "new man in Christ," which requires an apostolic man not a religion man, a *Christian*, not a secular anthropologist. In the study of religious phenomenology of this kind, there are two ways of *getting into the act* — one is by accepting it and readjusting one's theology to fit his new position, and the other is to come into actual encounter with it on the level of faith. Missiology today needs nothing more urgently than an adequate articulated methodology for confronting the dynamic resurgence of contemporary animism with the Christian alternative.

In this post-colonial era of mission, every cross-cultural missionary, therefore, needs a degree in anthropology sufficiently advanced to permit his doing field research; and upon retirement from the field after, say, 15 or 20 years, the home church should open the door for a select few of these men to be set aside for advanced research — men who, having worked for years outside their own language and culture, can continue their involvement in the dynamics of these cross-cultural phenomenological problems. Every mission field of the world is plagued with some form of syncretism, and every field should have some full-time experienced missionary-anthropologist studying the dynamics of their situation and making it available to the field missionaries. Someday, the Lord of the Vineyard will ask our boards and sending churches why they sent men into the vineyard without teaching them how first to care for vines and harvest the grapes, and why they opened fields at all for mission, which they were not prepared to research.

From these experienced missionary researchers, a limited number should serve as coordinators of the total research and the development of a body of *missiological theory* based on the field data. Our missiological theory is not yet adequate for the missionary task I anticipate our being confronted with in the next twenty-five years. On my recent visit to New Guinea, I was thrilled by certain evidences of indigenous Christianity, and yet appalled by the tragic loss of converts through cargo cults. Our missionary gosepl is a glorious one, but our methodology is far short of what the Lord of the Vineyard surely expects of his stewards.

Notes

1. I do not know what Dr. McGavran means by saying that missiology refers only to the adjustments on "new ground," that "adjustments which well-established churches make are no business of missiology," and that "when the *church* makes the adjustments, the process is no concern of missiology." Perhaps I do not read him correctly (ch. 2). I believe the continual adjustments required of the church are part of its mission — for only thus can it hope to bridge the generation gap within its own constituency; I cover this in *Verdict Theology* (1973:10-16), under the phrase "the inward dimension of mission." This paragraph of McGavran's mystifies me in the light of what he has written under the head of "biological growth."

2. In Dr. McGavran's first chapter we meet "secular culture," "modern culture," "each culture of the world," "our culture," "your culture," "a culture religion," "deistic culture," "gnostic culture" and "any culture." Sometimes it seems to be a culture pattern, sometimes a philosophy or religion, sometimes part of the pattern (without religion). It is sometimes anthropologically used and sometimes aesthetically.

3. Unless I misunderstand Dr. Beyerhaus (ch. 6), I think he underrates the importance of "making the large scale adaptations" in the first generation. Functional substitutions made 20 or 30 years later have been notably unsuccessful.

We are dealing with conversion from paganism. The very first fellowship of believers should be structurally and operationally recognizable as indigenous from the beginning; otherwise we are building in a cultural void for the indigenes and a "mission to church" problem for the missionary enterprise. I think that whatever indigenous features are to be adopted should be identified and possessed for Christ from the time of the initial people movement and its catechetical consummation.

4. Hoekendijk's first presentation (ch. 3) leaves us with non-western and western Christians alike "on different steps on the axis ladder" — reflecting an admittedly necessary humility on our part. However, the tendency to use some kind of scale like this to measure syncretism in a scientific manner is often used by researchers. It may be useful for measuring behavior, but when it comes to such things as faith or revelation it fails. Religious experience is so complex that we can never hope to identify the variables for experimental use, let alone eliminate them.

5. The reduction of the world to a global village to make a statistical point (Hoekendijk ch. 7) involves the writer in a false analogy. I do not dispute Hoekendijk's point, but I do challenge the model he uses to make it. It would have been better stated in simple percentages. The analogy assumes an even distribution of the condition (e.g., illiteracy) throughout the statistical universe — which is not so, some places being quite illiterate and others not at all so.

6. The exegesis of Mark 5 (Hoekendijk ch. 7) might well have become a point of debate among us because it implies the authority of a commentator to declare a biblical narrative to be a current heathen folk tale. This bears on our attitude to the nature of Scripture and its interpretation.

7. Hoekendijk's schema of Christianization (ch. 7) reflects medieval European history and is useful as a frame of reference for a particular set of circumstances in history, but it is not necessarily a universal pattern, neither does it mean that there is no other quite different frame of reference for analyzing the Christianization of Europe. It may well be that medieval church history will some day have to be written in terms of the dynamics of modern cross-cultural people movements.

8. Scientific humanistic self-sufficiency and the religio-philosophical incredibility of the idea of God can hardly be part of the same "system" as modern culture which "gives birth to a conviction that life is meaningless." Self-sufficiency and anomie are essentially different attitudes.

9. A worldview which is philosophically deist cannot, in my understanding, be equated with a culture. There is no "deistic culture." Such-and-such a culture may be orientated towards deism — but this is a very different thing. However, I agree with McGavran that when biblical faith is adulterated with the philosophy of deism (as he describes it), we shall have syncretism on our hands (ch. 1).

10. Ratu Epenisa Cakobau of Bau, known also as Cikinovu (Centipede) was probably the most famous cannibal chief of history and had reportedly devoured over a thousand human victims before his conversion to Wesleyanism in 1854, whereafter, his life was completely changed to piety and Christian leadership.

11. Ilaijia Varani (France) earned the name by destroying a French ship and massacring the crew. He was Cakobau's henchman and leader of the forces which upheld Bau. He had a remarkable conversion and lived to be a Christian negotiator and peacemaker of no mean order, eventually losing his life on a peace mission.

12. Ra Esekaia was the first-born son and heir of the Chief of Bua. He gave up his title when he became Christian as he knew he did not have the loyalty of the warriors and other heathen. However, he protected the small Christian party during the persecution period in Bua. It is hard to see how the Christians could have survived without his leadership.

13. Josua Mateinaniu was a petty chief of Fulaga and a dancing master of renown, who was taken to Tonga to teach Fijian war dances to the Tongans, and was converted there. He returned to Fiji with the first mission party and served as their herald. Thereafter, he was the spearhead of the Christian advance, preceding the missionaries in Rewa, Somosomo, Bua and other places.

14. Dr. Hoekendijk's objection to my use of the word "pagan" is a good example of our failure to communicate because of the "boxing" at the receptor end of the process. He does not (or maybe will not) give *my word* anything but *his meaning* and thus distorts the communication. (By the way, I only use this as

an example. We all do it.) This is one of the main problems we have in communicating the gospel. All through Dr. Hoekendijk's second paper his semantic problems are due to his "failure to understand" [his own phrase] and this is clearly because of his "matrix of the known." In his subliminal striving for meaning, he gives "pagan" (as also "possessio", etc.) a meaning from his own frame of reference. To people who have trouble over the meaning of the word "pagan", I would recommend their reading Maurier's *Theology of Paganism* (English translation 1968, especially pp. 22-24).

The same problem arose in Dr. Hoekendijk's response, to which I had no opportunity to reply, with respect to his use of the word "hope" as he set *his hope* over against our *security*. He says he *does not know* how we "could be so secure." Here he is in a particular theological "box" which seems to prevent his understanding my particular theology of the Christian hope in terms of assurance — "the full assurance of hope" *(endeiknusthai spouden pros ten plerophorian tes elpidos)*.

15. The gestaltists have developed the concept of "closure" to explain the psychological striving or straining towards the completion of an incomplete configuration. The tension is not relaxed until the missing part is realized and the gestalt thus closed.

16. Kirk & Talbot (1966), in an article "The Distortion of Information," described three different fundamental types of distortion, which they designated as *stretch, fog* and *mirage*. The analogies offer a useful frame of reference which might have been used for an analysis of the different forms of syncretism.

17. The older belief that New Testament Greek was peculiar was disposed of by Deissmann, who demonstrated its contemporary use in the secular world of New Testament times: for example, it was thought that Peter invented the term "Chief Shepherd." Deissmann reported a burial tablet describing the deceased by this term, and indicating the existence of a kind of shepherd guild of which one was chief *(Light from the Ancient East* 1927).

18. Neill's opening paragraph in *Call to Missions* (1970) reads: "The missionary work of the Christian Church is a fact of the modern world. We may like the fact or we may dislike it. That makes no difference; whether we will or no, it is just there. Not only so; it is a large and ever expanding fact."

CHAPTER TEN

Decisive Factors in the Cross-Cultural Communication Process

PETER BEYERHAUS

IT was a most thrilling experience to read and listen to the lectures of my colleagues in this Carter Symposium on Church Growth! We have been and still are discussing the central problem of missiology. The most important lesson I have learned from my Swedish teacher Bengt Sundkler is his definition of mission. He calls it the "constant tendency of the church to cross frontiers." He also can say: "Mission is translation." Christian mission, indeed, is the process by which the eternal gospel of Jesus Christ is communicated across the borders of his visible church. And it is the specific task of missiology scientifically to study the laws of this communication process and from Scripture and historical experience give guidance to Christians who are involved in this vital function.

At Milligan I listened to three distinguished experts presenting their theological views and personal experiences of apostolic communication across the borders of different religious cultures. And while I was listening, it struck me again: this process of communication is really a breath-taking event; in mission the eternal gospel of Jesus Christ on which the salvation of the world depends, passes through the critical phase of disembodiment and re-embodiment. For we cannot communicate the gospel to people of different languages and cultures in that incorporated form in which we ourselves have received it and are familiar with it. Christ, the eternal Word, became flesh once and for all. But the event of inverbation, i.e. the kerygmatic analogy to incarnation, must take place again and again whenever the gospel is introduced to people of different cultures.

Although we all agree on this in principle, each one of us has seen it from a specific angle and has given his particular contribution. Let me share my observations and reflections with you by answering three basic questions with regard to the different treatments of our symposium theme:

(1) How do we view the situation in which we discuss the communication problem?
(2) How do we view the target and the pitfalls in the communication process?
(3) Whom do we regard as responsible agents in the communication process?

THE PRESENT SITUATION:
HOW DO WE VIEW THE SITUATION IN WHICH WE DISCUSS THE COMMUNICATION PROBLEM?

All contributors to this symposium have emphasized the perennial and universal significance of the problem of translating the biblical faith cross-culturally. It has been there since the biblical God revealed himself within the movement of history, and it is encountered wherever the gospel is transmitted to a new realm. Our examples were drawn from the time when Israel conquered Canaan until the appearance of Bishop Robinson's *Honest To God,* and they stretched geographically across the oceans from the Fiji Islands via Mexico to Asia Minor and India.

I was especially intrigued by the magnificent historic sweep in Dr. McGavran's first chapter, where he analyzed three famous adjustments of Christianity to the dominating non-Christian religio-philosophical movements of its time. Here a McGavran presented himself who revealed dimensions of thought far beyond his usual concentrations on the laws and strategy of church growth. I wonder, however, whether in the light of the illustrations he selected he still can maintain that missiology is only concerned about those adjustments in the communication process which are made in the pioneering period, where the foreign missionary plays a decisive part. This is also the position of Dr. Hoekendijk, who even apologizes for intruding on other men's ground. We can, if we want, limit the sphere of missiology to such particular fields. But this would deprive our discipline of much of its theological dimension, and moreover of its vocation to be the integrating force in the concert of all theological disciplines. Personally, I consider missiology to be the bridgehead of the communication of the gospel to people of non-Christian religions and ideologies. It studies all the theological, linguistic, psychological and sociological processes which take place during this communication in both directions. Therefore, the Arian controversy, the crisis of faith in the age of Enlightenment and the confrontation between Christianity and humanistic secularism are, indeed, proper concerns of the missiologist as well, although not only his. When in July 1974 the International Congress on World Evangelization took place in Lausanne, we dealt with the problem of evangelistic communication in the American hippie sub-culture no less then with breaking new ground among untouched tribes in the Amazon forests. I agree that no single person is able to become expert in the multitude of such diverse situations with their specific problems. This is a new reason why we need closer cooperation and coordination among missiologists.

Dr. McGavran stated that he chose those examples also in view of liberating the indigenization complex from being tackled emotionally in the context of the Third World anticolonialist reaction. This is a real danger indeed. There is, today, the tendency sweepingly to ostracize the historic Christian faith as "western", and from there to usurp the right to develop new types of indigenous theology or forms of Christianity which, together with the outward forms, also change the very substance and the spirit of the apostolic faith.

And here lies my first main question to the other participants in this symposium: are we fully aware of the peculiar situation within the history of the Church Universal in which we are dealing with the adaptation-syncretism axis? Adjusting the forms of empirical Christianity to new cultures where it wants to take root is a timeless concern. But today it poses itself in a very particular and crucial way. This has been observed both by Dr. Tippet and by Dr. McGavran, who pointed out the remarkable analogy between gnosticism and theological modernism as perils to the biblical creed of the church. (Dr. Ulrich Wickert, church historian in Berlin, dramatically stated this parallelism with the following words:

> The heresy of the early church denied the humanity of Jesus; the modern heresy which now becomes a world-wide action program denies the godhead of Christ. The Christian faith is threatened by nothing less than the loss of heaven, of eternity, and even of God himself. This is the greatest menace which the church has had to go through since the gnostic heresy of the second century. Even the state of emergency against which Luther voiced his protest, was of less significance in comparison with this.)

What are the determining factors of this present situation in which we discuss the trans-culturation syndrome? I would mention five:

(1) In the world in which we live, there are no stable and specific cultures any more. We might find some relics of them in certain native reserves. But even they are rapidly drawn into the whirlpool of world-wide rapid social change, heading for the coming world society. Dr. Hoekendijk pointed this out already 25 years ago in his scathing criticism of the romanticism in the German missiological concept of "Volkstum" as the foundation and building material of national churches. I do not agree with the guiding ideas of the "theology of secularization," but it has made important observations which we should not bypass here.

(2) This process of change has also affected the Christian church, its beliefs, moral values, ecclesiastical order and theology. The development started already in the epoch of Enlightenment, when together with the philosophical demoliton of metaphysics, the authority of revelation and ecclesiastical dogma was also undermined. A new rational principle of hermeneutics was introduced, which gave birth to the historic-critical method of exegesis. It finally led to the dissolution of the unity of biblical teaching and the credibility of biblical accounts. Dr. M.M. Thomas approvingly quotes Harvard scholar Wilfred Cantwell Smith's statement that

metaphysical, philosophical and biblical theology has suffered a complete breakdown: "This has led to so much disunity, conflict and chaos in the Christian church that the old ideal of a systematic and unified Christian truth has been lost. For this even the ecumenical movement came too late." Dr. Thomas goes on to quote Cantwell Smith: "Christianity as a coherent historic structure will break into pieces, and it will, thereby, destroy any orthodoxy and, therefore, any heresy. There will remain only communities with a personal Christian faith which offers an open plurality of alternatives to select between."

(3) This process of dissolution of historic Christianity suits a third trend in our present history, i.e. the trend of *emancipation*. We encounter it in a variety of forms. In the West its main features are the anti-authoritarian and the sexualist vogues. Among underprivileged classes in North and South America, it is the cry for liberation and black power. In Africa it is the search for the African personality and the rediscovery of one's true identity. Here the consequences are different forms of syncretistic nativism, as I have described them in my first lecture, or even an open return to the old tribal religion. In the African state of Chad, even governmental forces are used to revive the old tribal initiation ceremony, and Christians who refuse to surrender are cruelly persecuted. Missionaries are expelled. This shows that the problem of accommodation does not pose itself in the former context of meeting an untouched traditional culture, but rather in a situation of a belligerent reaction which is anti-western and anti-Christian at the same time. And we have also to be aware that there are influential voices in the ecumenical movement which are prepared to go to any extent in meeting this colored quest for religio-cultural renaiscence and self-assertion. The extreme consequence of such attitude was drawn by the WCC-sponsored Barbados Consultation of January 1971. In the interest of liberating Latin-American Indians, the Barbados Declaration demanded "the suspension of all missionary activity." And the first reason given for this startling request was that evangelization is of "essentially discriminatory nature, implicit in the hostile relationship to Indian culture conceived as pagan and heretical."

(4) But emancipation is not the final word in the present process of world history. At the same time from many quarters, we hear the cry for a new universal integration. Philosophers, politicians and religious leaders are discussing plans for a coming world community. The reason is either the naked quest for human survival or the utopic vision of a future paradise on earth. Therefore, the main interest today is not so much to preserve the integrity of the different cultural traditions. Instead one wants these cultures to pull together and make their contribution to one common culture of mankind. Therefore, even the communication process is not evaluated so much any more by the question: how does it relate to the traditional conceptual world? Rather the ideal is that the missionary communication should be sensitive to those forces at work in all cultures that lead to a convergence in such an integrated world community.

(5) But what in fact is the common denominator by which all religious and secular movements are linked together? More and more leaders today are intrigued by a secular humanism which is strongly influenced by Marxism. It seems to lend itself readily as an integrating ideology that can inspire the action programs needed in the quest for a future world society. All traditional religions and primal cultures are reinterpreted in conformity with such socialist humanism. The religious terminology, which is employed then by way of adaptation or possession, condones the basically secularist and atheistic assumptions on which this Marxist humanism is constructed. But what is happening is that autonomous man is assuming control over the process of world history in which no divine intervention is expected any more.

Dr. McGavran has spoken of some theologians who demand a radically new type of Christianity. This is, indeed, what is going on within the ecumenical movement today. All confessional traditions are openly or secretly reinterpreted in the light of Marxistic humanism. The independent Ecumenical Institute of Chicago serves as an avant-garde in this process. It has created a number of outposts in the Third World. They provide crash courses for national church leaders and theologians to re-educate them for so-called church renewal. What is done is that both Christian and indigenous concepts are brought together, emptied and refilled by a syncretistic ideology of socio-political change in the Marxist sense.

I hope that these observations and reflections are not taken as a deviation from the proper theme of our symposium. I strongly believe that we cannot really deal with the task of missionary "possessio" and the problem of "syncretism" without being aware of that large-scale process of syncretistic possessio which right now is going on in all parts of the world. In due time it is bound to reach even the remotest local church on the mission fields which we may have in mind in our present deliberations.

AIM AND DANGER:
HOW DO WE VIEW THE TARGET AND THE PITFALLS IN THE COMMUNICATION PROCESS?

(1) The Target

Any process of communication implies two basic elements: (a) There is something essential which is to be communicated, the content of the message; (b) this message must be transmitted in such a way that it conveys meaning to the mind of the receiver.

If we see (a) and (b) together, then the target of missionary communication is a new church which expresses the essentials of the Christian faith in forms which are familiar and meaningful to its members. This we call indigenous Christianity, and on this we all agree. But I doubt whether our concepts of indigenous Christianity are really identical.

But in Christian missions there are and always have been two different emphases and schools. Dr. Tippett speaks of the apostolic-man and the religion-man as representing these two traditions. One could add that these two different approaches are not peculiar to missions. They are to be found in systematic theology as well. Some of the fiercest dogmatic battles have been fought on account of these two opposite approaches. The Barth-Brunner controversy of 1932 is one example.

I do not think that there is a proper representative of the religion-man approach in our midst. If we had one, it would have enlivened our symposium. We might have invited a representative of the "Christian Presence School" or of the ecumenical "Program of Dialogue with the Living Faiths and

Ideologies." Dr. Tippett rightly points out that these are old traditions reaching back to the age of the post-apostolic church.

Still, I wonder whether the present situation has changed the approach to non-Christian religions as well. The culture and religion of the non-Christian partner in dialog are not viewed so much as a given system of thought and social organization. Rather they are seen as a living movement, meeting with the movement which we represent ourselves. And in this encounter something new is born. It neither represents the former belief of our partner nor the belief which we have been witnessing about. It is something else which changes both of us.

It is in view of these new concepts that I have some questions for Dr. Hoekendijk. He defines as the goal of Christian mission the "obedience of faith" among the hearers of the message. This is St. Paul's well-known description of his apostolic ministry in Romans 1:5-6, which was also the central missiological concept of my teacher Walter Freytag. And he used to relate it to the regeneration of the conscience of the converts. Christ has become their supreme authority instead of their former heathen deities. Therefore, without external force they spontaneously change their way of life.

But here the questions begin: who gives enlightenment to the conscience so that the new Christians really are obedient to the will of Christ as their new Lord? To Paul the answer was quite clear. He not only invited his heathen listeners personally to surrender their lives to the living Lord Jesus. In the subsequent catechetical instruction he also revealed to them the whole counsel of God. He instructed them in the basic elements of the apostolic *paradosis;* he taught them how to order their congregational life, and he gave them in the oral and written way a clear ethical admonition. Only on this basis does the Pauline term "obedience of faith" become meaningful. The genitive "of faith" is both a subjective and and objective genitive: "believing obedience" and "obedience to the authentic faith." This includes the unchangeability of the essence of the apostolic message. And here I wonder whether Dr. Hoekendijk is quite in agreement with his fellow contributors. He does not appear particularly concerned about how the purity of the apostolic gospel is preserved. The idea of somebody believing he can administer *The* truth is rather ridiculed by his capitalizing the definite article *The*. For him no human being, no missionary, is a guarantor of truthful communication. Instead he appeals to the work of the Holy Spirit. He does so because he is considering the great variety of different cultural and historic situations in which the obedience of faith must find its concrete expression. If this first of all means that a variety of cultures contribute to a variety of indigenous churches, I could agree. But I wonder whether Dr. Hoekendijk does consider the indigenous church to be the immediate goal of missionary communication. From the nonchalance with which he speaks of counting Christian noses, I gather that to him the ideal of church planting and church growth takes second place to the concern for responding in a Christian way to the challenge of the historical situation, as it was practised, e.g. by the East Javanese churches during the anti-communist riots in 1965-66.

But here again we have to ask: by what standard can it be decided what proper Christian obedience in a certain situation looks like? Dr. Hoekendijk seems inclined to consider that if headhunting is not possible, then at least corporate suicide may be a proper Christian decision. The *judicium fidei* is left to God alone. But was the apostolic church of New Testament times not quite certain as to the nature of the divine offer and of the requirements placed upon man for salvation? And are we not responsible to spell this out to present-day inquirers and believers as well?

Unlike Dr. Hoekendijk, the participants from Fuller Theological Seminary very sternly and emphatically state that there is an unchangeable core of the gospel which under all circumstances must be preserved in the act of communication and indigenization. It is merely the outward form of the gospel which may and should be recast to make the message meaningful to people of the different cultural backgrounds. On these principles I wholeheartedly agree with them. Yet even here there is room for arguing. Is it already decided what belongs to the eternal core and what to the transitory form of Christianity? By whom is it decided, and on what ground is it decided?

Dr. McGavran has challenged each of us to give a clear statement of what we regard to be the core of the Christian religion. And he has drawn up such a statement himself in his first chapter. He states three basic elements: (a) belief in the Triune God; (b) belief in the Bible as infallible rule of faith and practice; (c) the central facts, commands and ordinances which are so clearly set forth in the Bible.

Now there are two things which I fail to understand. One is the difference between points (b) and (c). If I believe in the infallibility of the Bible, I automatically believe in the infallibility of its instructions. If this is the case, I do not understand, secondly, how there can be a degree of elasticity in regard to part (c). If it simply means that these ethical commandments and instructions about order are put in a way that make them applicable in a different way in different situations, I understand. For the Bible does not always give binding instructions as to how to practise its rules and commandments. But Dr. McGavran stretches the alleged elasticity of the biblical ordinances to such a degree that he even tolerates the total omission of the two great sacraments, baptism and the Lord's Supper, which are so solidly based on a clear command of Jesus Christ. Paying high respect to the spirit of Christian love shown by the Friends, I simply cannot agree that their community fulfills the biblical standards of a true Christian church. Personally I hold that where the Bible sets forth clear standards of Christian faith, behavior and ecclesiastical order, they have to be regarded as the unchanging core of the Christian religion. Where, however, the Bible leaves a degree of openness as to how to give expression to a certain principle of ecclesiastical order or social behavior, a synthesis has to be found between the basic principle and the situational condition. And this situational synthesis is what we call *indigenization*. It has to be sought by our reason motivated by the Holy Spirit, guarded by the clear descriptions and prohibitions of the word of God and guided by the experience of the Christian church in former times and in other parts of the world.

Which are the realms where such indigenization is to be performed, and what is the material which can be used in this process? Dr. Tippett gives the widest indication and the most detailed description. I agree with him that the *vernacular language* must become the vessel of the word of God; that the *worship* must be conducted in forms which are spontaneous expressions of the new faith; that *church buildings* should be erected with the help of indigenous arts and crafts, and that the new belief should be expounded in a way which gives *meaningful answers* to the basic needs of the people. By his plastic illustrations from the work of the London Missionary Society on the Fiji Islands, he has rescued our discussion from tumbling in vague generalities as so often is the case when this adaptation complex is discussed. I would agree with a good many of his conclusions. The question whether indigenous rhythm, dance and music can be adopted for Christian use must be answered discriminatingly. There must be a selection between the suitable and the unsuitable.

(2) The Pitfalls

Still it is exactly at this point that we ought to go into greater detail and to dig deeper. Is it enough to state: "Where Scripture is iconoclastic, it is the faith formulation and not cultural form that is under attack?" Is the faith formulation always using the way of verbal communication, where rhythm, music and gesture are only accompanying elements? Or are there non-verbal message and impulses which can make use of subliminal influences? We know that shamanism in all parts of the world uses certain techniques of falling into trance. It is in this trance that spiritual possession takes place. Taking drugs, getting emotionally upset by hard beating rhythm or listening to enchanting melodies are some common forms of it. Modern beat music originates from the ecstatic rituals of the African tribal religion. It has an enrapturing effect also on the souls of western youth. Is it legitimate if beat music is made the vehicle of Christian evangelism and edification if the words being underlaid are Christian and the result is enthusiastic rapture? Is this a genuine way of experiencing the presence of the Holy Spirit, or could this adaptation possibly lead to demon possession with a Christian service? How do we explain that there are cases of former narcomaniacs who have fallen back into their addiction after they were evangelized by Jesus People with the aid of beat and rock music? Is there still something in certain cultural forms which predestines them to become vehicles of the spirits rather than of the Spirit?

I want to ask the same question with regard to the techniques of eastern meditation, Zazen, Yoga and Transcendental Meditation. I am quite certain about the latter. It is an adapted form of ancient Hinduistic Mantra Yoga, in which short spells are used to invoke the deity and to draw from its metaphysical force. The Mantras of Transcendental Meditation are all names of Hindu gods, and the result of practising Transcendental Meditation is occult oppression and the syncretistic deformation of the Christian faith. I am inclined to voice the same reservation also with regard to practicing the Asanas of Hata Yoga and the sittings of Zen Meditation. Both are ancient religious roads which, if practised according to instructions, automatically lead to the desired encounter with the transcendent reality, and this reality will not be different if the practitioner happens to be a Christian.

I have pointed out a few possible pitfalls in the process of faith transformation. My colleagues have mentioned other risks. Dr. Tippett has described the possibility that whole clusters of animistic concepts and practices may survive side by side with the professed Christian creed, because it has not been related to the elementary needs of the primal culture. This harmonizes largely with my analysis of the reason for the emergence of nativistic movements in Africa.

I am especially grateful that both Dr. McGavran and Dr. Tippett have pointed out one pitfall which has become specially significant today again. It is that traditional Christian terms are used, but secretly filled with a completely different meaning. Dr. McGavran refers to it by the name of "morphological fundamentalism," and Dr. Tippett draws a most illuminating parallel to the anti-gnostic struggle of Irenaeus. What has happened here is the very reverse of missionary translation. Instead of conquering the concepts of the non-Christian culture and filling them with a new biblical significance, the biblical concepts are captured and filled with a non-biblical meaning. It is not so much due to an error in Christian communication as to a deliberate assault on Christianity by an anti-Christian force.

This leads me to my final reflection in response to my colleagues.

AGENTS AND RESPONSIBILITIES:
WHO ARE THE AGENTS AND WHAT PART DO THEY
PLAY IN THE COMMUNICATION PROCESS?

The guiding question posed to the participants of this symposium was: "As Christianity spreads into the myriad cultures of the earth, it must correctly adjust to each culture, but what are the limits to such adjustment?"

The question states that *Christianity* spreads and that *it* adjusts. But now we have to ask further: who exactly is the agent in spreading, and who does the adjustment? As I have studied the papers of my colleagues, I found that they answered this question differently. Dr. McGavran, on the one hand, made his position clear from the outset that he wants to treat our topic as a missiological theme and that, for him, the primal interest lies with the foreign missionary and his role. He is the one commissioned to communicate the gospel to receptive populations across the borders of cultures. And he is responsible to see that this communication is done in such a way that the integrity of the essential core of the gospel is preserved. He has to adjust it to the recipients' cultural conditions as far as this is needed and permissible. McGavran also reckons with the fact that the indigenous church later makes further adjustments as far as historic challenges and changes demand them, but most of the adjustments have to be made in the second phase of mission history, where the great mass movements occur, a phase which is described by Dr. McGavran as the really formative period. Still, many of the adjustments which Dr. McGavran describes in his first chapter are those which were made by the established churches in much later times.

I'm afraid that to Dr. Hoekendijk this conception falls under the verdict of a missio-centric view, of which he accuses both Walter Holsten and Werner Gensichen in his first chapter. Dr. Hoekendijk emphatically states that there are no prima donnas in the *Opera Dei* of mission. And in his historic description of the spreading of Christianity in Indonesia, he has not many commendatory remarks about the role of the foreign missionaries. Insofar as they dominated in the earlier periods, they made almost every possible mistake of commission and omission. And when Christianity started really to spread spontaneously in recent dramatic movements, there was no noticeable role for foreign missionaries. I believe that it is possible seriously to challenge Dr. Hoekendijk on this description. I am sure that it is not only the study of the historical facts, but also his preconceived theological understanding of the *Missio Dei* which has inspired his presentation. There have, indeed, been remarkable figures of foreign missionaries in the history of Christian mission in the Dutch East Indies. They exercised a determinative influence when adjustments in view of the emerging indigenous Christianity were made. I am thinking of the famous work of the Dutch missionaries Dr. N. Adriani and Dr. A.C. Kruyt among the Toradja people on the Minahassa peninsula on Sulawesi. There was also Ludwig Ingwer Nommensen, the "apostle of the Batak people" of the Rhenish Mission and his famous adjustment to the unwritten traditional code of *adat*. I would finally mention Dr. Hendrik Kraemer with his historic contribution to the indigenization of the churches on Java. I quite agree that the missionaries have neither made nor written the whole story of missions in Indonesia. Especially during the last nine years of the widely acclaimed revival and mass movement on East Java, Timor and North Sumatra, there is such a close interaction of different factors that is is impossible to disentangle them for an objective description of the real events.

Dr. Hoekendijk refers to this by the term *Missio Dei*, and he expressly states that the Holy Spirit is the *true factor in the story*. But this is not to be understood in such a way that we could observe clear evidences of the divine *ordo salutis*, i.e. vocation, illumination, regeneration and sanctification, or remarkable demonstrations of spiritual gifts — as they have been reported rather sensationally from the revival on Timor. According to Dr. Hoekendijk, the work of the Holy Spirit cannot really be identified. It can only be believed as the decisive factor within the rather bewildering interaction of psychological, political, social, religious and other forces playing their parts in world history. Therefore, he comes to the conclusion that the missiologist must be satisfied with "humble agnosticism" about what really is taking place.

Dr. McGavran and Dr. Hoekendijk represent opposite positions in their respective views of the communication and adaptation process. The former believes that the spreading of Christianity is based on a clear personal commission by the divine Lord, and that it is conditioned by laws and factors which can be studied and controlled scientifically. He has established the Institute of Church Growth where this is practised to a remarkable extent. Dr. Hoekendijk, on the other hand, has his sharp reservations about such a view. I guess he considers it as a pragmatical and antropocentric interference into the sovereign initiative of God. He stresses the divine factor to such a degree that very little is left to human responsibility and almost nothing to the control of the foreign missionary. His final advice is: "Let God happen."

Now this apparent opposition reminds us that we must, indeed, become aware that there is an interaction between human and divine factors in the process of Christian communication. This interaction is very clearly stated in the Great Commission: "Behold, I am with you," and it is described in the first history of missions in Luke's Book of Acts. The church called it the *Acts of the Apostles,* but according to Luke's true intention it should rather have been called "The Acts of the Lord through the Apostles." Roland Allen and Harry R. Boer have described how any decisive event in the history recounted in this work was initiated by the Holy Spirit which almost visibly guided the apostolic messengers and opened or closed the doors for them. But this means that to the New Testament authors the work of the Holy Spirit in mission is not done anonymously and beyond human perception. The Holy Spirit gives clear directions to the messengers; he works miracles which cause the Christians to praise the Lord, he sets the pattern of genuine missionary procedures, which later are followed faithfully by ecclesiastical missionaries who do not experience his interference in such an ostentatious way anymore.

I believe that the interaction between the efficient work of the Holy Spirit and the responsible obedience of the Christian witness — whether he is a foreign missionary or a national believer — is the true clue to the solution of the communication problem. It is false to believe that God pursues his redemptive mission in history independently of the ministry of his church. But it is also wrong to believe that God has entrusted the whole cause into our hands so that it is solely dependent on our missiological skill whether there is true communication and indigenization in church growth or not. I do not say that my colleagues represent these extreme positions, but I see certain tendencies tempting them into these opposite directions.

Yet in order to get a proper theological perception of the communication process, it does not suffice to point to these two agents: The Holy Spirit and the missionary. We have to go further in our analysis of contributing factors, and the participants in this symposium are aware of this.

On the *human* side we have to study the distinct parts played by the cooperation between the foreign missionary and the local church moving towards better adjustment to its cultural background. Dr. Tippett has given a good example of a convincing adaptation which was made by a conscious policy of British missionaries in Fiji. He also reported on an indigenization which came about almost automatically by the development of a young church in Guatemala. I believe that the approach to the adjustment problem is different insofar as it normally comes about spontaneously on the side of the local church, whereas it is done deliberately from the side of the foreign mission. Becoming indigenous is simply a sign of the vitality of vigorous young Christians who express their faith in the form most natural to themselves. But the foreign missionary has to approach the problem by way of reflection and discernment. He acts as a professional messenger whose duty it is to translate the faith entrusted to him. He is responsible to see that it remains identical and still becomes intelligible to the people to whom he is sent. The office of the missionary is also to act as a representative of the church universal. Therefore, he sees to it that the indigenous church develops doctrinally in accordance with the faith once for all delivered to the saints. Still, he is not to decide alone whether the process of translation and adaptation has been successful. He is dependent on the testimony of the national converts to know whether a new indigenous expression of Christian faith and ethics is in harmony with their exclusive loyalty to Jesus Christ and, at the same time, natural to their cultural feelings.

Still, the main agent of communication is neither the missionary nor the local church. That the Christian message is really understood and accepted cannot be secured by any perfection of missionary translation and accommodation. It is the work of God himself. It is he who by his mysterious grace opens the door both to entire social groups and to the individual heart. The central role of the Holy Spirit is strongly emphasized by Dr. Hoekendijk, and I agree with him in principle. In my travels around the world I have found that I could communicate instantly with Christians of most different cultural backgrounds and social standards. The reason was that there existed a divine bond of fellowship, of common relation and experience which transcended our conceptual frameworks as conditioned by our cultures.

But in our present ecumenical theology, the concept of the Holy Spirit working in cross-cultural communication has developed in an ambiguous way which gives cause for serious theological concern. There is the new strange notion that the Holy Spirit or Christ is at work saving, not only through the ministry of the church in the means of grace, but also in the systems of religious thought and in the ideological movements of our time. The work of the Holy Spirit within and through the church is even belittled in the name of his alleged work *"extra muros ecclesiae."* Dr. McGavran rightly has expressed concern about the idea of the indwelling Christ, who independently of his word acts as our "inner light", or through our experiences and encounters with other people. I would call this modern ecumenical pneumatology a kind of secularized and syncretized pentecostalism. For in pentecostalism, too, the emphasis is on the work of the Holy Spirit through immediate inner experience and direct revelation apart from the written word of God. Conservative pentecostalism, however, limits the work of the Spirit to the realm of the Christian fellowship and, at least, claims conformity of its experiences with the biblical standard. Ecumenical spiritualism has universalized the working of the Spirit. Here Christ or the Holy Spirit is held to be equally present within the process of universal history, within our non-Christian partners in dialog and within us Christians. Therefore, Dr. Samartha challenges us in dialog to become sensitive to the work of the Holy Spirit within the other religions and the secular ideologies. Another representative of modern ecumenism, Dr. W. Hollenweger, demands of the Christian missionary in dialog to venture his whole existence and even his faith in order to be open for the rediscovery of the nature of the gospel and the person of Christ. He seriously considers the possibility that such an experience might lead us to discard the doctrines of the Trinity of God and of the two natures of Christ. Accordingly, the Christological ideal of Ram Mohan Roy, the founder of the Brahmo Samaj, is held to be a hopeful expression of indigenous theology in India, which unfortunately was quenched by the insensitivity of the conservative Anglican missionaries in the beginning of the last century. I wonder whether Dr. Hoekendijk has something similar in mind when he states: "It is safe to assume that what has been documented as curious deviation, syncretism, Christopaganism or even heresy might very well have been the undetected beginnings of an indigenous theology." How, in any case, does Dr. Hoekendijk make out whether it is God who is at work in a specific current movement within or towards Christianity?

To me this question becomes all the more disquieting as I have come to the impression that the whole ecumenical concept of history is a monistic one. No distinguishing line is drawn between world history and church history any more, because the same divine force is seen at work in both. All particular processes in the world are regarded as convergent. By the divine movement efficient in all religions, ideologies and political groups, they are bound to meet at the point Omega (Teilhard de Chardin), or the coming universal brotherhood of all men, or the classless society.

In sharp opposition to such a view, I want to draw the attention of this symposium to the fact that besides God there is still another metaphysical force at work in the processes of history. It is the Prince of this World, who also wants to play his part in the communication process in order to change it into his own game. In my second chapter, I showed that St. John attributed the syncretistic teachings of the gnostic heretics to the work of the devil, which made them forerunners of Antichrist. I was greatly encouraged to find in Dr. Tippett's second chapter that this notion was preserved in the post-apostolic church, and that it was expressed again in the anti-gnostic struggle of Irenaeus. In fact, it could be shown that all later heresies occurring in the history of the church were explained in the same way by the defenders of the faith.

This shows, that while we definitely have to stress the work of the Holy Spirit as the decisive factor in missionary communication, we cannot be satisfied with leaving everything to him and relaxing confidently in an attitude of "humble agnosticism." The initiating part played by the Holy Spirit calls for a close interaction between the divine and the human factor. And it is the specific responsibility of the missiologist to use his theological and anthropological discrimination to assist so that this interaction is not disturbed but is carried out in obedience to the revealed will of God.

CHAPTER ELEVEN

Universality and Freedom in Mission

J.C. HOEKENDIJK

INTRODUCTION

YOU all know, by now, what "professors" are. Let's try two current definitions: (a) A professor is *a person with a different opinion:* a dis-senter. Therefore, this peculiar species of the human race feels compelled to write books and to give lectures to prove their identity. (b) Or the word has to do with *pro-fessio:* a person who feels called to speak out *(fessio)* in public *(pro-)* for the whole world to hear.

These etymologies are, perhaps, not quite correct. But we all know that wrong derivations are often clues to find truth, *a-letheia,* opening up, dis-closure of reality as it happens to us.

I hope that my colleagues will not be offended because in this third round, I will not spend much time in producing different opinions. I am not trying to be defensive about the ecumenical movement nor offensive against the Frankfurt Declaration. Everybody who wants to do this is, of course, welcome to do so.

Rather I want to make my *pro-fessio.* That is, to respond to you, who have been so patient during this weekend, listening. A confession of my faith in the missionary God, who continues his *Missio Dei.* This, again, might be heard as a "different opinion"! That is your choice. In order to make clear that we are all in this thing together, I should like to conclude with an experimental translation of a passage of the New Testament that seems to me relevant to get our minds, hearts, expectancies together. It will be bad English, but it is delivered to us in bad Greek *(koine)*.

So, again, three points: (1) A brief reaction to my colleagues, who were up here; (2) An attempt to dialog with my colleagues down there; (3) Romans 8:14-27 with a couple (only a few) footnotes.

BRIEF REACTION

Let me preface these few remarks with a quote I found the other day in an article by one of the outstanding Roman missiologists of our time. He referred to me as a "Calvinistic-Pentecostal." I am sure that neither the Calvinists nor the Pentecostals will be very happy with this surprised ally. As for myself, I have given up all respect for labels. Maybe, some time after retirement, I will collect them to show that they "include each other out." So, *no party line!*

Therefore, my first reaction to my colleagues is simply a question: "How can you be so secure?" You will remember the distinction in Reformation theology: certainty *(certitudo)* vs. security *(securitas)*. The first lives by promises. A sense of security is anchored in guarantees. I am not talking about the chapters of this symposium. These are only texts in a wider context of publications, speeches, etc.

Let me try to specify. Dr. McGavran is sure that we live in a pre-Christian era. I only spoke of a post-Christendom era, which is altogether different. I was talking about what happened to the well-established churches in China (Nestorians, Ricci, C.S.), Japan (the Christian Century), North Africa, etc. I was thinking, for instance, of Luther, who admonished his fellow German Christians: "The Gospel is like a rainstorm, it pours down, . . . then it is gone!" For this reason I am rather skeptical about David Barrett's (who took his doctor's degree at Union Theological Seminary) predictions. What is promised is that there will be "a little fold sent in the midst of wolves"; a fold with a Shepherd; that should be enough.

Dr. Tippett keeps talking about "pagans", who are no longer there in a post-Christendom period. The processes of "Christianization" are far more diverse and complex, it would seem to me, than he suggested. The idea of a future projection, or even of a couple of alternative projections of church growth, I as an historian of Christian missions do not understand.

Dr. Beyerhaus has a precise concept of "present ecumenical theology," of which I am not aware, unless he simply means recent pronouncements of the World Council of Churches, but that is a quite different story. He is right in asserting that I am not very excited about ecclesiocentric missionary work (defined as moving from one church to the next!), but, of course, the *ekklesia* is "a sign, instrument and sacrament" of God's universal plan; and God has elected, chosen this "ground personnel" to carry out his/her purpose.

But enough; all these people "holding another opinion" have expressed these opinions in varieties of ways during, let's say, the last forty years.

DIALOGUE WITH MY OTHER COLLEAGUES

To you, the patient participants of this symposium, I want to make my *professio*. The first day I looked around in this chapel and estimated how much experience of this communication process was present here. I do not want to offend you, but my minimum guess was 1000 years. Probably more.

Cross-cultural communication of the gospel. We all know that one does not have to go overseas to be involved, although our rhetoric was full of the old "salt-water mythology" (K. Bridston). In New York I have only to cross a street to be in a different sub-culture. Kraemer distinguished between "communication with" (sit where people sit), and "communication of" (message). We have mainly dealt with the second aspect, and deliberated about the "pure" or the "essential gospel": the irreducible minimum. I am not sure this was right. To proclaim to the lame that "the blind man can see" is no good news, although, of course, correct. It can be footnoted as correct orthodoxy, but not gospel. In order to communicate a message, one has first to communicate with: to be in "communion with."

Even in the New Testament we find four Gospels for different situations. In other words, the story is *situation variable*. God has graciously decided to be *Emmanuel* (with humankind). Not only generally, universally — Jesus as the pioneer and initiator of a new humanity — but also particularly, specifically.

As long as we remain imprisoned in general formulae, however sound they are, we do not fulfill the gospel (Rom. 15:19) nor take it wherever it is destined.

What is the gospel about? About Jesus, of course. A Christian is a person "obsessed by Joshua of Nazareth."

What does this *historia Jesu* initiate? Let's use the good old word, *salvation,* and add two postscripts:

(1) Salvation happens (as is recognized now in recent missiology [Gensichen]) along two main lines: (a) *Liberation.* Exodus symbol: to be free from . . .; (b) *Blessing.* To be free for . . . others, for the future, and for God. These two lines converge in the word: *shalom.* "Steadfast love and faithfulness will meet." "Righteousness and peace will kiss each other." ". . . will go before the Lord and make his footsteps a way" (Ps. 85:10-13).

(2) In history we find a reduction of *shalom* (all relations of life) to *soteria* (in the New Testament mainly in relation to God) and to *salus* (ultimate destiny of the faithful).

The only point I want to make is that people who try to recover the richness, the pluriformity of *shalom* are not, necessarily, secular humanists, with all the bad connotations Dr. Beyerhaus suggests. They can also be radical Christians, who go back to the *radices,* the roots, knowing that the Messiah is the Prince of Shalom or, in New Testament terms, Christ is our peace.

ROMANS 8:14-27

Let us try together to recover this biblical vision. The two foci of the gospel are *universality* (this is good news for everybody) and *freedom,* or, more dynamically, liberation.

The horizon of Romans is universal, but the theme, the dominant motif, the thesis, is freedom. In chapters 5-7 Paul begins his argument with a loud stroke on the gong of freedom. He "hammers out freedom all over the land." Freedom from sin (5), freedom from death (6), freedom from law (7). He summarizes it in 8:2: "Now you are released from the law of sin and destruction" (death).

The *horizon:* all humankind.

The *theme:* liberation, freedom.

The dominant factor in this new age beyond slavery is the Spirit. That is the background of the text I should like to read with you in a kind of experimental translation.

(1) The Translation

14. All who are moved by the Spirit of God are children of God. 15. For you did not get back an old master-slave relationship *(pneuma douleias),* based on fear; what you got is a parent-child relationship *(pneuma huiothesias),* in which we are entitled to call God: *Abba.* 16. This Spirit (of God) bears united witness with our spirit, that we are children of God. 17. Since we are God's children, we will, one day, also inherit, we will possess the blessings God keeps for the people and we will share with Christ (as joint heirs) what God has kept for him; if we share Christ's suffering, we will also share God's glory *(doxa).*

18. I consider (think, reckon, figure: *logizomai)* that whatever we suffer now, cannot be compared at all with the splendor *(doxa)* as yet not revealed, which is in store for us. The created universe is waiting on tiptoe (eagerly longing) for the children of God, to show what they are (to be revealed). *(Cotton Patch Version:* "In fact, the fondest dream of the universe is to catch a glimpse of real live sons of God.") 20. The creation is in the grip of frustration/futility *(mataiotes).* Not by its own choice; God made it so. (God has arranged it this way) and (therefore) there is always hope *(eph'elpidi)* that one day the universe will be set free from the shackles *(douleia)* of mortality/decadence and share the glorious freedom (freedom and glory) of the children of God. 22. As we all know up to the present time, the creation in all its parts *(pasa)* groans with pain like the pain of childbirth. 23. But not just *creation alone* (groans); we ourselves, although we have tested already the *apéritif* of the Spirit *(aparche:* first fruits only, more to come) we groan (inwardly, silently, within ourselves) (because we are still) anticipating childship and (or, that is) the full liberation *(exodus)* of our human existence *(soma).* 24. For (let us be realistic) *we must be content to hope that we shall be saved* – our salvation is not yet in sight; if it were, we should not have to be

hoping (who hopes for something that is seen?) 25. We must hope for what we do not yet see and it takes patient endurance (*upomone*) to wait for it.

26. Now then (*hosautos*): In the same way the Spirit also comes to help us, weak that we are. We do not even know how to pray properly. (The Spirit has to do the job for us.) The Spirit (itself: *auto*) expresses our pleas in a way that could never be put into words.

27. And (God) who X-rays our hearts, understands (knows: *oiden*) what the Spirit means (*to phronema*) because it pleads for God's own people (*hagioi*) in God's own way (*kata theon*).

(2) A Few Footnotes

(a) Martin Luther in commenting on this passage once said: "Evidently we have to put our eyes into our ears to understand what all this is about," things as we see them are not decisive, they keep *ta blepomena* away from *ta elpizomena*: things we hope for. Hoping has priority over seeing. Listen to this cosmic symphony (cacophony) of groaning; you will hear the loud cry for liberation of the universe "in all its parts" and the continuous intercession of the Spirit on behalf of God's own people, who really do not know what to say. Put your eyes into your ears and listen: we are not required to be "where the action is," but we are within listening distance of the groaning, of the agonizing.

(b) Note that the *whole* creation is not the scene, the arena *for* the children of God to do *their thing*. For some mysterious reason (it was not by its own choice, Paul says, God arranged it this way) the universe is historicized, rather futurized, it stretches itself beyond its present frustration and futility; it is "infected with hope." It is in *provolution*: turning itself away from the *status quo*, moving forward, ahead (*pro*). This pro-volution is, so to speak, the creational reflex to God's promise (*pro-missio*). The universe and the children of God find themselves in the same history.

(c) Evidently the creation has only one *locus* to look for the "glorious freedom" it desires: the children of God . . . fantastic!

(d) It is even more fantastic when we remember that these children of God are not on an isle of bliss; they are not the "saved", serving out their gifts to the "non-saved". They are (and I quote) groaning, waiting, hoping children who still anticipate adoption, not yet emancipated in their human existence; they have only tasted the *apéritif* of the Spirit and do not know how to pray properly. There is not a bit of triumphalism.

What could *missionary participation* possibly mean? Perhaps involvement in a pro-missionary way *(sub specie promissionis,* in the perspective of promise). Things are not fixed, established, here to stay; they are rather open-ended: so-called "facts" are simply processes leading toward liberation; men are not caught in any kind of bondage *(douleia)* but already set free towards "future and hope."

Missionary participation is, it seems to me, not believing our eyes *(ta blepomena,* things as we see them), but trusting our ears, hearing promises which kindle hope and acting accordingly, expectantly within the world-wide horizon of hope.

CHAPTER TWELVE

The Adaptation-Syncretism Axis

DONALD A. MCGAVRAN

THE position of the last contributor, commenting on the offerings of his three colleagues in regard to the acceptable limits of adjustment and adaptation is particularly difficult.

Nevertheless, the differences of opinion between the four of us — and especially between Dr. Hoekendijk and the other three — have been obvious. We have all stated well-considered positions. Those of you who know Drs. Tippett, Hoekendijk, Beyerhaus and myself have no doubt all the way through been saying, "How typical of each man are these chapters and responses." The value of these twelve chapters is, I think, that they have brought together four major ways of considering the adjustment-syncretism axis.

Each man has written in a consistent fashion. Each has developed his thought skillfully. What a rich offering. What a contrast. What a complex process. What signs of hope! What signals of despair! What warnings and rebukes! What exposure of Marxist and agnostic presuppositions! Exciting, inviting and dangerous possibilities open up before us. The whole missionary movement will be much more aware of the real situation because the Carter Symposium has brought this unusual audience together and induced the four of us to give untold hours to the preparation of these papers.

I express special thanks to Dr. Hoekendijk. He holds views on revelation , the propagation of the gospel, the multiplication of churches, syncretism and possessio quite distinct from those of the rest of the team. It must have been difficult for him to bear with us. He has gone straight ahead, however, and stated his convictions modestly and courageously. Since his views are widely held by a large number of avant-garde thinkers on mission, his exposition has added a valuable dimension to the discussion. That I disagree with his position does not diminish from the fact that it needs to be heard. The adaptation process is ambiguous and complex. Christians need to see the various solutions being proposed and judge which is acceptable and which unacceptable.

Further discussion on the adaptation-syncretism axis, however, will have to be on two tracks. The presuppositions and assumptions of the three of us, on the one hand, and of Dr. Hoekendijk, on the other, are so different that it is confusing to cast them all in one conversation and to use the same terms for very different realities. Dr. Hoekendijk shares few of the basic positions held by Drs. Tippett, Beyerhaus and myself. Joint discussion will yield little fruit. For example, his translation of Romans 8:14-27 I understand, but there is so much on the other side. This mysterious passage is overwhelmed by so much more that is not mysterious but, on the other hand, is clear and readily understandable. Both strands are needed in understanding the Scriptures. To focus merely on the mysterious is to misunderstand what God is saying. Even in this one passage, the words of Paul must be seen in the light of how he used them in other passages.

Dr. Hoekendijk holds existentialist, mystical and cosmic opinions. He says his views of inspiration are "very weak." He humorously calls himself a Calvinist Pentecostal and avers that neither Calvinists nor Pentecostals will be happy to own his position as theirs. He dispenses with revelation — save as that which takes place like a flash of lightning in any man's consciousness. He proposes to "let God happen," apparently untrammelled by the Bible. All this demands separate treatment at considerable length. Perhaps Dr. Yamamori will arrange a separate symposium to consider on strictly biblical grounds just this one unusual way of looking at the Bible. We are all biblical people. What the Bible really says, that we will do. But we must be convinced that the Bible — the whole Bible — really says it.

I have been pleased with the urbanity of the exchange. We prepared chapters independently and did not know what the others were going to say. Naturally considerable differences have surfaced as a Methodist, a Presbyterian, a Lutheran and — you will forgive me — A Christian have expressed themselves in many matters concerning the heart of the Christian faith.

As we saw the differences, some penetrating questions have been asked. Dr. Tippett has appended some footnotes of dissent. Dr. Beyerhaus has differed vigorously with Dr. Tippett, Dr. Hoekendijk and myself at several points. We are all richer for his frankness. The tremendous issues are so rich with possibilities and so fraught with danger that plain speaking is demanded.

Readers benefit by Dr. Beyerhaus' skillful evaluation of the various theological emphases made by the other three speakers. The Christian missionary movement needs a great deal more frank disagreement. This is ecumenical conversation at its best. The grave issues which Dr. Hoekendijk's second and third chapters brought before us demand considered answers. That they have not come in the last round is due to the suddenness with which they came before us and to the fact that they cannot be discussed on ordinary presuppositions. Answers will be given, of course, in other publications. The issues are too important to let them lie unchallenged.

Be that as it may, many major problems and aspects of adaptation and possessio have been spread out to be seen. We have illustrated them profusely. We have explained what they mean in many different situations. We have looked at the axis from many angles. Readers judging where the truth lies, will take those aspects of adaptation which fit their situation and build on them. Men and women gathered here come from and go out to all six continents — Asia, Africa, North America, South America, Europe and Oceania. I am confident that readers will find in this symposium much with which they will agree, much which will be new, much which they can use, some which they will doubt and some which they will strongly controvert.

Probably the most helpful thing I can do is to call attention to four main dimensions of the axis: the geographical-historical, the anthropological, the theological and the ecclesiastical. To the first of these I now turn.

THE GEOGRAPHICAL-HISTORICAL DIMENSION

The adaptation-syncretism axis must always be seen as a characteristic of a particular geographical-historical situation. There is no axis in general. All that exists is a series of particular adaptations. All that really exists is one kind of embodied Christianity at one specific time and place, making one adjustment to one particular religion and one particular culture. Indeed, usually the adjustment is made not to one religion and one culture, but to that religion and that culture as practised by a small group of highly selected individuals. In short, the geographical-historical dimension is an essential part of the picture. Much of the confusion which surrounds the subject is due to the grandiose world-embracing pronouncements in which it is set forth. These are almost certain to be in error. The greater the generalization the more certain the error. If the generalization has a degree of validity in Africa, it has none in regard to the churches arising among Japanese intelligentsia. If it sounds right in universities in North America, it sounds wrong to the proletariat in urban India.

My esteemed colleague Dr. Hoekendijk has done the symposium a favor in his careful historical description of the Indonesian scene of adjustment. As he dipped back into the sixteenth, seventeenth and early eighteenth centuries and laid bare the geographical-historical context in which empirical Portuguese and Dutch churches found themselves, we could see clearly how impossible it is to project back into that scene our contemporary thinking about adjustment. Obviously what the Protestant chaplains were attempting in the fortified trading posts where they lived was closely limited by the fact that they were employees of an all-powerful state church, which in its homeland was coextensive with the state, and was locked in mortal combat with the other (heretical) politico-ecclesiastical system. A premise they never questioned was that all the

subjects of a Roman Catholic prince should be Roman Catholics
and of a Protestant prince should be Protestants. Naturally the
task in the forts and factories established by Holland and
Portugal was to practice the precise form of Christianity which
each state church authorized, and to bring the Asian subjects of
Portugal and Holland into conformity with the religion of the
kings of Portugal and Holland. Had the chaplains been asked,
"Is this not imperialistic?" they would have answered with a
cheerful "yes — we intend to be imperialistic and are doing right
in being so. It is the only possible course of action."

Another example of the geographical-historical setting is seen
in the last 18 chapters of the book of Acts. Missionary work —
which always involves adjustment and is always in danger of
syncretism — was there being carried out in a context radically
different from both the seventeenth century Indonesian scene
and the twentieth century Asian and African scenes. The early
church was carrying out mission from a have-not nation to the
political and military rulers and the intellectual elite of the
Mediterranean world. Mission went from the "ignorant and
unlearned" Christians of Jerusalem and Antioch to proud
Athens and to imperial Rome. Inevitably it made its entry along
that one thin extension of Palestine which found form in the
synagogue communities of the urban centers. The missionaries
were unpaid. There was no missionary society. Missiology
would not be born for nineteen hundred years. There was no
temptation to civilize before Christianizing. The Jewish
Christian missionaries had no particular status in the lands to
which they went. If they were stoned or beaten or thrown into
prison, no Jewish consul took up the matter with the
government. While the distances concerned were shorter, the
time it took to get to the field was greater. In short, the
geographical-historical circumstances were unique. That
particular axis had marked dissimilarities from today's axes.

As I developed this dimension of our problem, I asked myself:
as men and peoples become Christian today, are there certain
stages through which they pass? And do adjustments take place
more in one stage than another? I answer yes to both questions.
Adaptations of embodied Christianity to new cultures take place

during a definite time span. Whether it takes a dozen years or a hundred, discipling a given homogeneous unit usually occurs in three stages which I spread out before you.

First, come those years in which a few individuals out of the culture become Christians. Whether they leave the non-Christian culture to join the new Christian churches, or remain as oddballs and eccentrics within their former culture, makes little difference. In either case, they affect the culture but slightly. They do carry out, as it were, a series of exploratory adaptations, translate portions of the Bible and hymns into the new language and demonstrate what has to be given up and what can be retained. They show what men of that tribe or caste look like when they become disciples of Christ. They blaze not highways but paths through the forest.

During this first stage, the scales are loaded in favor of the older forms of embodied Christianity. The advocates — the missionaries — inevitably know best their own kind of Christianity. As they portray Christ and persuade men to become his followers, of necessity they speak of the Christianity they know. The few individuals who become Christian join congregations in which they are always incoming novices. Their inclination and the political weightage of the situation fairly well guarantee that they learn existing patterns rather than create adaptations and adjustments to their former religion and custom.

Missiologists who have served in congregations which have arisen as converts one by one across several decades came to Christian faith, have much to say about the need for more indigenization, adaptation and cordial welcome to other cultures. Yet in these first-stage conglomerate congregations and denominations, little real adaptation *can* occur, even if missionaries see the need for it and work hard for it.

Second, come those years during which a people movement sweeps through that unit. Large numbers in natural groups become Christian, live on in their ancestral homes and earn their living in traditional ways. They become Chrstian without social dislocation. During stage two, major adaptations take place. The scales are loaded in favor of the culture. Indigenization takes place whether the missionaries want it or not. The hard problem is neither to make the church indigenous, nor to give the culture a chance. The hard problem is to make the church Christian, to communicate the essential gospel, to prevent Christopaganism from developing. Here ministers of the growing church and missionaries who have thought their way through the adaptation-syncretism process can make significant contributions. They can suggest adaptations and adjustments which transmit the Christian faith intact and dress it in the beautiful garments of the new culture.

During the early years of people movement growth, the new church is leadable, anxious to do that which Christians do. It is close enough to the traditional culture to be able to mold it to the will of Christ. For example, among the Bataks an early decision to accept the tribal *adat* (customary law) as that which Christians would follow helped the movement enormously. Christians were free to concentrate attention on the heart of the Christian religion. While they did change the *adat* here and there, most matters of conduct were judged according to its accepted strictures.

It is, of course, desirable during this second stage that adaptations be accepted by the people as their own decisions. This does not mean that the missionary plays no part and stays quietly in the background while the new converts decide whether ancestral tablets, for example, be burned, or modified, or hung in the church! New converts cannot make such decisions.

Often they have read little of the Bible or may, indeed, be unable to read it. They know nothing of the great sweep of Christian history. The missionary is an essential part of the picture. His role cannot be played by some elder who was recently baptized, and has stumbled through parts of the Gospel of Mark. But the missionary should be sensitive to the culture in which he works. He should carry his people with him. He should associate new Christians with himself.

Since by the time of the second stage, it often happens that ministers recruited and trained from people converted in stage one are available, the ministers too play an important part in working out adaptations essentially Christian and culturally correct. Perhaps more than anyone else they are in position to advocate courses of action true to the Bible and congenial to the culture.

Stage three is made up of those decades during which churches are multiplying through the whole people concerned, and adjustments worked out during stages one and two are being further modified and institutionalized. Major adaptations seldom occur during this stage. The church is already indigenous. The Christian way is simply burned still further into the consciousness of the Christians.

Occasionally during stage two some needed adjustment was *not* made. In such cases, changes need to be made during stage three. The example given by Dr. Tippett in his first lecture fits here. As the Indians of Latin America via the people movement route became Roman Catholic Christians, they were *not* instructed and *were* allowed to make adaptations which betrayed the gospel. They became Christopagans. During stage three, Roman Catholic leaders should have led them on to renounce their old gods, obey the Bible and have a personal experience of Christ. When this did not happen, evangelical missionaries came in to initiate a radical change, a conversion out of the syncretistic faith to genuine Christianity. This became stage one in the movement to biblical faith.

Unless the Church of Rome in Latin America rapidly presses forward with the reconversion within itself of Christopagans to biblical faith, the present small beginning of an evangelical stage one will grow into large evangelical people movements in stage two, and will spread throughout each Indian tribe in stage three.

During stage one of the Aymara and Quechua movements to evangelicalism, small numbers are affected, and the embodied Christianity developed is loaded in the direction of Mestizo and North American Christianity. In stage two great opportunity will open for an embodied Christianity which is at once soundly biblical and thoroughly Indian. Many Roman Catholic and Indian features could be brought across intact. For example, there is no biblical reason why the excellent system of godfathers and godmothers (*compadres* and *commadres*) should not become a bulwark of all evangelical congregations.

THE ANTHROPOLOGICAL DIMENSION

We live in a world and an era where the anthropological dimension of life is ever before us. For many the divine dimension has faded out of view. Most men in modern Eurica and the elite of Latrica also are incurably secular. They are all anthropologists and think and talk as if the only reality was that which can be seen and measured.

Consequently, all four of us have taken naturally to the unspoken assumption which has underlain most of our presentations — namely, that the adaptation-syncretism axis was something which men do. It proceeds according to anthropological and sociological laws. Cultural compulsives make certain adaptations almost inevitable. "Afro-messianism," Dr. Beyerhaus says, "is the outcry of a community which has broken down in the cultural clash." Dr. Tippett asserts that the nature worship of Juan's fellow villagers was "the survival of a discrete cultural unit, an animistic cohesive cluster of both faith and practice." In my second chapter I called attention to the fact that the first few individuals to become Christian always join congregations in which they are novices, and usually are a tiny minority. "Their inclination and the political weightage of the situation guarantee that they learn existing patterns, rather than create adaptations and adjustments to their former religion and custom." Numerous other examples can be given. All of us write as if the whole matter of adapting empirical Christianity to each culture into which it flows were something that missionaries did. Converts did. Congregations did. Non-Christians did. In short, that men did. This is the anthropological dimension.

It is a useful dimension, though we should remember that it is not the only one. Men do act according to laws of human behavior. Regularities occur in their actions. Certain ways of response are statistically probable. As the sciences of man — psychology, sociology and anthropology — mature it becomes more and more possible to see what men do in the light of these laws. Madison Avenue knows that if fifty million people are exposed to such and such a stimulus, Z number of them will buy a certain product. Or, to change the illustration, every man acts on the basis of a network of typifications which are formed by his predecessors, his circumstances, his contemporaries as appropriate tools for coming to terms with things. For example, the universe of every person is experienced in the form of types — trees, houses, students, teachers, plumbers, professors, cattle and among the last Holstein cows. There are types of artifacts such as tools, cars, typewriters and chairs. There are types of social roles such as politicians, taxpayers, legislators and laborers. All these typifications are taken for granted. Language is full of them. They are part of the anthropological dimension and they help us predict what will happen. Sophisticated anthropological thinking simply carries this typification a step further and refines and qualifies it and makes prediction somewhat more certain.

All this has a great deal to do with missionary adaptation. Adaptation is partly determined by conscious decisions on the part of Christian leaders; and partly by the laws of communication, of social structure, of innovation and of other ways of human behavior. Typifications and what Alfred Shutz calls domains of relevance greatly influence what adaptations should be and can be made. The homogeneous unit plays a very important part in church growth. Many adaptations which ought to be made are not made because the homogeneous units concerned are not recognized.

Knowledge of the laws of human behavior described by anthropology and other social sciences helps minister and missionary establish churches which fit the culture and feel good to people of that culture. Such knowledge is part of the working equipment of all missionaries. In times past they have acquired it by living in it, observing it and forming an accurate opinion of how the people of this caste or that tribe regularly behave. But today, extensive researches on almost every segment of mankind, if studied by the missionary and minister, place at their disposal expert opinion and mountains of evidence concerning how the people they are evangelizing think and act. Today adaptation can proceed in the light of knowledge. There is less excuse for a funbling approach. Much less time is needed to become effective communicators of the grace of God.

Above all, the wealth of anthropological detail should enable those seeking to embody Christianity in the thought forms, logic, understandings and customs of any given people, to achieve substantial indigeneity without sacrificing any part of the core of Christianity.

THE THEOLOGICAL DIMENSION OF ADAPTATION

These conversations on adjustment and adaptation have been greatly enriched by Dr. Beyerhaus, who has called our attention so effectively to the fact that the spread of the Christian faith into every culture is God's will and must take place in accordance with God's revelation. All the speakers have, it is true, stressed this, but Dr. Beyerhaus probed the depths and laid the missionary movement under deep indebtedness. Unless the process of adaptation is seen in God's perspective and circumscribed by his regulations, it soon degenerates into syncretism.

It would be impossible in a short summary statement to review adequately the treasures Dr. Beyerhaus has spread before us. I shall not attempt the task. I intend rather to select three emphases which typify his contribution and thus attempt to recapture the flavor of the whole.

The theological dimension discerns that many adaptations have feet of clay. They are not culturally *necessary*. They did not arise because Christians in this culture have to make this adaptation. Rather they arose as a natural response of unregenerate man. If he happens to be in North America, his response appears in the guise of American culture; if in Japan, in the guise of Japanese culture; if in Nigeria, in the guise of some Nigerian culture. But in all three cases the response may be not so much cultural as sinful. Missiologists should beware of idealizing all responses of Christians in other cultures than their own. The Korean missionary to Los Angeles should not assume that all American responses are, by virtue of being American, the outcome of a pure heart! The missionary from India to South Africa would be a simpleton, indeed, were he to believe that every Christian in South Africa acts exclusively from brotherly and loving motives, or that South African cultural responses are necessarily good responses.

For example, many an agnostic in North America — heart of the agnostic culture — disbelieves in the resurrection of the dead and, therefore, in the resurrection of Jesus Christ. He thinks it a quaint tale. He fancies himself a hard-headed secularist. He knows that when men are dead, they are dead and never rise from the grave. But such an agnostic should not deceive himself that the culture of the twentieth century will not allow belief in the resurrection of the body. It was equally difficult for the disciples who had seen the cold stiff dead body of the Galilean leader to believe that he had risen. The culture is not to blame. Unregenerate man in any culture finds it easy to deny the resurrection. He excused himself saying "my education, my culture, my worldview, my science really makes it quite impossible for me to believe." The fact of the matter, of course, is that once he gives himself to Christ, the intellectual difficulties in any culture which prevent faith simply disappear.

Similarly, in India the minister must not assume that the Hindu who believes on Christ and wants to go on worshiping Ganesh is compelled to such action by Indian culture. It is much more likely to be lack of real belief in God the Father Almighty, who has commanded "Thou shalt have no other gods before me." The Indian church is continually faced with adjustments worked out by individuals and congregations. While welcoming all moves which make Christianity in India more Indian, the church should not stupidly close its eyes to the possibility that a fair number of adjustments will prove on inspection to be neither good nor really Indian.

What this symposium is saying to us is that the theological dimension of the adjustment-syncretism axis helps us see that man is not solely a creature of culture. He is also regenerate or unregenerate as the case may be. This must be taken into account.

In the second place, the theological dimension helps us see that since mission always involves translation, the adjustment process is always affected by the quality of the exegesis, hermeneutic and translation. If any of the three go wrong, faulty adaptation results. Careless exegesis fails to discern what the Bible really says. A slipshod hermeneutic distorts the meaning

— generally in the direction of the unconscious or unconfessed sinful drives of the interpreter. Incompetent translation fails to put into the heart language of the receptors the exact meaning of the message. Let us take an example from North American Indian culture. This cordially receives those teachings concerning the Holy Spirit which accord with Indian beliefs of a vague spirit power which can be very dangerous or, when guided and controlled by the shaman, can heal and benefit men. Since pre-Christian Indians know nothing about the Holy Spirit who is the Third Person of the Triune God, and guides the church into all truth, the idea of definitive revelation given by the Holy Spirit is strange to them. The following is not a message for which American Indians are culturally prepared: "No prophecy of scripture is a matter of one's own interpretation, because no prophecy ever came by the impulse of man, but men moved by the Holy Spirit spoke from God (II Peter 1:21). Indians know of the vague Spirit World, but not of the indwelling Spirit who transforms the Christian into the image of Christ — the image which has been revealed in the Scripture and can be compared with and checked by the Scripture, the Christ who is the same yesterday, today and forever.

In the third place, the theological dimension reminds us sharply that the African Confession, the Indian Confession and the Korean Confession toward which the church in those lands is undoubtedly trending will do two things. First, it will affirm the faith in terms understandable by men in those cultures, congenial to their thought forms (though not necessarily congenial to them) and conveying exactly the meanings which God has revealed in the Bible. Second, it will expose the misunderstandings of God's word which missionary and national translators have unwittingly exhibited and denounce the misunderstandings which unregenerate men, both in the church and out of the church, have loaded onto the pure gospel.

For example, when we think about adaptation from the theological point of view, we think about it *as it looks to God who has spoken to us in his word*. We remember that throughout the Bible God demands respect for his majestic position. He expects Israel to give him exclusive loyalty. I am God, he declares, and there is no other. You shall have no other gods before me. This position, so impressively stated in the Old Testament, is diametrically opposite to pantheism, universalism and the easy opinion that all concepts about God are about equally right. This position grates on the ear of secular relativistic men. They do not like it. It sounds narrow and exclusivistic. But there it stands, like a rock. God *is* a jealous God. He tolerates no other conception of God than the one he has revealed. There is no other Name by which men can be saved. There is no other way to reach God the Father. God's self-disclosure was for all men. Speaking in the Hebrew culture and the Hebrew language and the Greek culture and the Greek language, he intended to disclose his purposes and his nature to the whole of mankind. He intended to be adored by men of all nations.

This theological dimension which forms such a clear and substantial part of the Scriptures means that as the Christian Confession forms in every culture, it is jealously guarded by God to see that it conforms to his true nature as revealed in the Bible. The American Confession of today must speak in terms understandable by Americans.

THE ECCLESIOLOGICAL DIMENSION OF ADAPTATION

Adaptation takes place in a particular geographical-historical situation, according to the laws which govern human behavior, under the sovereign power of God and governed by his written word, and always manifests itself as a churchly phenomenon. Adaptation cannot be done by a single isolated Christian. It is something a church does. It has to do with congregational life, with how Christians live together, with the regulations governing their relationship to other Christians and non-Christians. It is an ongoing process within the *ecclesia* of God.

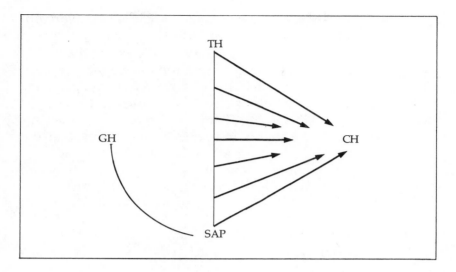

The above diagram will help us see the situation. Let GH represent a precise geographical-historical situation. Let TH represent the theological dimension, the biblical given, the message which must be transmitted intact, the divine self-disclosure which it has pleased God to give in the Bible and in Jesus Christ. Let SAP represent the sociological-anthropological-psychological context in which the gospel is advancing. Let CH represent the church forming on new ground. The arrows reaching out from various parts of the line TH — SAP toward CH represent adaptations or adjustments which carry forward into the new congregations and the new denomination elements of the SAP culture and the TH biblical given. The mixture in each arrow is different. In the arrows nearest SAP, the mix contains much of the culture and little of the theological given. The lowest arrow, let us assume, represents how the Christians out of that precise situation (GH) earn their living. After becoming Christians they continue to earn their living in very much the say way they did before they became Christians. Hence the arrow goes out from the line very near SAP.

The top arrow represents the God the Christians worship. Here the mix heavily favors TH not SAP. They have left their old gods and have believed on Jesus Christ and come to the Father through him. The second arrow from the top might represent how they worship. They use their own SAP language. They gather for worship in one of their SAP houses. They come dressed in their SAP clothing. They sing according to the SAP tunes they know. All this is indicated by the position of the arrow down from TH toward SAP. But in worship they address their adoration, penitence and offering to God as they are coming to know him in Christ according to the Scriptures. This is indicated by the position of the second arrow toward the top of the line, near TH.

If it be borne in mind that any diagram has severe limitations and illustrates only a few things, much may be learned from this one.

Note first that what we loosely call "an adaptation" is in reality a cluster of adaptations. In actual fact each new congregation demonstrates thousands of adaptations. Most come over from the previous culture very little changed. That is why the diagram shows many more arrows at the SAP end than at the TH end. Each separate cultural component makes, so to speak, a mix of its own. Or, to speak theologically, God calls into his new church thousands of cultural components substantially as they existed in the pre-Christian population.

Note second that each separate adaptation has a mix of its own. It is composed of a different proportion of SAP and TH. Even such a neutral element as language, which might be expected to be the same for Christians and non-Christians, is found to be different for Christians. They purge their language of idolatrous, perverse and hateful words. A high caste Hindu feudal lord once said to me of a group of low-caste Christians who worked for him, "They use much better language now that they have become Christians. Better language in fact than we do." One expects that Christians will treat their animals better, educate their children more carefully, pay their debts more conscientiously and keep their houses cleaner. In general, however, it may be said that the closer to SAP, the less change is to be expected in cultural components, and the closer to TH, the greater change is expected.

Note third that the ecclesiological dimension insists that, in regard to any proposed mix, an essential question is the pragmatic one: does it work? Does a church form out there at CH?

An adjustment which is theologically correct, or anthropologically correct, and does not take shape in an ongoing church is an irrelevancy. Armchair theorists can discuss these things at great length and waste incredible amounts of time doing so. Gunpowder is that mix of charcoal, saltpeter and sulfur which goes off bang. An adaptation is that mix of Christian conviction and existing culture which produces a growing, thriving church. It is quite useless for anyone to advocate a wonderful adaptation which produces church decline. If the operation is successful, the patient must not invariably die.

Let me illustrate the last point. In August 1973, I was in Nigeria conducting a church growth seminar and heard that black missionaries of the Nigerian church had gone to the islands in Lake Chad, settled there as humble cultivators of the soil and had, in a quiet way, evangelized the dominantly Moslem population. The Christians, finding everyone on the islands worshiping on Friday and gathering for prayer five times each day according to the Moslem custom, had themselves gathered for prayer to God-in-Christ five times a day, and for weekly worship on Friday when the Moslems were in their mosques. Earnest evangelism, as it so frequently does, won converts. Moslems became believers in Christ. They continued to pray five times a day — but now at Christian places of worship and to God in the name of Christ. Weekly worship on Friday suited their culture and they continued this joyfully. Back in the United States I reported this interesting incident at a meeting.

I was somewhat dismayed, however, when I heard one of my disciples advocating this adjustment to Moslem custom as one of the great new breakthroughs of missiology. Theoretically it is an adjustment about which much may be said both for and against, but that is not the point. Before that adjustment is worth serious consideration, it must lead thousands of Moslems into ongoing Christian churches. And that, I fear, is not the case on the Lake Chad islands. There, I seriously question whether the Moslem converts who commune on Friday number more than a handful — maybe they have not even been baptized. On the other side of the question, more than 100,000 Moslem converts who have been baptized in East Java, have apparently come into all kinds of churches, and followed all kinds of orders of worship from Pentecostal to Reformed, and all have done so *on Sunday*.

In short, it has yet to be proved that an adjustment to Moslem custom which consists in prayers five times a day and weekly worship on Friday is a good adjustment. So far it has not developed anything out there toward CH. It has not "worked".

On the other hand, the Jews for Jesus Movement, led by Moishe Rosen, has proved that when American Jews are offered the option of becoming followers of the Messiah without leaving their Jewish culture, without eating pork, without losing their sense of Jewish identity, without traitorously abandoning their people, it has enabled some hundreds of them, perhaps by now some thousands of them, to accept Jesus Christ as God and Savior. They call themselves fulfilled Jews or Jews for Jesus. In the case of the Jews for Jesus, adjustment to Jewish culture which is still true enough to TH to satisfy the most meticulous, passes the pragmatic test. It works. It is not ivory tower conversation. It is actual church-multiplying evangelism. To use Dr. Hoekendijk's terminology, it establishes "new units of shalom" in a formerly non-Christian territory. The congregations do not look like any existing denomination, but they are made up of disciples of Christ, followers of the Way. They are as Christian as were all Jesus' disciples from the day of Pentecost till about A.D. 50.

As missiologists consider adaptations, possessions, accommodations, they must make sure that the resulting church is still Christian. Nothing is gained by promoting a series of syncretisms. Nothing is gained by watering down the Christian faith till it can mix with any other faith or non-faith: that is a sure formula for syncretism. Equally, nothing is gained by adding to the Christian faith elements from other faiths or non-faiths so that the new church is not Christian at all. Syncretisms which are gained by reducing Christianity or by adding to it are equally to be eschewed.

At the same time, missiology should beware of any adaptation which does not help the church grow on new ground. That is the purpose of adaptations — that they sweep away non-biblical obstacles. As men and women confront Christ, they must face and overcome biblical obstacles: the scandal of the cross, the difficulty of penitence, the renunciation of self, the abandonment of idols. But the church must be careful not to place non-biblical obstacles in the way of would-be believers. Just as the early Christians became baptized followers of Jesus Christ while still remaining culturally Jews, so it must be increasingly possible for men of all nations, languages and cultures to become baptized followers of Jesus, while still remaining culturally Maasai, culturally Russian, culturally Brahmins, culturally factory workers or culturally university professors. This is the next great frontier for the Christian faith. How to achieve that end while remaining simply, honestly and thoroughly biblical is an exciting adventure. That it can be achieved, I do not doubt. It is in fact currently being achieved. All the signs are that it will be achieved more and more in the years ahead.

The cultural diversity of the Christian faith will increase tremendously. The essential unity of the church will, if I am any prophet, also increase. One Lord, one faith, one baptism, one God and Father of us all — this is the unity of the Body. This is what the one Book, the one Church, the One Holy Spirit help to bring about.

Successful achievement of cultural diversity within an unbreakable unity will accompany a surge of growth such as the church has never seen. We stand at the beginning of a great expansion of the Christian faith in all six continents. It may well be that the Carter Symposium will have played a part in helping to bring about that unprecedented spread of the liberating gospel.

Concluding Thoughts

CHARLES R. TABER

IN this brief concluding essay, I cannot hope to summarize all of
the significant contributions of the four participants in the Carter
Symposium; they are too numerous and too varied, and are in
any case better stated in the authors' own words. Nor can I even
hope to highlight all of the differences between them, ranging as
they did from nuances right down to conflicting starting
assumptions. Again, the authors have done this much better
than I could. Finally, I do not want to emphasize personal
differences, though readers who know the four contributors or
who attended the symposium know how much these
differences, though always expressed in a Christian spirit,
enlivened the proceedings.

Rather, it is my intention to isolate a very small number of
what seem to me to be key issues on which the participants
differed, whether explicitly or implicitly; issues to which they
made significant contributions, but which remain in need of
further thought. In order to save space, I will present these
issues — with apologies to the authors, who so ably emphasized
the importance of "embodying" them — in a rather disincarnate
manner.

Though the symposium topic was rather broadly stated, the
aspect of it which, in fact, was the major focus of attention was
the following question: given a community of people, a doctrine
or a custom, which claims to be Christian, is it possible to

validate or to invalidate that claim? If so, how? What are the criteria, and who is in a position to apply them? To each of these questions, sharply divergent answers are offered.

One point of view on the major question is that the judgment is easy to make, both in principle and in practice. Proponents of this view cite numerous cases, and confidently decide in each case whether or not the phenomenon under investigation is Christian. The opposite point of view is that the whole enterprise is both impossible and illegitimate. This sharp disagreement, it turns out, rests crucially on divergent views both of the criteria to be applied and of how and by whom they can be applied.

What kind of criteria might be used? Differences here concern both the formal properties of the criteria and their substantive contents. The position that it is easy to decide whether or not people, beliefs or practices are Christian rests on the assumption that the criteria are structured according to a binary, yes-no metric which can be directly applied to the data. The opposite position uses the metaphor of a ladder, on which everyone who claims to be Christian occupies one or another rung, but on which there is no sharp cut-off point.

With respect to the substantive contents of the criteria, one position makes the following claims: (a) there is such a thing as a "pure gospel," a "non-negotiable faith once for all delivered"; (b) that gospel is supracultural, i.e. it is independent of particular cultural features and is universally applicable; (c) that gospel is for all practical purposes isomorphic with a set of abstract propositions about God (especially the doctrine of the Trinity), and the Scriptures which are ultimately based on the Bible but which are more directly derived from the decisions of the early ecumenical councils, especially Nicea and Chalcedon; and (d) any putatively Christian group that believes that faith and proclaims that gospel is Christian, whereas any group that alters that faith and that gospel is not Christian but Christopagan.

The counter-argument takes the form of two questions, which are not made fully explicit in the present papers but which are clearly implicit in the logic of the position. (a) Granting, as all four contributors do, that theology is made by theologians who are conditioned by the thought patterns of their own cultures, what is the justification for exempting the historic creeds from this process and giving them a privileged position of supracultural universality? Are they not, in fact, expressions of one strand of western Christian tradition, the one that turned out to be politically victorious in the western church? Are they not, in other words, *ethnotheology* on the same footing as other theological statements and, therefore, incarnate in particular cultural forms, rather than being universal and supracultural? Is not the very idea of a proposition both *formulated* in the words of a language and also *supracultural* a contradiction in terms? (b) *Is* the gospel, the Christian faith, in its *essence* to be identified with a set of propositions to be believed, however they may have been derived and formulated? Or is it not rather a "reality" which "happens to people" and *"becomes* truth"? The conflict arises, of course, out of the emphasis, on the one hand, on a faith intellectually conceived, in the Reformed tradition; and on the other hand, on faith as arising out of an existential encounter with God. If one accepts the first position, including the assumption of supracultural status for the creedal formulation, it becomes in principle possible to make the judgment we are discussing. If we opt for the second position, the judgment at once becomes moot, since a person's spiritual experience is not directly accessible to others.

So far we have been focussing on the criteria in the abstract, but specifying criteria is a purely academic exercise unless we can make satisfactory provision for their application to real cases. At this point we come to the third crucial disagreement between the four authors. Someone, some human being, must apply the standard and make the evaluation. The question, in concrete terms, is this: is a foreigner, whether missionary or missiologist, in a position to make the decision? One view confidently asserts the competence of the foreigner, with various provisos (anthropological training, consultation with and consent of indigenous Christians, etc.). Proponents of this position place heavy emphasis on the maturity of the foreigner, on his special knowledge of the Bible and theology, and on the other properties which distinguish him and make him able to exercise a valid judgment. In other words, the foreigner is assumed to be to some extent, like the Nicene Creed, in a special and privileged position.

The opposite position is summed up in one question: "How can you be so secure?" Implicit in this question is an emphasis on the fact that the missionary is no less subject to the normal pressures of enculturation than anyone else, and also on the fact that history demonstrates ad infinitum the extent of that conditioning. Those who believe in the competence of the foreigner all mention his enculturation but, say their opponents, they do not give it enough weight.

In other words, if I may sum up these positions rather starkly, one side holds that a judgment on the question that concerns us is not only possible but necessary. The criteria consist of a distillation of the great creeds, which are universally valid, and the foreigner (missionary or missiologist) can apply these criteria as a binary metric and confidently decide whether or not a given phenomenon is Christian. The opposite side argues that the judgment is impossible and illegitimate, because faith is found in a dynamic encounter with God, which is not available to scrutiny by outsiders, rather than in belief in a set of sentences; and because all sets of sentences and all possible interpreters of sets of sentences are inextricably involved in and conditioned by specific human cultures, which makes them incapable in principle of occupying a supracultural position. Therefore, the judgment *(judicium fidei)* must rest with God; men presume to make it at their own spiritual peril.

Where does this debate leave us? What questions are raised for further study? I will mention three, two which arise directly out of the present symposium, and one which was barely touched on except in Dr. Tippett's last chapter.

1. The first is this: what is the relation between creedal statements and biblical faith? Though this is a very broad theological question which transcends missiology, it becomes crucially relevant to missiology, as can be seen from the present discussion, because it relates to the anthropological problem of the close link between language and culture, which becomes especially apparent each time a new cultural boundary is crossed. This link would seem to jeopardize claims to supracultural status for any verbal formula. Under what

conditions, if any, might a *text* embodied in a human *language* attain supracultural and universal status? If such conditions can be satisfactorily specified, this would tend to support the "faith-is-creed" position; conversely, failure to specify such conditions would tend to undermine the position.

2. The second question is quite brief, but of extreme importance: what is the role of human enterprise and ingenuity in cross-cultural mission, and what is the role of the Holy Spirit? Or, to rephrase the question more dynamically, in what way do human messengers and the Spirit of God cooperate to achieve the work of God?

3. The third question is practical and programmatic: how can I in my missionary endeavors lead people, from wherever they are at present, towards Truth? How can I avoid misleading them, or leading them into sterile digressions? This, it seems to me, is at once more useful and less onerous than the the question which was chiefly discussed: more useful because it spells out a concrete task; less onerous because it removes from us the burden of making a retrospective judgment which, even if possible, can be seen as invidious, and which is not obviously helpful. Might we not make a more practical use of whatever historical insight we have if we asked, not whether a given phenomenon was or was not Christian, but whether a given method or approach led towards Truth or away from Truth? In other words, might we not both achieve the real purpose of the "faith-is-creed" proponents, to foster genuine biblical faith, and also admit the human limitations under which we must work, if we thought less in terms of a static concept of position and more in terms of a dynamic concept of direction?

Bibliography

Abineno, J.L. Ch., 1956. *Liturgische Vormen en Patronen in de Evangelische Kerk op Timor*. Doctoral thesis, Utrecht.

Addison, J.T., 1936. *The Medieval Missionary*. London: IMC.

Aldenfels, W. (SJ), 1973. Review of Ruetti, *Zur Theologie der Mission*, In *Priester und Mission*, 4:201-217.

Anderson, Gerald H., n.d. *Bibliography of the Theology of Missions in the Twentieth Century*.

Anderson, Rufus, 1875. *Foreign Missions, Their Relations and Claims*. Boston.

Andersson, E., 1958. *Messianic Popular Movements in the Lower Congo*. Uppsala: Studia Ethnographica Upsaliensia XIV.

Aubin, P., 1962. *Le problème de la conversion*. Paris: Beauchesne.

Ayer, J.C., 1952. *A Source Book for Ancient Church History*. New York: Charles Scribner's Sons.

Baëta, C.G., 1962. *Prophetism in Ghana. A Study of Some "Spiritual" Churches*. London.

Bakker, D., 1969. *Da'wah*. Ev. Miss. Zeitschrift.

Bangkok Assembly, 1973. Minutes and Reports of the Assembly of the Commission on World Mission and Evangelism of the World Council of Churches. December 31, 1972 and January 9-12, 1973.

Barber, B., 1941. "Acculturation and Messianic Movements," *American Sociological Review*, 6:663-669.

Barnett, Homer G., 1953. *Innovation: The Basis of Cultural Change.* New York: McGraw-Hill Book Co.

Basileia (Freytag Festschrift), 1959. Stuttgart Evang. Missions Verlag.

Bavinck, J.H., 1964. *An Introduction to the Science of Missions* (trans. D.H. Freeman). Philadelphia: The Presbyterian & Reformed Publishing Co.

Beaver, R. Pierce, 1962. *The Ecumenical Beginnings in Protestant World Mission.* New York: Nelson.

Belshaw, C.S., 1964. *Under the Ivi Tree: Society and Economic Growth in Rural Fiji.* London: Routledge & Kegan Paul.

Berglund, A.I. 1966. "The Rituals of the Independent Church Movement and Our Liturgy," in *Our Approach to the Independent Church Movement in South Africa.* Issued by the Missiological Institute, Lutheran Theological College, Mapumulo, Natal, pp. 113-125.

Beyerhaus, Peter, 1956. *Die Selbstaendigkeit der jungen Kirchen als missionarisches Problem.* Wuppertal/Barmen: Verlag der Rheinischen Missionsgesellschaft.

_____, 1964. "Unüberwundenes Heidentum als innere Bedrohung der afrikanischen Kirche," *Evangelische Missionszeitschrift,* 1964:114-131.

_____, 1972. "Missions and Racism," in *Shaken Foundations. Theological Foundations for Mission.* Grand Rapids: Zondervan Publishing House, pp. 89-102.

Beyreuther, Erich, 1957. *Francke und die Anfaenge der oekumenischen Bewegung.* Hamburg.

Bijlefeld, W.A., 1959. *De Islam als Na-Christelijke Religie.* Doctoral thesis, Utrecht.

Blauw, Johannes, 1962. *The Missionary Nature of the Church.* London: Lutterworth Press.

Boland, B.J., 1971. *The Struggle of Islam in Modern Indonesia.* 's Gravenhage: H.H.L. Smits.

Brisbois, J., 1972. *Apostolat, religion, eschatologie.* Doctoral thesis, Paris.

Cary, William, 1792. *An Enquiry into the Obligations of Christians to use means for the Conversion of the Heathens.* London: Hodder & Stoughton.

Cooley, Frank L., 1961. *Altar and Throne in Central Moluccan Societies.* Doctoral thesis, Yale.

_____, 1968. *Indonesia: Church and Society.* New York: Friendship Press.

_____, 1973. "The Revival in Timor," *South East Asia Journal of Theology,* Vol. 15.

Cronin, Vincent, 1959. *A Pearl to India: the Life of Roberto de Nobili.* New York: E.P. Dutton

Cross, F.L. (ed.), 1957. *Oxford Dictionary of the Christian Church.* London: Oxford University Press.

Dammann, E., 1965. "Das Christentumsverständnis in nachchristlichen Kirchen und Sekten Afrikas," in E. Benz (ed.), *Messianische Kirchen, Sekten und Bewegungen im heutigen Afrika.* Leiden: Brill, pp. 1-21.

Daniélou, Jean, 1964. "Christianity in the Non-Christian Religions," in J. Daniélou (ed.), *Introduction to the Great Religions.* Notre Dame: Fides Publications.

Deissmann, G. Adolf, 1927. *Light from the Ancient East.* New York: George H. Doran Co.

Durkheim, Emile, 1951. *Suicide: A Study in Sociology.* New York: The Free Press (1st edition in French 1897).

East Asia Christian Conference, 1966. "The Confessing Church in Asia and its Theological Task," *International Review of Missions,* 55:199-204.

Enklaar, I.H., 1947. *De Scheiding der Sacramenten op het Zendingsveld.* Doctoral thesis, Utrecht.

Filson, Floyd V., 1973. "New Testament History," *Encyclopedia Americana,* Vol. 3.

Fisher, G.P., 1945. *History of the Christian Church.* New York: Charles Scribner's Sons.

Freytag, W., 1961. "Der Islam als Beispiel einer nachchristlichen Religion," *Reden und Aufsätze,* 2:53-62.

Garbe, Richard, 1959. *India and Christendom*. La Salle, Ill.: Open Court Publishing Co.

Gensichen, H.W., 1960. "Were the Reformers Indifferent to Missions," in *History's Lessons for Tomorrow's Mission*. Student World.

_____, 1971. *Glaube für die Welt: Theologische Aspekte der Mission*. Gütersloh: Mohn.

Giddens, Anthony (ed.), 1972. *Emile Durkheim: Selected Writings*. Cambridge: The University Press.

Grapevine (JSAC), 1972. "Mission in an International Age," Feb. 1974.

Green, M., 1970. *Evangelism in the Early Church*. Grand Rapids: Eerdmans.

Gunkel, Herrmann, 1903. *Zum religionsgeschichtlichen Verständnis des Neuen Testamentes*. Göttingen.

Hallencreutz, C.F., 1966. *Kraemer Towards Tambaram*. Doctoral thesis, Uppsala.

Handbuch theologischer Grundbegriffe, 1962.

Häselbarth, H., 1966. "The Zion Christian Church of Edward Lekganyane," in *Our Approach to the Independent Church Movement in South Africa*. Issued by the Missiological Institute, Lutheran Theological College, Mapamulu, Natal.

_____, 1972. *Die Auferstehung der Toten in Afrika*. Gütersloher Verlagshaus Gerd Mohn.

Hazard, Paul, 1953. *The Crisis of the European Conscience*. London: Hollis (original French title *La Crise de la conscience européenne* 1680-1715).

Herskovits, M.J., 1937. "African Gods and Catholic Saints in New World Religious Belief," *American Anthropologist*, 39:635-643.

_____, 1951. *Man and His Works*. New York: Alfred A. Knopf.

Hogerwaard, T., 1953. "Het Aandeel van de Amberi-gurus in het Zendingswerk," in F.C. Kamma (ed.), *Kruis en Korwar*. den Haag: Voorhoeve, pp. 258-265.

Hollenweger, Walter, 1973. *Evangelisation Gestern und heute.* Stuttgart: J.F. Steinkopf Verlag.

Holsten, W., 1949. *J.B. Goszner: Glaube und Gemeinde.* Goettingen: Vandenhoek und Ruprecht.

_____, 1953. *Das Kerygma und der Mensch.* München: Kaiser.

Howson, John S., 1872. *The Metaphors of St. Paul and Companions of St. Paul.* Boston: American Tract Society.

Hunter, M., 1964. *Reaction to Conquest. Effects of Contact with Europeans on the Pondo of South Africa.* London.

Irenaeus, 2nd Cent. *Against Heresies* (Hardy's Trans.), in C.C. Richardson (ed.), *Early Christian Fathers.* Philadelphia: Westminster Press (1953).

Käsemann, Ernst, 1964. "Einheit und Vielfalt in der neutestamentlichen Lehre von der Kirche," in *Exegetische Versuche und Besinnungen,* Vol. 2, Göttingen.

Khodre, George, 1972. "Das Christentum in einer pluralistischen Welt — das Werk des Heiligen Geistes," in *Dialog mit anderen Religionen.* Frankfurt am Main.

Kidd, B.J., 1922. *A History of the Christian Church to A.D. 461.* Oxford: Clarendon Press, Vol. 2.

Kirk, John R. and G.D. Talbot, 1966. "The Distortion of Information," in Alfred E. Smith (ed.), *Communication and Culture.* New York: Holt, Rinehart & Winston, pp. 308-321.

Koper, J., 1956. *Enkele Aspecten van het Vraagstuk der missionaire Bijbelvertaling in het bijzonder in Indonesie.* Doctoral thesis, Utrecht.

Kraemer, H., 1938. *The Christian Message in a Non-Christian World.* London: The Edinburgh House Press.

_____, 1958. *From Mission Field to Independent Church.* The Hague: Boekencentrum.

_____, 1959. *Religion und christlicher Glaube.* Göettingen (original English title: *Religion and the Christian Faith.* London and Beccles, 1956).

_____, 1960. "Synkretismus," in F. Little and H. Walz (eds.), *Weltkirchenlexikon*. Stuttgart, pp. 1416-1419.

_____, 1962. "Synkretismus," in *Religion in Geschichte und Gegenwart*,[3] Vol. 6:563-568.

Kraft, Charles H., 1973a. "Toward a Christian Ethnotheology," in Alan R. Tippett (ed.), *God, Man and Church Growth*, Grand Rapids: Eerdmans Publishing Co., pp. 109-126.

_____, 1973b. "Church Planters and Ethnolinguistics," in Alan R. Tippett (ed.), *God, Man and Church Growth*. Grand Rapids: Eerdmans Publishing Co., pp. 226-249.

_____, 1973c. "Dynamic Equivalence Churches," *Missiology*, 1:1:39-57.

Kvist, Gustav, 1957. *Intet annat namn*. Helsinki: Missionen in Bibelns ljus.

Latourette, Kenneth Scott, 1966. *The Thousand Years of Uncertainty*. New York: Harper & Row (Vol. 2 of *The History of Expansion of Christianity*).

Latuihamallo, 1966. *Indonesia Raja*. Bad Salzuflen: Missionsverlag.

Lietzmann, Hans, 1932. *Geschichte der Alten Kirche* I. Berlin und Leipzig.

Linton, Ralph, 1936. *The Study of Man*. New York: Appleton-Century-Crofts (Paperback 1964).

_____, 1943. "Nativistic Movements," *American Anthropologist* 45:230-240.

Lowie, Robert H., 1952. *Primitive Religion*. London: Peter Owen.

Luzbetak, Louis J., 1963. *The Church and Cultures: An Applied Anthropology for Religious Workers*. Techny: Divine Word Publications.

Madsen, William, 1957. *Christopaganism: A Study of Mexican Religious Syncretism*. New Orleans: Middle American Research Institute, Tulane University.

Malinowski, Bronislaw, 1927. "The Problem of Meaning in Primitive Languages," Suppt. I in Ogden & Richards, *The Meaning of Meaning*. New York: Harcourt Brace & Co., pp. 296-336.

_____, 1948. *Magic, Science and Religion*. New York: Doubleday & Co.

_____, 1949. *The Dynamics of Cultural Change*. New Haven: Yale University Press.

_____, 1965. "The Anthropology of Changing African Cultures," in *Methods of Study of Culture Contact in Africa*. Oxford University Press for International African Institute.

Manecke, D., 1972. *Mission als Zeugendienst*. Wuppertal: Brockhaus.

Margull, Hans-Jochen and Stanley Samartha, 1972. *Dialog mit anderen Religionen*. Frankfurt am Main.

Martin, M.L., 1964. *The Biblical Concept of Messianism and Messianism in Southern Africa*. Morija/Lesotho.

Maurier, Henri, 1968. *The Other Covenant: A Theology of Paganism*. Glen Rock: Newman Press (translated from French by Charles McGrath).

Mbiti, John S., 1969a. "Eschatology," in K.A. Dickson and P. Ellingworth (eds.), *Biblical Revelation and African Beliefs*. Maryknoll: Orbis Books, pp. 159-184.

_____, 1969b. *African Religions and Philosophy*. London, Ibadan, Nairobi: Heinemann.

_____, 1971. *New Testament Eschatology in an African Background*. London: Oxford University Press.

McGavran, Donald A., 1955. *The Bridges of God*. London.

McGavran, Donald A. (ed.), 1972. *Eye of the Storm: The Great Debate in Mission*. Waco: Word Books.

Moeller, Wilhelm, 1893. *History of the Christian Church in the Middle Ages*. London: Swan, Sonnenscheim & Co.

Mqotsi, L. and Mkele, N., 1946. "A Separatist Church: Ibandla lika-Christu," *African Studies*, 2:120-132.

Mulders, A., 1962. *Missiologisch Bestek*. Hilversum: Brand.

Müller-Krüger, Th., (ed.), 1960. *Indonesia Raja*. Bad Salzuflen: Missionsverlag.

_____, 1968. *Der Protestantismus in Indonesien*. Stuttgart Evang. Verlag.

Musurillo, Herbert, 1962. "Athanasius," *Encyclopaedia Britannica*, Vol. 2.

Mykelbust, O.G., 1955-1957. *The Study of Missions in Theological Education*, Vols. 1, 2, Oslo: Egede Instituttet.

Neill, Stephen C., 1964. *A History of Christian Missions.* Harmondsworth: Penguin Books.

_____, 1970. *Call to Mission.* Philadelphia: Fortress Press.

Neill, W.T., 1973. *Twentieth - Century Indonesia.* New York: Columbia University Press.

Nettleton, Joseph, n.d. *John Hunt: Pioneer Missionary and Saint.* London: Chas. H. Kelly.

Nida, Eugene A., 1959. "The Role of Cultural Anthropology in Christian Missions," *Practical Anthropology*, 6:110-116.

_____, 1960. *Message and Mission: The Communication of the Christian Faith.* New York: Harper & Bros.

Ohm, Th., 1962. *Machet zu Juengern alle Voelker.* Freiburg: Wewel.

Oosthuizen, G.C., 1966. "Isaiah Shembe and the Zulu World View," in *Our Approach to the Independent Church Movement in South Africa.* Issued by the Missiological Institute, Lutheran Theological College, Mapumulu, Natal.

_____, 1967. *The Theology of a Bantu Messiah.* Leiden and Cologne.

_____, 1968. *Post-Christianity in Africa.* London: C. Hurst & Co.

Opler, Morris E., 1946. "Themes as Dynamic Forces in Culture," *The American Journal of Sociology*, 51:198-206.

Pannenberg, Wolfhart, 1967. "Erwägungen zu einer Theologie der Religionsgeschichte," in *Grundfragen Systematischer Theologie*. Gesammelte Aufsätze pp. 252-295.

Pfitzner, Victor C., 1967. *Paul and the Agon Motif.* Leiden: E.J. Brill.

Plattner, F.R., 1955. *Pfeffer und Seeler.* Einsiedeln: Benzing.

Pozas, Ricardo, 1962. *Juan the Chamula: An Ethnological Re-creation of the Life of a Mexican Indian* (trans. Lysander Kamp). Berkeley: University of California Press.

Proctor, Francis, and Frere, Walter. n.d. *A New History of the Book of Common Prayer*. London: Macmillan and Co.

Proksch, Otto, 1950. *Theologie des Alten Testamentes*. Gütersloh.

Radin, Paul, 1937. *Primitive Religion* (1957 edition). New York: Dover Publications.

Ramm, Bernard, 1973. "Divorce and the Lord's Command," in *Theology News and Notes*, Pasadena: Fuller Theological Seminary, Dec. 1973.

Reyburn, Wm. D., 1957. "The Transformation of God and the Conversion of Man," *Practical Anthropology*, 4:185-194.

Richardson, Alan, 1961. *An Introduction to the Theology of the New Testament*. London: SCM Press.

Riesenfeld, Harald, 1969. "Translating the Gospel in New Testament Time," in P. Beyerhaus and C.F. Hallencreutz (eds.), *The Church Crossing Frontiers*. Uppsala.

Rivers, W.H.R., 1922. "The Psychological Factor," in *Essays on the Depopulation of Melanesia*. Cambridge: The University Press, pp. 84-113.

Roloff, J., 1965. *Apostolat-Verkuendigung-Kirche*. Gütersloh: Mohn.

Rosin, H.H., n.d. *Missio Dei*. Leiden: Missiological Institute.

Ruetti, L., 1972. *Zur Theologie der Mission*. Greifswald: Kaiser.

Sapir, Edward, 1949. *Language*. New York: Harcourt, Brace & Co. (Originally published 1921).

Schlosser, K., 1958. *Eingeborenenkirchen in Süd- und Südwestafrika*. Universität Kiel.

Schmidt, W.J., 1966. *Ecumenicity and Syncretism*. Doctoral thesis, Union-Columbia University.

Schreiner, Lothar, 1972. *Adat und Evangelium*. Gütersloh: Mohn.

Sherif, Mustafer, 1936. *The Psychology of Social Norms*. New York: Harper & Bros.

Smalley, William A., 1955. "Culture and Superculture," *Practical Anthropology*, 2:58-71.

Smith, R.G., 1966. *Secular Christianity*. London: Collins.

Sumner, Wm. G. and A.G. Keller, 1927. *The Science of Society.* New Haven: Yale University Press. 4 vols.

Sundkler, B.G.M., 1961. *Bantu Prophets in South Africa.* London: Oxford University Press.

Taylor, J.V., 1963. *The Primal Vision.* London: S.C.M. Press.

Tellenbach, n.d., Bibliography in *Evang. Kirchen Lexicon,* Vol. 4.

Tempels, P., 1959. *Bantu Philosophy.* Paris: Présence Africaine.

Tippett, A.R., 1963. "Initiation Rites and Functional Substitutes," *Practical Anthropology,* 10:66-70.

_____, 1967a. "Religious Group Conversion in Non-western Society," Research in Progress Pamphlet, Pasadena, School of World Mission.

_____, 1967b. *Solomon Islands Christianity: A Study in Growth and Obstruction.* London: Lutterworth Press.

_____, 1970. *Church Growth and the Word of God.* Grand Rapids: Eerdmans Publishing Co.

_____, 1971. *People Movements in Southern Polynesia.* Chicago: Moody Press.

_____, 1972. "Possessing the Philosophy of Animism for Christ," in D.A. McGavran (ed.), *Crucial Issues in Missions Tomorrow,* pp. 125-143.

_____, 1973. *Verdict Theology in Missionary Theory.* South Pasadena: Wiliam Carey Library (2nd edition).

Turner, Harold W., 1960. "Searching and Syncretism: A West African Documentation," *The International Review of Missions,* 189-194.

van Akkeren, Ph., 1970. *Sri and Christ, A Study of the Indigenous Church in East Java.* London: Lutterworth, World Studies of Churches in Mission.

van Andel, H.A., 1912. *De Zendingsleer van G. Voetius.* Doctoral thesis, Kampen.

van Boetzelaer, C.W.Th., 1947. *De Protestantsche Kerk in Nederlandsch Indie.* 's Gravenhage.

van Leur, J.C., 1934. *Beschouwingen betreffende den ouden Asiatischen Handel.* Doctoral thesis, Leiden (English trans. *Asian Trade and Society,* 1955).

Väth, A., 1932. *Das Bild der Weltkirche.* Hannover.

Visser, B.J.J., 1925. *Onder Portugeesch-Spaansche Vlag.* Amsterdam.

_____, 1934. *Onder de Compagnie.* Batavia.

Visser't Hooft, W.A., 1963. *No Other Name: The Choice Between Syncretism and Christian Universalism.* Philadelphia: Westminster Press (German version *Kein anderer Name.* Basel: Basileia Verlag, 1965).

von Harnack, Adolf, 1906. *Die Mission und Ausbreitung des Christentums in den ersten drei Jahrhunderten,* Vols. 1, 2. Leipzig.

von Rad, Gerhard, 1963 and 1969. *Theologie des Alten Testaments,* Vols. 1, 2. Evangelische Verlagsanstalt Berlin.

Wallace, Anthony F.C., 1956. "Revitalization Movements," *American Anthropologist,* 58:264-281.

_____, 1966. *Religion: An Anthropological View.* New York: Random House.

Wand, J.W.C., 1954. *A History of the Early Church.* London: Methuen & Co.

Warren, Max, 1971. *A Theology of Attention.* Madras: Christian Literature Society.

Welbourn, F.B., 1961. *East African Rebels.* London: SCM.

Welbourn, F.B. and B.A. Ogot, 1966. *A Place to Feel at Home.* London: Oxford University Press.

Wells, Ann E., 1971. *This Their Dreaming.* St. Lucia: University of Queensland Press.

Wessels, C., 1926. *De Geschiedenis de RK. Missie in Amboina.* Nijmegen.

Whitman, Walt, 1959. *Complete Poetry and Selected Prose,* Jas. Miller, Jr. (ed.). Boston: Houghton Mifflin Co.

World Council of Churches, 1968. Draft for Sections, Uppsala 68. Geneva.

Wright, Fred H., 1953. *Manners and Customs of Bible Lands.* Chicago: Moody Press.

Yinger, John Milton, 1964. "On Anomie," *Journal for Scientific Study of Religion,* 3:158-173.

Other Books by the William Carey Library

General

Church Growth and Group Conversion by Donald A. McGavran $2.45p

The Evangelical Response to Bangkok edited by Ralph D. Winter $1.95p

Growth and Life in the Local Church by H. Boone Porter $2.95p

Message and Mission: the Communication of the Christian Faith by Eugene Nida $3.95p

Reaching the Unreached: A Preliminary Strategy for World Evangelization by Edward Pentecost $5.95p

Verdict Theology in Mission Theory by Alan Tippett $4.95p

Area and Case Studies

Aspects of Pacific Ethnohistory by Alan R. Tippett $3.95p

The Baha'i Faith: Its History and Teachings by William Miller $8.95p

A Century of Growth: the Kachin Baptist Church of Burma by Herman Tegenfeldt $9.95c

Church Growth in Japan by Tetsunao Yamamori $4.95p

A New Day in Madras by Amirtharaj Nelson $7.95p

People Movements in the Punjab by Margaret and Frederick Stock $8.95p

The Protestant Movement in Italy by Roger Hedlund $3.95p

Protestants in Modern Spain: the Struggle for Religious Pluralism by Dale G. Vought $3.45p

The Religious Dimension in Hispanic Los Angeles: A Protestant Case Study by Clifton Holland $9.95p

Taiwan: Mainline Versus Independent Church Growth by Allen J. Swanson $3.95p

Understanding Latin Americans by Eugene Nida $3.95p

Theological Education by Extension

Designing a Theological Education by Extension Program by Leslie D. Hill $2.95p

An Extension Seminary Primer by Ralph Covell and Peter Wagner $2.45p

The World Directory of Theological Education by Extension by Wayne Weld $5.95p

Textbooks and Practical Helps

Becoming Bilingual: A Guide to Language Learning by Donald Larson and William A. Smalley $5.95xp

God's Word in Man's Language by Eugene Nida $2.95p

An Inductive Study to the Book of Jeremiah by F.R. Kinsler $4.95p

Bibliography for Cross-Cultural Workers by Tippett $3.95p $5.95c

Principles of Church Growth by Weld and McGavran $4.95xp

Manual of Articulatory Phonetics by William A. Smalley $4.95xp

The Means of World Evangelization: Missiological Education at the Fuller School of World Mission edited by Alvin Martin $9.95p

Readings in Missionary Anthropology edited by William Smalley $4.95xp